D1178946

THE

INVESTMENT
TRUSTS
HANDBOOK

2019

Every owner of a physical copy of this edition of

THE INVESTMENT TRUSTS HANDBOOK 2019

can download the eBook for free direct from us at Harriman House, in a DRM-free format that can be read on any eReader, tablet or smartphone.

Simply head to:

ebooks.harriman-house.com/itshandbook19

to get your copy now.

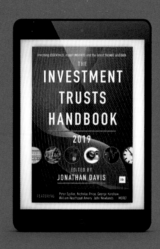

THE
INVESTMENT
TRUSTS
HANDBOOK

2019

*Investing essentials, expert insights and
powerful trends and data*

EDITED BY
JONATHAN DAVIS

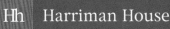 Harriman House

www.ITHB.co.uk

HARRIMAN HOUSE LTD
18 College Street
Petersfield
Hampshire
GU31 4AD
GREAT BRITAIN
Tel: +44 (0)1730 233870

Email: enquiries@harriman-house.com
Website: www.harriman-house.com

First published in Great Britain in 2018.
Copyright © Harriman House Ltd.
Original chapter text and photographs remain copyright © of individual authors or firms.

The right of the authors to be identified as the Authors has been asserted in accordance with the Copyright, Design and Patents Act 1988.

Hardcover ISBN: 978-0-85719-736-8
eBook ISBN: 978-0-85719-737-5

British Library Cataloguing in Publication Data
A CIP catalogue record for this book can be obtained from the British Library.

All rights reserved; no part of this publication may be reproduced, stored in a retrieval system, or transmitted in any form or by any means, electronic, mechanical, photocopying, recording, or otherwise without the prior written permission of the Publisher. This book may not be lent, resold, hired out or otherwise disposed of by way of trade in any form of binding or cover other than that in which it is published without the prior written consent of the Publisher.

No responsibility for loss occasioned to any person or corporate body acting or refraining to act as a result of reading material in this book can be accepted by the Publisher, by the Authors, or by the employers of the Authors.

Hh   Harriman House

www.ITHB.co.uk

CONTENTS

CONTENTS

ACKNOWLEDGEMENTS

Compiling *The Investment Trusts Handbook 2019* has again been an intensive and collective effort. Thanks are due to all those who have helped to bring it to fruition, whether as contributors or handmaidens to the production process.

At Harriman House: Chris Parker, Stephen Eckett, Myles Hunt, Sally Tickner and Tracy Bundey.

Contributors: Robin Angus, John Baron, James Burns, Geoffrey Challinor, Sandy Cross, Mark Dampier, Max King, John Newlands, Peter Spiller, Alex Denny, Claire Dwyer, Charles Cade, Alex Davies, George Kershaw, Richard Curling, William Sboczak, Tony Yousefian, James Anderson.

Research: Charles Cade, Simon Elliott, Kieran Drake, Emma Bird, Christopher Brown, Alan Brierley, Annabel Brodie Smith, David Elliott, Richard Pavry.

At the publishing partners: Alex Denny, Claire Dwyer and Nicholas Price (Fidelity), Derek Stuart, Billy Aitken and Kartik Kumar (Artemis), Piers Currie (Aberdeen Standard Life), Toni Craig (Jupiter).

INTRODUCTION

||||||||||||||||||||||||||||||||||||||||||||||||||||||||||||||||||||||||||||||||||||

W E HAVE MADE a number of changes to the content of *The Investment Trusts Handbook* since last year's successful first edition. Although we have retained some of the general introductory sections, on the basis that they have timeless value, we have made sure that every section has been thoroughly revised and updated to take account of events and market movements since the last edition was published. John Baron, for example – well-known to many private investors for his monthly columns in the *Investors Chronicle* – has not only revised his comments from last year, but added an entirely new section on how to put together a portfolio of investment trusts. Mark Dampier, Sandy Cross, Alex Denny and James Burns have also refreshed and updated their contributions, offering a range of perspectives from professional practitioners.

There is also a host of newly commissioned content which is designed to round out the content of this year's edition. We have interviews with both the longest serving trust manager (Peter Spiller of CG Asset Management) and the youngest recently appointed one (Kartik Kumar at Artemis). Charles Cade, head of investment trusts at Numis Securities – regularly feted as one of the best investment trust analysts in the City – answers a host of questions about the state of the trust industry as we head towards and into 2019. Historian John Newlands commemorates the launch of the first Scottish investment trust in 1873 with a piece about the role of Robert Fleming in making Dundee a centre of investment trust expertise (a role which it continues to perform in some measure to this day). Fund manager Nicholas Price makes the case for investing in Japan, one of my favourite markets for the longer term, while James Anderson, co-manager of the UK's largest trust, SCOTTISH MORTGAGE, explains how some fascinating pioneering academic research on stock market returns has influenced the distinctive way that the trust now invests. Robin Angus describes how the board of PERSONAL ASSETS divides responsibilities with its investment adviser. Further insights into the critical role of trust directors is provided by

George Kershaw, co-founder of Trust Associates, a headhunting firm that specialises in recruiting non-executive directors for investment companies.

We have a section on how a ratings firm goes about analysing investment trusts, and another that explores the reasons that trusts which manage concentrated portfolios often perform better than most (it is not that surprising to us, though beware of concluding that a concentrated portfolio is a certainty to outperform, which is not the same proposition). Next comes a Q&A with the investment trust team at Fidelity about the role that trusts could play in attracting the interest of millennials. Turning to the subject of trusts that invest in alternative assets, Max King provides a rounded introduction to the subject, fund manager Richard Curling explains how he uses this kind of trust to generate cash for his monthly income fund and analysts from Winterfloods, another of the top-rated City broking firms, explain what investors need to look out for when considering putting their money into three of the most important sub-sectors of this mostly new genre (property, infrastructure and debt). We then have two pieces on the case for investing in venture capital trusts and how this important tax-efficient sub-sector of the market has developed over the past 12 months.

Finally I have revised and updated the 65-page section on analysing investment trusts that makes up the second half of the book. This covers the most important metrics that anyone looking deeper into the available choices needs to consider when doing their research. If you aren't quite sure what gearing or a z-score is, this is the place to look. In response to feedback from readers of last year's edition, we have transferred most of the detailed listings section to the handbook's website (www.ithb.co.uk), where it can be regularly updated. It will also include a library of relevant articles and data sources. For handy reference, we have retained in print a simple list of all trusts with a market value in excess of £100m as at the last week of October. The ticker symbols will help you on your way to further research online. On the handbook website you will also find links to my private circulation notebook (see www.independent-investor.com for more details) in which I comment regularly, among other things, on investment trusts and investment strategy.

Whatever 2019 holds for you, I wish you the best of luck with your investments.

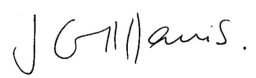

EDITOR'S NOTES

A REVOLUTIONARY BREAKTHROUGH?

I T HAS LONG been a matter of faith among fans that investment trusts deliver superior performance to their open-ended fund equivalents. This statement is regularly trotted out as fact and there is no doubt that you can point to a number of specific examples where you can directly compare the performance of two funds – one an investment trust, the other open-ended – which are managed by the same fund manager. In these direct comparisons the investment trust typically comes out on top handsomely over time. A good example would be the two Japanese funds managed by the recently retired Sarah Whitley at Baillie Gifford, one of our most impressive – and impressively unshowy – firms in the business. Charts that illustrate the superior record of investment trusts are regularly produced by investment company research analysts (see page 248 for an example).

But how robust is that general finding that investment trusts outperform open-ended funds? And if that is indeed true, which features of the trust structure are responsible for the divergence in performance? Given that we all know how misleading statistics can be, you can imagine the interest that greeted the news earlier this year that academics at Cass Business School in London had formally tested the hypothesis and found some robust evidence that it is indeed true. The headline results of this research were presented at a conference in London in June 2018. You can see a short video summarising the event on the event website (www.mip-fit.com).

This appears to have been the first time that such a rigorous academic analysis of trust performance has been undertaken; apart from the lingering mystery of the persistence of closed-end fund discounts (a non-issue, in our view – see page

273), investment trusts have remained of surprisingly little interest to academia. So this could potentially be a big deal. Yet frustratingly, at the time of writing, the formal academic research paper which sets out the results of the analysis has still to be published. (It was originally promised for Q4 2018, but I am told by the authors that it is now more likely to see the light of day in 2019.)

It is impossible therefore to do more than summarise the reported findings. Professor Andrew Clare and Dr Simon Hayley, who carried out the research, say that they found that directly comparable investment trusts outperformed their open-ended equivalents by an average of 1.4% a year between 2000 and 2016, taking net asset value (NAV) performance as the measure. (Previous studies have tended to look at share price performance, which is more volatile because of discount movements, rather than NAV performance, which is a truer measure of fund management skill.) The analysis excluded specialist sectors, such as private equity, where there were insufficient cases to study. The final study pitted 134 trusts against 1,200 open-ended funds with similar mandates, admittedly not the largest of samples. Professor Clare commented that the extent of the 1.4% per annum gap – which, while modest at first sight, would translate into significantly higher returns once compounded over several years – was unexpected.

The results suggest, he said, that the structural factors behind the superior performance included:

1. the bias trusts historically have towards holdings of smaller companies, which tend to outperform larger stocks

2. the closed-end structure, which saves managers of investment companies from having to buy and sell stocks at inopportune moments

3. the ability of trusts to buy back their shares at a discount to their real value

4. to a very limited extent, the use of gearing to amplify investment returns.

Noting a recurrent problem with many less rigorous statistical studies, Prof Clare said he wanted to do further work to make doubly sure that the results had not been skewed by 'survivorship bias' (the fact that poorly performing funds tend to be closed down, reducing the sample size and the robustness of the findings, unless appropriate adjustments are made).

So the Cass team are now updating the study and extending the data set back to 1994 and forward to 2018. But he did add, tellingly, "what we can tell at the moment is the level of fund manager skill tends to be higher in investment trusts compared to comparable open-ended funds". He estimated that, even after allowing for the structural factors listed above, the average trust still

We strive to explore further.

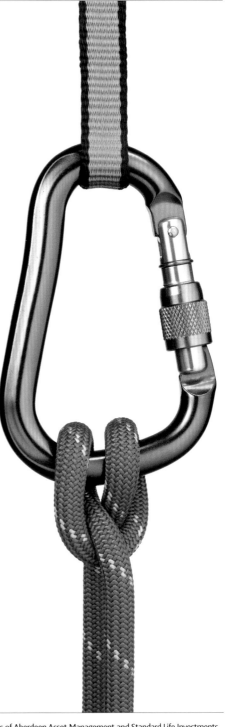

Aberdeen Investment Trusts
ISA and Share Plan

We believe there's no substitute for getting to know your investments face-to-face. That's why we make it our goal to visit companies – wherever they are – before we invest in their shares and while we hold them.

With a wide range of investment companies investing around the world – that's an awfully big commitment. But it's just one of the ways we aim to seek out the best investment opportunities on your behalf.

Please remember, the value of shares and the income from them can go down as well as up and you may get back less than the amount invested. No recommendation is made, positive or otherwise, regarding the ISA and Share Plan.

The value of tax benefits depends on individual circumstances and the favourable tax treatment for ISAs may not be maintained. We recommend you seek financial advice prior to making an investment decision.

Request a brochure: **0808 500 4000**
invtrusts.co.uk

Aberdeen Standard Investments is a brand of the investment businesses of Aberdeen Asset Management and Standard Life Investments. Issued by Aberdeen Asset Managers Limited, 10 Queen's Terrace, Aberdeen AB10 1YG, which is authorised and regulated by the Financial Conduct Authority in the UK. Telephone calls may be recorded. aberdeen-asset.co.uk

THE INVESTMENT TRUSTS HANDBOOK 2019

outperformed open-ended equivalents by 0.84% per annum in NAV terms and an equivalent index fund by 0.58% per annum.[*] That conclusion may not be news to many of us who have followed the sector for years, but if it survives unscathed from the inevitable scrutiny that the results will attract when published, it is obviously good news for the investment trust business.

NOT MUCH GOOD TO SAY ABOUT THE FCA

One wonders however what impact, if any, this research will have as and when it filters through to the offices of the Financial Conduct Authority (FCA), the industry's regulator. You don't have to travel far round the City or Edinburgh before you will hear the complaint that the FCA has little or no interest in investment trusts and in subtle ways is failing to ensure a playing field between trusts and the much larger universe of open-ended funds. As noted here last year, the FCA's successful campaign to remove the longstanding scandal of commission-driven bias in fund selection amongst financial advisers has been rightly welcomed by investment trust fans. Yet it is impossible to shake off the conviction that the FCA is more interested in advancing the cause of passive investment solutions than it is in creating a genuinely free market in which both active and passive investment firms can compete for business on equal terms.

With their long history and seemingly robust claim to superior performance, you would think that investment trusts would be of much greater interest to the FCA as a solution for informed investors than they are. As Alex Denny notes on page 167, it is bizarre enough that it appears impossible for anyone with a defined-contribution pension to allocate any part of their pension fund to investment trusts. (You can only do so if you switch to, or start, a self-invested personal pension.) Research by Lang Cat published this year also found that many financial advisers are still working with professional industry platforms that make it difficult or even impossible for them to invest in investment trusts for their clients.

---

[*]   If you assume that a broad equity market index fund will grow at an average of 7% per annum, in line with the long run historical return, an additional 0.58% per annum of return will add an additional £27,000 to the value of an initial £100,000 portfolio after ten years.

For this and other reasons – ignorance, bias, the impact of holding costs – five years after the Retail Distribution Review, which was designed to eliminate commission bias in adviser behaviour, just 5% of the money on adviser platforms is invested in investment trusts.[*] With two such important financial channels – defined-benefit pension schemes and financial adviser platforms – difficult or impossible to access, it is not really a surprise that the investment company sector remains only a quarter the size of the open-ended fund business, despite having a 60-year head start and (so we continue to believe) a superior performance record.

The FCA's reputation will not have been enhanced by the bizarre episode of the KID, or 'key investor document', which became mandatory in January 2018 for every investment trust to produce, alongside its own factsheets and other literature. Most platforms also now feel obliged to provide them. This new requirement is part of a wider EU regulatory initiative that imposes what are known as PRIIPS rules on investment products sold to retail investors.[†] Like most regulation it is well-intentioned but heavy-handed and patently vulnerable to the law of unintended consequences. (A distinguished American professor named George Stigler was awarded a Nobel Prize as far back as 1982 for his part in demonstrating that the long-term effects of regulation are often perversely to achieve the opposite of what was intended when first introduced.)

As the industry's trade association, the AIC has protested to the FCA about several aspects of these new rules, including the requirement for KIDs to include standardised risk ratings and estimates of future performance under a range of different scenarios. The way that both the ratings and the estimates are produced ensure that in both cases they generate outcomes that can only be described as absurd. Professor John Kay splendidly held up the whole process to ridicule at the annual conference of the AIC in March.[‡] Similarly, the analyst team at Numis produced a detailed study illustrating some of the anomalous results and blatant inconsistencies produced by the mandated formula imposed by the authors of the PRIIPS rules. According to the AIC, more than 50% of trusts, for example, are projected to make a positive return even in "unfavourable" market conditions. Venture capital trusts, which invest in highly risky early-stage businesses, have an average risk rating that is lower than conventional listed equity trusts. Such distortions make the new regulations both pointless and – worse – potentially misleading.

---

[*]   Source: AIC, 'Market bias, prohibitive costs and "sketchy knowledge"', press release, 3 July 2018.

[†]   PRIIPS stands for 'packaged retail and insurance-based investment products' – don't bureaucrats just love their acronyms…

[‡]   You can read Prof Kay's initial denunciation of the new rules on his website johnkay.com, in an article 'Risk, the retail investor and disastrous new rules', dated 22 January 2018.

It is silly enough that regulators who insist on including the statement that 'past performance is no guide to the future' in all fund marketing literature should at the same time introduce a new set of rules which mandates firms to publish estimates of future returns which are explicitly derived from past performance. Because boards have no discretion over whether to produce these documents, we have witnessed the unusual spectacle of some investment firms warning their shareholders that the projections they have produced under duress are over-optimistic – an expression of self-effacement for which the financial services industry is not renowned.

To add insult to injury, the date on which the new rules are required to be introduced by UK open-ended firms has been set two years later than the requirement imposed on UK investment companies – a competitive disadvantage. The reason given is that open-ended funds are already subject to a set of EU rules known as the UCITs regime and those rules are not scheduled to be updated until January 2020. (UCITs funds confusingly have to produce something called a KIID, but it does not have the same requirements or content as the KID, which trusts are required to produce.) It may of course be relevant that the closed-ended fund is a largely unknown phenomenon on the Continent. It is true that the PRIIPS rules are an EU initiative, rather than one sourced in the UK, but the FCA has been an instrumental participant in the process and, even if it wished to do so, has clearly been powerless to prevent this particular idiocy coming into force.

CLARITY AND CONFUSION OVER COSTS

If you can be reasonably certain that the KID in its current form will eventually be killed off, for being both unworkable and misleading, it is equally certain that the PRIIPS rules will continue to play a part in another development to which investment trusts – rightly in this case – are having to respond. This is the relentless pressure on all fund providers, be they investment trusts or open-ended funds, to make fuller and better disclosure of the costs of ownership to their investors. The irresistible rise of the humble low-cost index fund and more recently the widespread adoption by institutional investors of its sister product, the ETF (exchange-traded fund), poses a powerful competitive threat to all exponents of active investment management, not just investment trusts.

Our *hunters* scour the map for hidden PROFITS.

When Profits are scarce in one part of the world, they can often abound elsewhere. That's why our hunters spend their lives carving through the atlas. Relying on their keen eyes and sharp reactions to bag far-flung Profits that others have failed to find. Leaving no stone – or page – unturned.

ARTEMIS
The PROFIT Hunter

0800 092 2051   investorsupport@artemisfunds.com   artemisfunds.com

The value of investments may go down as well as up and you may not get back the amount you originally invested. Issued by Artemis Fund Managers Limited which is authorised and regulated by the Financial Conduct Authority. For your protection calls are usually recorded.

The fees on index funds have fallen so far and have become so cheap that it is putting relentless downward pressure on all other types of fund. That is clearly to the advantage of investors in actively managed funds as well, since costs compound as inexorably as returns, and many funds historically have been able to extract handsome excess profits despite indifferent performance. That has undoubtedly been helped in no small measure by the lack of full disclosure of what those costs are. So by insisting on greater disclosure, the regulators in this case are pushing at what has become an open door. The annual management charges for investment trusts have been falling steadily for some time, and I am not aware of any cases where the external managers of a trust have decided to hand back their management contract because the viability of their contract is under threat from lower fees.

The problem here, though, is that fuller disclosure is not necessarily as helpful to the end user as you might think. Instead of clarity, sometimes the result can simply be more confusion. True to form, the PRIIPS regulations introduced by the EU adopt a different method of disclosure to that adopted elsewhere. They require funds to use a method known as 'reduction in yield' (RIY), which is designed to illustrate how much the return from a fund over a given time period will be reduced as a result of the costs owning the fund. This is in contrast to methods such as the total expense ratio (TER) and the ongoing charge ratio (OCR), which both attempt to calculate the current cost of ownership. In theory the figures should be broadly comparable, but in practice often they are not.

All methods of calculating the cost of ownership suffer from two defects – differences in the type of cost that are included and differences in the assumptions made about the future. Without going into all the technical issues involved (it is not the most exciting subject), suffice it to say that the PRIIPS method appears to be the worst of all worlds. Not all firms calculate the figures in the same way. In some cases the formula results in firms showing – absurdly – negative costs. In others it appears to overstate the costs, making trusts appear more expensive than they are when compared to open-ended equivalents. One fear for the trust sector is that wealth managers, who are now required to include these cost figures in reporting to their clients (even if they are inaccurate), may be deterred from adding trusts to client portfolios as a result. As wealth managers are amongst the biggest buyers of investment trusts, this could make a significant difference to the health of the sector.

The AIC's official advice about KIDs is "burn before reading" and we would endorse that advice. The EU is due to review the regime in 2019. It does not mean that the cost of ownership is irrelevant – on the contrary, it is one of the most important criteria to look at when buying any kind of fund – but you do need clear and consistent data for comparisons to be of any use, and for now at least the OCR seems like the better option when doing your research. Faced with a chorus of complaints, the FCA has since conceded that trust boards are free to provide additional information if they feel that the return and cost projections in the KIDs they are mandated to produce are misleading.

ADAPT OR DIE

The investment trust business has changed dramatically in the last two decades. Gone, to all intents and purposes, are the opaque and potentially dangerous split capital trusts which once were a defining feature of the sector, but mercifully failed to survive the dismal experience of the 'split capital trust scandals' of 2001–02.* In has come a host of alternative asset funds offering handsome yields for income-seeking investors starved of income by the fallout from the global financial crisis of 2007–08. Coupled with some overdue regulatory and governance changes, and the subsequent emergence of activist investors looking to enforce change, the crisis has helped to transform the way that trusts are priced and managed, entirely for the better.

One consequence of a more bracing competitive environment, however, is that these days the need to 'adapt or die' is more relevant for an investment trust than it was in days gone by. Faced with the need to compete against a new generation of passive low-cost investment vehicles (index funds and ETFs) and still easier-to-market actively managed open-ended funds, investment trusts have to work harder to justify staying in business. They have been helped by the strong performance of most types of investment since the low point of the crisis and earlier legal and regulatory changes which make it much easier than before for boards to to issue new shares and raise awareness of their existence through marketing. It has also become much easier for private investors to research and buy trusts through cheap execution-only platforms.

As Charles Cade has addressed many of the most important issues facing the sector in his Q&A, I see no need to address them here in any more detail. Suffice it to say that if 2017 was an exceptional year for the equity market and

---

* To be clear, split capital trusts fulfilled a useful function for knowledgeable investors, but became toxic as a result of mis-selling, poor disclosure and unseemly collusion between a number of industry providers.

an excellent one for alternative assets – both extremely helpful developments for the investment trust sector – then 2018, at the time of writing, is shaping up to be a more mundane experience. Ten years on from the collapse of Lehman Brothers, the point at which the global financial system threatened to implode, much has changed, but fears of a further systemic collapse and a worldwide deflationary crisis have receded. As always, however, there are no shortage of opinions as to how the global economy and the financial markets will develop from here. The election of President Trump and the seemingly never-ending saga of the Brexit negotiations both pose challenges to those attempting to employ conventional analytical methods to determine the outlook.

One encouraging trend in 2018 has been the revival of conventional equity trust IPOs. As we noted last year, most of the new launches in previous years – by number at least – have been from alternative asset funds looking to tap into investor demand for income. There are some signs that, as far as renewable energy, infrastructure and specialist property funds are concerned, this phenomenon might now be getting close to saturation point. The infrastructure funds took a knock early in 2018 when the collapse of Carillion added to existing nervousness about what a Corbyn government bent on nationalisation and ending PFI contracts might do. Other types of alternative asset trusts, however, continue to be launched: among the past year's crop of IPOs, BIOPHARMA CREDIT, which provides credit to biotech companies, and HIPGNOSIS, which is looking to exploit rights to recorded music, stand out as being particularly innovative. It is important to remember that the rationale for investing in alternative assets is not just about income, but also about diversification. There are good reasons for thinking that the returns of many types of alternative asset trust could be uncorrelated with equity markets – a useful defensive feature if we do see a market downturn in due course.

While bigger, more established equity investment trusts with strong performance records have been able to continue growing by making regular secondary issues of shares – the aforementioned SCOTTISH MORTGAGE has issued more than £600m of new shares in the last two years alone – it has proved harder to generate sufficient support from investors for new conventional equity offerings. Nick Greenwood, the manager of Miton's fund of investment trusts, examines this issue in his article on page 139. This year, however, has seen several interesting new equity trust launches, among them Baillie Gifford's new North American fund, a distinctive Japanese trust managed by Asset Value Investors, and a second global equity investment trust from Terry Smith's Fundsmith group. The latter, called SMITHSON, proved so popular that it raised more than

TESTING NAPPIES. THE LENGTHS WE'LL GO TO FOR A BETTER INVESTMENT.

LET'S TALK HOW.

It may sound odd that nappy absorption could have an impact on one of the investment trusts from our global range, but it did. When researching two manufacturers in Asia, we questioned why one of them had declining sales. Management told us it was a marketing issue, but was it something more fundamental?

We ran an independent test and found their nappy just didn't hold water, which put them out of the running Hands-on local research helped us make a better investment decision.

Our 375 investment professionals across the globe always dig deeper by cross-checking facts, asking the difficult questions and sometimes even testing nappies. We believe this gives us stronger insights across the regions and markets our investment trusts cover.

Fidelity's range of investment trusts

- Fidelity Asian Values PLC
- Fidelity China Special Situations PLC
- Fidelity European Values PLC
- Fidelity Japan Trust PLC
- Fidelity Special Values PLC

This information is not a personal recommendation for any particular investment. If you are unsure about the suitability of an investment you should speak to an authorised financial adviser. The value of investments and the income from them can go down as well as up and you may get back less than you invest. Past performance is not a reliable indicator of future results. Overseas investments are subject to currency fluctuations. Investments in small and emerging markets can be more volatile than other overseas markets. Some trusts invest more heavily than others in small companies, which can carry a higher risk because their share prices may be more volatile than those of larger companies. The trusts may also use financial derivative instruments, which may expose them to a higher degree of risk and can cause investments to experience larger than average price fluctuations. Research professionals include both analysts and associates. Source: Fidelity International, 30 June 2018. Data is unaudited.

Let your investment benefit from our robust research. Visit fidelity.co.uk/research or speak to an adviser.

Money
Observer.net
TrustAwards
2018

Highly Commended
Premier Group Award
Fidelity International

The latest annual reports and factsheets can be obtained from our website at www.fidelity.co.uk/its or by calling 0800 41 41 10. The full prospectus may also be obtained from Fidelity. Fidelity Investment Trusts are managed by FIL Investments International. Issued by Financial Administration Services Limited, authorised and regulated by the Financial Conduct Authority. Fidelity, Fidelity International, the Fidelity International logo and F symbol are trademarks of FIL Limited. UKM0818/22367/SSO/1218

£800m from investors, making it the largest equity trust launch ever. Two former managers of well-known trusts, Mark Mobius and Stuart Widdowson, have also reappeared at the helm of smaller vehicles offering the same strategy as their former employers,* while a new fund management company, Merian – owned and run by the highly regarded former equity management team at Old Mutual – were working on a mixed private and listed equity offering as I finished these notes.

TOWARDS A NEW MARKET ENVIRONMENT

There is, however, a growing sense that the environment for investing to which investors have become accustomed in recent years may finally be beginning to change. The last ten years have been characterised by below-trend economic growth, unprecedented amounts of monetary stimulus, record low interest rates and a bull market in equities that has continued to climb the traditional 'wall of worry'. With money so cheap, value investing has been comprehensively trumped by growth, and momentum strategies and small-cap funds have done better than large-cap equivalents. The search for income in a low-interest-rate world has meanwhile produced what by historical standards are numerous anomalies.

There is a reasonable chance, however, that 2018 will go down as the year when some at least of these trends finally started to reverse. Bond yields have been moving upwards and more importantly real yields (yields adjusted for inflation) have edged back into positive territory in the United States, though not yet in the UK. Negative real yields sit uneasily with the way that capitalist economies are meant to behave, and the sooner we can return to a world where sensibly invested money can earn an honest return, the sooner we can return to a world in which investors can hold fast once more to traditional investor nostrums. Whether that in turn is enough to moderate the surge in populist and anti-establishment political movements across the globe is open to question. There is little evidence of that so far.

While nobody in their right mind can forecast the short-term direction of markets, my suspicion for what it is worth is that while we are not yet at the end of the current market cycle, we have certainly advanced a good way

---

* The MOBIUS INVESTMENT TRUST and ODYSSEAN INVESTMENT TRUST respectively.

towards its eventual demise. It remains to be seen whether the Federal Reserve's desire to raise interest rates over the next couple of years can be fulfilled, but with unemployment at generational lows, wages starting to rise after years of stagnation, and quantitative easing in the US replaced by quantitative tightening, the benign conditions of the last ten years look unlikely to persist indefinitely. If you think that zero interest rates have helped to inflate the price of most financial assets, then it is only logical to assume that a reversal in the interest rate regime will bear down on lofty valuations. It would be no surprise in these circumstances to see some new market trends emerge – including a revival of value as an investment style, some rotation from small- to large-cap market leadership and in due course at least a temporary setback in the equity markets as profits weaken, the discount rate rises and politicians look to the owners of capital for more revenue. Investment trusts inevitably will not be immune from these effects, should they happen. With discounts so narrow by historical standards, it is inevitable that there will be periods when widening discounts and heightened market volatility test the resilience of boards that have introduced discount controls and the nerves of investors in those trusts where no such regime exists. Such an outcome, as we noted last year, will be both a challenge and an opportunity for investors who follow the sector closely.

At the time of writing, equity markets have experienced three significant sell-offs in 2018 – in February, April and October. Such episodes provide prima facie evidence as to which trust sectors are most vulnerable to corrections if a bear market were to develop. In that sense they provide a more meaningful measure of risk than any regulatory-inspired formula. In the first two weeks of the October sell-off, for example, the list of biggest fallers included all the trusts with big holdings in technology and biotech companies, the same stocks that have been leading the market higher for many months. Small-cap specialist trusts also sold off more sharply than their larger counterparts, as you would expect. The decline in most alternative asset sectors, on the other hand, was more modest, reflecting their more defensive nature. It is not so easy to measure how they will be affected if we get a more enduring downturn in the markets, let alone another deep bear market, since they are mostly too new to have relevant historical experience to fall back on.

Hedge funds and private equity trusts were very popular in the run up to 2008, but their share prices were savaged during the global financial crisis because of their high levels of gearing, and while you can argue that circumstances today are very different – gearing levels in private equity trusts are generally lower, for example, and the hedge fund trusts have almost all disappeared – there can be no certainty how investors will react in a different future environment. In particular there must be a question mark over how long investors will be prepared to stick with those alternative asset trusts which are mandated to invest in illiquid assets as and when trouble next comes around. The price of their shares may well fall to testing levels as demand reduces.

The flipside of all this is that sudden sell-offs also create opportunities. Investor behaviour tends to be herd-like and that, combined with the defensive measures taken by market makers when prices move against them, can often produce anomalous share prices. Discount movements can amplify this further. That is the cue for the most knowledgeable trust investors to move back in. A good example came earlier in 2018 when fears of nationalisation and the collapse of outsourcing company Carillion clobbered the shares of infrastructure funds. That created an attractive entry point for those capable of cooler analysis. If you have been frustrated by the premiums at which many otherwise attractive high-yielding funds have tended to trade over the last few years, it may be that at this stage you should be looking forward to market downturns rather than fearing them. Experience suggests, however, that only a minority of investors have the patience and the discipline to wait for such moments to come around. In the later stages of the market cycle, where we are today, the harder part still is to have the courage and the foresight to build up reserves of liquidity and wait so that you have the cash to deploy when the next big buying opportunity comes around. Younger readers may find the perspective of the trust sector's longest serving manager, Peter Spiller, helpful in this context.

In our view, however, there is only limited reward to be had from spending a lot of time trying to work out how the global macro-economic environment is going to pan out. Even if you get the direction right, it is hard to get the timing right as well. As with Brexit, there are still too many unknowns to make predicting the future path of the global economy anything other than an educated guess. As Warren Buffett has pointed out on many occasions, investors are best served by focusing on the things that they can understand and control, and using diversification to protect themselves against things that they cannot. If you have a strong view about politics, the path of bond yields and the imminence of a recession, and sufficient conviction to back your judgement, well and good. For most of us, however, as closely as we may try to follow events, that certainty is hard to obtain.

My personal experience over four decades in the markets is that investors are generally best served putting most of their effort into finding a few well-managed funds where the managers have both long experience and retain a close alignment with your own interests (see 'Skin in the Game' on page 282). Once you have

DIRECTION

Some follow. We take our own investment path.

At Jupiter, we encourage our fund managers to follow their convictions and actively look for new investment opportunities.

For over thirty years, this culture of freethinking and individuality has allowed us to search for the best investments, as we look to grow our clients' money. We believe it's this confidence to go our own way, that sets us apart. Today we manage over £47 billion* on behalf of our clients, offering a broad range of actively managed investment strategies.

Market and exchange rate movements can cause the value of an investment to fall as well as rise, and you may get back less than originally invested.

Discover the Jupiter difference. Visit **jupiteram.com** or search **JUPITER ASSET MANAGEMENT**.

VISIT **JUPITERAM.COM**

JUPITER
Asset Management

This advert is for informational purposes only and is not investment advice. We recommend you discuss any investment decisions with a financial adviser, particularly if you are unsure whether an investment is suitable. Jupiter is unable to provide investment advice. Jupiter Asset Management Limited, registered address: The Zig Zag Building, 70 Victoria Street, London, SW1E 6SQ is authorised and regulated by the Financial Conduct Authority. *Jupiter, as at 30.09.18. MKT00214-02-1018 found them, your bias should be to stick with them and, in the absence of a clear regime change in market conditions, only change your portfolio if the reasons you bought them in the first place cease to be valid, or some more compelling newer alternative presents itself. This does happen periodically, sometimes because of unjustified discount movements. It may be prudent to rebalance your holdings once every one or two years and of course to review what you own should either your personal circumstances or tolerance for risk materially change, as they might well be doing after the strong returns of the last decade.

In January 2017, as an experiment, I put together a short list of trusts, all of which I own myself, that in my view met this general test – ones I would be happy in principle to own indefinitely. The names are set out in the table on the opposite page. (Not knowing your personal circumstances or risk appetite, dear reader, I hope it is clear that you should not interpret this as a recommendation that you should also necessarily invest in these particular trusts – they are just among my personal favourites.) Since I first created the list I have – unusually – already made a number of changes in response to events (see subsequent tables). I have essentially moved in the direction of greater defensiveness and more exposure to value as a discipline. I propose to continue monitoring the way that this portfolio changes and performs over time.[*] However the markets pan out, I shall be disappointed if the long-term results are at odds with the findings of the Cass Business School academics, and more than happy if your own experience as a trust investor turns out to be even more fruitful than mine in the uncertain times that (as ever) lie ahead.

JONATHAN DAVIS
Oxford, 2018

JONATHAN DAVIS *MA, MSC, MCSI is one of the UK's leading stock market authors and commentators. A qualified professional investor and member of the Chartered Institute for Securities and Investment, he is a senior external adviser at Saunderson House and a non-executive director of the Jupiter UK Growth Trust. His books include* Money Makers, Investing With Anthony Bolton *and* Templeton's Way With Money. *After writing columns for* The Independent *and* Financial Times *for many years, he now writes a private circulation newsletter and is researching two new books. His website is: www.independent-investor.com.*

---

[*]   Go to www.independent-investor.com for more details.

Some personal favourites

DATE	TICKER	NAME	FOCUS	RATIONALE
Ten original holdings				
Jan-17	JEO	Jupiter European Opportunities	Europe	Outstanding fund manager: conviction portfolio.
Jan-17	BGFD	Baillie Gifford Japan Trust	Japan	Consistent outperformer over 30 years.
Jan-17	TRY	TR Property Investment Trust	Property	Property specialist with experienced management.
Jan-17	HSL	Henderson Smaller Companies Inv Trust	UK equities	One of several excellent small-cap trust managers.
Jan-17	WWH	Worldwide Healthcare Trust	Global healthcare	Exposure to global growth sector.
Jan-17	FCSS	Fidelity China Special Situations	China	A play on the rise of China.
Jan-17	CGT	Capital Gearing Trust	Multi-asset fund	Veteran Peter Spiller has outstanding track record.
Jan-17	RCP	RIT Capital Partners	Multi-asset fund	Set up and overseen by Lord Rothschild.
Jan-17	TEM	Templeton Emerging Markets Inv Trust	Emerging markets	One of the first and for many years one of the best emerging market investment trusts.
Jan-17	IIT	Independent Investment Trust	Mainly UK equities	Idiosyncratic portfolio run by experienced Max Ward.

Original portfolio (4 January 2017)

Seed capital: £100,000 – ten roughly equal holdings.

Changes since January 2017

DATE	TICKER	NAME	FOCUS	RATIONALE
New or added to holdings				
Mar-18	HICL	HICL Infrastructure	Infrastructure	Oversold post Carillion collapse; good entry point.
Aug-18	CGT	Capital Gearing Trust	Multi-asset fund	Ultra-defensive holding – markets overbought, so reducing risk.
Aug-18	HGT	Hgcapital Trust	Private equity	Outstanding record and private equity still attractive.
Oct-18	TMPL	Temple Bar Investment Trust	UK equities	Shifting into value, UK large-cap stocks.
Oct-18	SSON	Smithson	Global equities	Bought at IPO – backing Terry Smith's global equity strategy.
Holdings sold				
Aug-18	TEM	Templeton Emerging Markets Inv Trust	Emerging markets	Departure of key fund managers.
Mar-18	IIT	Independent Investment Trust (50%)	Mainly UK equities	Unsustainable premium: director share sales.
Oct-18	IIT	Independent Investment Trust (50%)	Mainly UK equities	Unsustainable premium: director share sales.
Holdings reduced				
Oct-18	HSL	Henderson Smaller Companies Inv Trust	UK equities	Reduced to fund other purchases – still excellent fund manager.

Value at 30 October 2018: £131,249

Includes dividend income of £3,056
13 holdings: largest CGT, JEO, BGFD, TRY

TRUST
BASICS

"INVESTMENT COMPANIES CAN INVEST IN A MUCH WIDER RANGE OF INVESTMENTS THAN OTHER TYPES OF FUND. IN FACT, THEY CAN INVEST IN ALMOST ANYTHING."

INVESTMENT TRUST BASICS

For first-time investors in trusts, here is an overview of investment trusts – what they are and how they invest – from editor JONATHAN DAVIS.

What is an investment trust?

I NVESTMENT TRUSTS, ALSO known as investment companies, are a type of collective investment fund. All types of fund pool the money of a large number of different investors and delegate the investment of their pooled assets, typically to a professional fund manager. The idea is that this enables shareholders in the trust to spread their risks and benefit from the professional skills and economies of scale available to an investment management firm.

Collective funds have been a simple and popular way for individual investors to invest their savings for many years, and investment trusts have shared in that success. Today more than £180bn of savers' assets are invested in investment trusts. The first investment trust was launched as long ago as 1868, so they have a long history. Sales of open-ended funds (unit trusts and OEICs) have grown faster, but investment trust performance has generally been superior.

How do investment trusts differ from unit trusts and open-ended funds?

There are several differences. The most important ones are that shares in investment companies are traded on a stock exchange and are overseen by an independent board of directors, like any other listed company. Shareholders have the right to vote at annual general meetings (AGMs) and vote on the re-election of the directors. Trusts can also, unlike open-ended funds, borrow money in order to enhance returns. Whereas the size of a unit trust rises and falls from day to day, the capital base of an investment trust remains fixed.

What are discounts?

Because shares in investment trusts are traded on a stock exchange, the share price will fluctuate from day to day in response to supply and demand. Sometimes the shares will change hands for less than the net asset value (NAV) of the company. At other times they will change hands for more than the NAV. The difference between the share price and the NAV is calculated as a percentage of the NAV and is called a discount if the share price is below the NAV and a premium if it is above the NAV.

What is gearing?

In investment gearing refers to the ability of an investor to borrow money in an attempt to enhance the returns that flow from his or her investment decisions. If investments rise more rapidly than the cost of the borrowing, this has the effect of producing higher returns. The reverse is also true. Investment trusts typically borrow around 10–20% of their assets, although this figure varies widely from one trust to another.

What are the main advantages of investing in an investment trust?

Because the capital is largely fixed, the managers of an investment trust can buy and sell the trust's investments when they wish to – instead of having to buy and sell simply because money is flowing in or out of the fund, as unit trust managers are required to do. The ability to gear, or use borrowed money, can also potentially produce better returns. The fact that the board of an investment trust is accountable to the shareholders can also be an advantage.

Another advantage is that investment companies can invest in a much wider range of investments than other types of fund. In fact, they can invest in almost anything. Although many of the largest trusts invest in listed stocks and bonds, more specialist sectors, such as renewable energy projects, debt securities, aircraft leasing and infrastructure projects such as schools, have also become much more popular in recent years. Investment trusts offer fund investors a broader choice, in other words.

And what are the disadvantages?

The two main disadvantages are share price volatility and potential loss of liquidity. Because investment trusts can trade at a discount to the value of their assets, an investor who sells at the wrong moment may not receive the full asset value for his shares at that point. The day-to-day value of the investment can also fluctuate more than an equivalent open-ended fund. In the case of more specialist trusts, it may not always be possible to buy or sell shares in a trust at a good price because of a lack of liquidity in the market. Investors need to make sure they understand these features before investing.

How many trusts are there?

According to the industry trade body, the Association of Investment Companies, there are currently around 400 investment trusts with more than £180bn in assets (as at the end of September 2018). They are split between a number of different sectors. The largest trust has approximately £5bn in assets.

How are they regulated?

All investment companies are regulated by the Financial Conduct Authority. So too are the managers the board appoints to manage the trust's investments. Investment trusts are also subject to the Listing Rules of the stock exchange on which they are listed. The board of directors is accountable to shareholders and regulators for the performance of the trust and the appointment of the manager.

How do I invest in an investment trust?

There are a number of different ways. You can buy them directly through a stockbroker, or via an online platform. Some larger investment trusts also have monthly savings schemes where you can transfer a fixed sum every month to the company, which then invests it into its shares on your behalf. If you have a financial adviser, or a portfolio manager, they can arrange the investment for you.

What do investment trusts cost?

As with any share, investors in investment trusts will need to pay brokerage commission when buying or selling shares in an investment trust, and also stamp duty on purchases. The managers appointed by the trust's directors to make its investments charge an annual management fee which is paid automatically, together with dealing and administration costs, out of the trust's assets. These management fees typically range from as little as 0.3% to 2.0% or more of the trust's assets.

What are tax wrappers?

Tax wrappers are schemes which allow individual investors, if they comply with the rules set by the government, to avoid tax on part or all of their investments. The two most important tax wrappers are the Individual Savings Account (or ISA) and the Self-Invested Personal Pension (SIPP). The majority of investment trusts can be held in an ISA or SIPP. There are annual limits on the amounts that can be invested each year (currently £20,000 for an ISA). Venture capital trusts (VCTs) are a specialist type of investment trust which also have a number of tax advantages, reflecting their higher risk.

Where can I find more information?

The best place to start is with the website of the Association of Investment Companies (AIC), which has a lot of basic information, as well as performance and other data. The *Money Makers* website has detailed tables summarising the main features of the most important trusts. Most online broker platforms, such as Hargreaves Lansdown, Fidelity Funds Network and The Share Centre provide factsheets, performance data, charts and other information. Most trusts now have their own websites too.

Independent research sites, such as FE Trustnet, Interactive Investor, Citywire, DigitalLook, Morningstar and periodicals such as the *Financial Times, MoneyWeek, Money Observer* and *Investors Chronicle* also regularly provide updates and recommendations on investment trusts. Citywire has a dedicated online investment trust newsletter. *Investment Trusts* is an independent subscription-only newsletter.

Lastly, head to www.ithb.co.uk for our official handbook website – where a wealth of valuable content and data can be accessed.

SOME USEFUL SOURCES OF INFORMATION

Industry information

The Association of Investment Companies | www.theaic.co.uk

Data, news and research

The Investment Trusts Handbook official website | www.ithb.co.uk

Morningstar | www.morningstar.co.uk

FE Trustnet | www.trustnet.co.uk

Citywire | www. citywire.co.uk

DigitalLook | www.digitallook.com

Platforms

Interactive Investor | www.iii.co.uk

Hargreaves Lansdown | www.hl.co.uk

The Share Centre | www.share.com

Fidelity International | www.fidelity.co.uk

Alliance Trust Savings | www.alliancetrustsavings.co.uk

Sponsored research

Edison | www.edisoninvestmentresearch.com

QuotedData | www.quoteddata.com

Trust Intelligence (Kepler Partners) | www.trustintelligence.co.uk

Specialist publications

Investment Trust Newsletter (McHattie Group) | www.tipsheets.co.uk

Investment Trust Insider (Citywire) | www.citywire.co.uk

Money Observer (regular supplements) | www.moneyobserver.com

Publications that regularly feature investment trusts

Financial Times | www.ft.com

Investors Chronicle | www.investorschronicle.co.uk

MoneyWeek | www.moneyweek.com

"WAITING FOR A BETTER LONG-TERM BUYING OPPORTUNITY COULD MEAN MISSING YEARS OF STEADY RETURNS WITH NO BANK INTEREST TO COMPENSATE."

TAKING THE PLUNGE

Investment trust expert MAX KING *offers advice to private investors on how to benefit from closed-end funds.*

A SIGNIFICANT PROPORTION OF the financial service sector operates on the assumption that savers are neither capable nor willing of looking after their own investments and so need help from the 'experts'. Inevitably this help and all the regulatory encumbrances that accompany it are costly, eating into investment returns.

There is often a strong bias towards sacrificing returns for what the professionals regard as lower risk, but which is, in reality, only a reduction in short-term price volatility.

People are accustomed to taking significant financial decisions such as buying a property or a car without paying for advice so why do they not take the same view of their investments? Taking the DIY plunge requires confidence and nerve, but it soon becomes much easier. The greatest dangers lie in getting carried away by success or despondent about disappointment, in letting personal emotions get in the way of sensible decisions and in being influenced by people whose job it is to entertain, scare or impress you, but not to make you money.

The best advice for all would-be investors was carved on the lintel of the doorway to the temple of the Delphic oracle thousands of years ago: "Know yourself". What works in investment varies from person to person. It takes time, experience and some uncomfortable mistakes to learn the rules which you are best suited to follow.

Long ago I realised that I was happier investing my own money in funds rather than directly in stocks, bonds or private companies, despite the tax advantages of the latter. Many investors successfully combine all three, but investment funds have some distinct advantages so should form at least a significant part of most portfolios.

Firstly, they encompass a broad spread of underlying investments making them less vulnerable to individual stock disasters. Secondly, they are managed by professionals who are better able to keep abreast of corporate developments, their markets and the broader economy. Finally, with the professional manager taking the individual stock decisions, the investor in the fund can leave well alone, just monitoring its performance and keeping an eye out for signs of trouble.

Inevitably, there are costs attached to this, which means that if you pay a wealth manager to invest in funds for you, you are paying twice over. There is little more satisfying than picking a stock market winner based on an insight the professionals have missed – and few more salutary lessons, on the other hand, than seeing the value of an investment wiped out. Investing in funds reduces the incidence of either extreme.

Having decided to invest in funds, your decision to go for investment trusts or other closed-end investment companies rather than unit trusts (now called open-ended investment companies or OEICs) is an easy one. Numerous studies have shown that over all time periods, closed-end funds nearly always outperform comparable open-ended funds in each sub-sector of the market, even when the funds are run side by side by the same manager.

There are several reasons for this: firstly, closed-end funds tend to have lower costs. Secondly, their managers can take advantage of gearing, borrowing for investment when opportunities are attractive and raising cash when they are not. Thirdly, fund managers find it easier to manage a fixed pool of money than a variable one. When an open-ended fund is doing well, new money floods in, forcing the manager to invest even though prices may be unsustainably high. When the market drops, money floods out and managers have to sell into falling prices. The risk of this also constrains the manager's ability to invest in less liquid but perhaps highly attractive opportunities.

Another major advantage is that closed-end funds are governed by a board of non-executive directors who are independent of the management company. The management company may be more interested in growing funds under management and in keeping fees high than in performance, but the directors won't be. If the performance is poor, they can negotiate a fee reduction, a change of manager or a move to another investment company. They will issue new shares only if it is to the advantage of all investors but can also buy in shares if they are cheaply priced. Finally, they scrutinise performance, cross-examine the managers and keep them on their toes far more effectively than happens under the internal governance of OEICs.

Of course, there are some excellent open-ended funds while some interesting segments of financial markets are poorly or not at all served by closed-end funds. On the other hand, there are some areas of the market where open-ended funds with daily liquidity simply don't work because the underlying assets are too illiquid. Examples include funds investing in private equity, property and the fast-growing area of alternative assets.

Alternative assets encompass funds investing in infrastructure, loans, aircraft, alternative energy and a growing list of other tangible or intangible assets. These funds generally offer a high yield, moderate dividend growth and the prospect of some capital appreciation. This makes them attractive relative to cash, corporate or government bonds and their consequent popularity has led to a flood of new issuance in recent years.

After a slow start, equity issuance in 2018 has accelerated but is unlikely to exceed the 2017 record. As last year, little of it is in the conventional equity space. Investors need to be wary of stock issuance whether for new or established funds as it is often opportunistic, driven by current investor fashion and of more benefit to the sponsors and managers than the investors. As shown in recent years by WOODFORD PATIENT CAPITAL and PERSHING SQUARE, the more popular the new issue, the worse the subsequent performance. But wariness should not extend to a full aversion; BAILLIE GIFFORD US has risen 30% since its flotation early in 2018.

Fund flows are far from being one way but good performance and low discounts mean that buybacks and liquidations are diminishing. Funds reach the end of their pre-determined lives, continuation votes are voted down, boards decide that the investment thesis no longer works and so wind up the company, or boards – whether of their own volition or at the instigation of activist shareholders – return capital to investors. In closed-end funds, disappointing performance usually leads to action but in open-ended funds it often leads only to stagnation.

A key indicator of disappointing performance, or merely that the fund's investment focus is unappreciated or out of fashion, is the appearance of a discount to net asset value in the share price. Clearly, this cannot happen in an open-ended fund but in a closed-end fund it reflects an excess of sellers over buyers and it makes the share price somewhat more volatile than the net asset value.

For existing investors, a widening discount is a problem, at least in the short term, as it constitutes a drag on the share price. For boards, it may represent an opportunity to enhance performance by buying in shares cheaply, and for new investors, an opportunity to buy the shares cheaply. However, investors should regard a sizable discount as enhancing the case for purchase but not the main reason for purchase.

Maybe the fund, the sector or the market is currently unpopular but will soon bounce back, with the discount disappearing again, but maybe the discount reflects structural issues which cannot be easily addressed. Many good investment trusts habitually trade at a premium but are still worth buying, while discounts will not necessarily narrow if performance is good. That said, there is a long-term trend towards narrowing discounts so that the sector average is now only 2%.

Getting access to information and good research is becoming less of a problem for private investors. Reports and accounts, interim reports and monthly fact sheets are usually available on websites and these contain details of past performance. Click the professional investor/financial adviser tab on the website rather than the private individual one as the latter gives access to much less information.

Comparative information on investment companies is available on the AIC website, together with helpful information on them generally and links to research notes. These have usually been sponsored and paid for by the companies so are not independent but they are a good source of information – and it's in nobody's interest for the writers of them to be less than honest.

Many funds and management companies go to considerable length and expense in marketing, providing updates from the manager, podcasts, links to media coverage and easy access to statutory information. There is some very good coverage in the financial press – including, I hope, my own modest contributions in *MoneyWeek*. Finally, it is always worth turning up to annual general meetings, even if you can't vote in person. These almost invariably include a presentation by the manager and an opportunity to ask questions either in public or face-to-face afterwards.

Time, however, is not necessarily on the investor's side. Opportunities can be fleeting so there is little time for homework. Waiting for a setback in the share price or the market or for any discount to asset value to widen is nearly always a mug's game. Remember the response of Nathan Rothschild when asked the secret of his success: "I never buy at the low and I always sell too soon." Expect the share price to dip after your purchase and be pleasantly surprised if it doesn't.

As important as picking good funds is putting together a coherent portfolio. This should include core generalist funds as well as specialist thematic funds. It makes sense to invest in technology, smaller companies, emerging markets and so on but not to have too much in any one niche. It's good to have a reasonable level of income but this usually involves some sacrifice of total return. A bird in the hand is more highly valued than two in the bush but you may prefer the latter.

Investing in cheap trusts on wide discounts or in unpopular, undervalued areas of the market can be lucrative but be careful; 'reassuringly expensive' trusts often perform much better than ones that are visibly cheap. Everyone loves a bargain but real value is reflected in long-term prospects while wide discounts reflect serious trouble as often as investor short-sightedness.

The most difficult question of all is when to sell. As Warren Buffett said, "My favourite holding period is forever." You don't need to sell or take some profit in good investments unless you need the cash. I still hold the shares I bought on the flotation of WORLDWIDE HEALTHCARE TRUST at launch in 1995, and have only added to the holding along the way. I was sorely tempted to sell out of BLACKROCK WORLD MINING a few years ago but the share price doubled in the next year. I missed selling out of POLAR CAPITAL TECHNOLOGY in 2000, but can't be sure I would have bought it back lower down.

Many investment sages point out that nobody ever went bust taking a profit. True; they went bust selling winners and reinvesting in losers. Sell if the investment thesis changes or you have made a mistake but don't assume that the departure of a good manager is your cue for an exit. The directors are not fools and will be rigorously looking for a worthy replacement.

But isn't the stock market heading for another meltdown? Isn't this the time to hold cash and wait for the bargains that litter the bottom of a bear market? The Jeremiahs worry that the economic up-cycle and the bull market have continued for longer than normal and must surely die of old age. At the start of 2018, many pundits predicted that the technology sector and the US market would suffer a setback as the rest of the world caught up. In fact, the reverse happened with the technology sector pushing historic US outperformance ever higher.

As always, there are reasons for concern. Monetary policy is being progressively tightened, especially in the US, and bond yields are pushing remorselessly higher. Emerging economies have, at best, hit bumps in the road, at worst are in crisis. Growth in the eurozone has fizzled out and the political tremors are worsening. The UK looks committed to a bungled Brexit.

Against this, the signs of euphoria and complacency which normally mark market peaks are conspicuously absent. Valuations, barely 16 times forward earnings in the US and lower elsewhere, are not stretched by historic standards and look cheap relative to cash or government bonds. There is no sign of the recession which would send earnings tumbling in the US, Europe or almost anywhere else. After the first decade of the new millennium saw two of the four worst equity bear markets in 100 years, caution and nervousness still prevail. A setback, as seen earlier in 2018, is always possible but more than that looks unlikely.

Geopolitical concerns abound but their impact on markets is highly uncertain. Though the long bull market in government bonds is surely over, the constraints on banks that prevent another credit boom and consequent bust look unlikely to be lifted. This should keep inflation and interest rates moderate by historic if not recent standards. Waiting for a better long-term buying opportunity could mean missing years of steady returns with little bank interest to compensate.

Nick Train, manager of FINSBURY GROWTH TRUST, likes to tell investors each year that he is bullish; he points out that markets rise in three years out of four so that is the smart way to bet. Even if next year turns out to be the one in four, don't panic. Buying at the high is not the biggest mistake an investor can make - selling at the low is. In time, markets recover and setbacks become barely visible interruptions of the long trend upwards.

MAX KING *was an investment manager and strategist at Finsbury Asset Management, J O Hambro and Investec Asset Management. He is now an independent writer, with a regular column in* MoneyWeek, *and an adviser with a special interest in investment companies. He is a non-executive director of three trusts and has a number of pro bono commitments.*

TRUSTS AND THE PRIVATE INVESTOR

MARK DAMPIER, *research director at Hargreaves Lansdown, the UK's largest and most influential online platform, says that investment trusts can make good choices for self-directed private investors.*

A LTHOUGH I ONLY own shares in a handful of investment trusts myself, I do sit on the boards of two trusts and have had the chance to observe them from both sides of the fence. In some respects, trusts are an ideal investment vehicle for the DIY investor. Many of the principles of investing in unit trusts and OEICs apply equally to investment trusts, but it is undeniable that they are slightly more complicated and harder to explain, which can be a deterrent.

Not that it seems to be deterring an increasing number of private investors from taking an interest, if our experience at Hargreaves Lansdown is any indication. Of the one million plus clients who now use our platform, around 150,000 hold at least one investment trust. In many cases these may be holdings that they held before they transferred their assets to us, but we are also seeing an increase in transactions as well. As you might expect, the wealthier and more sophisticated the client, the more likely they are to hold an investment trust.

How investment trusts differ from unit trusts is that they are (a) closed-ended and (b) trade on the stock exchange. This means that to start life they need to raise money through a public offering of shares (an IPO, in technical jargon) and this gives them a fixed amount of starting capital. Unlike unit trusts, which create or cancel units at will, they can't grow or reduce their capital anything like as easily as a unit trust can, although it has become easier to do so in recent years.*

The net asset value of an investment trust generally rises and falls in line with the market and the expertise of the fund manager. Consequently, whereas the price of a unit in an open-ended fund should nearly always track its net asset value very closely, this is not so with investment trusts, whose share price is influenced by supply and demand.

If the trust is in fashion, or performance is stonkingly good, the shares may stand at a premium to net asset value. If you buy shares in the trust in these circumstances, you will be paying more than its current assets are worth. If on the other hand demand is poor or non-existent, and performance has been indifferent or worse, the trust's shares may well slip to a discount. The share price will then stand below the net asset value of the trust; now when you buy the shares, you will be paying less than the underlying value of its assets.

Got that? I can assure you that it isn't as complicated as it sounds. In simple terms, buying shares in an investment trust when they are at a discount is broadly a good idea – akin to something being in the January sales. Buying at a premium, however – certainly if it is more than say 3% to 5% – is usually a poor idea in the long run. There are some nuances behind this simple formula, however!

It depends a lot on why the discount has come about. If it is because the fund manager is no good and the trust's performance reflects that, the case for buying is weak, even if the price is a bargain-basement one. But if it is because the whole sector is unfashionable and unloved, it can often be an indication of genuine value and you should investigate it as a potentially contrarian buying opportunity. Even in the first case, it may be worth keeping an eye on the trust as the board of directors always has the power to change the fund manager for someone better. If this happens, you will tend to see the discount start to narrow, though rarely immediately, which may still give you time to get on board.

When a trust is trading at a very large premium, it may be because the fund manager is exceptionally good, or more often it is an indication that the sector the trust invests in has become highly fashionable and therefore at risk of a sudden or dramatic change in sentiment. When a trust is trading at a premium of over 10%, it strongly suggests to me that you should not be buying it. It really has to go some in order to justify that kind of fancy rating. Even top-quality fund managers can see shares in their trust go from a premium to a discount. In

---

* What they can do is issue more shares from time to time, either by buying them in and reissuing them, or making what is called a C-share issue. It is still a more cumbersome process.

those cases, however, they can often go back to a premium again, so keeping a watching brief on the share price and discount can be worthwhile, since from time to time it can throw up attractive opportunities.

One of the best examples of that phenomenon over the last decade has to be the case of FIDELITY CHINA SPECIAL SITUATIONS. The story includes one of the UK's best fund managers, a sector that has drifted dramatically in and out of favour, and the impact of huge media exposure. The trust was born when Anthony Bolton, who had successfully run unit and investment trusts for Fidelity for more than 25 years, decided after a brief retirement that he wanted to move to Hong Kong in order to run a China fund for his old firm.

Given his track record and high profile in the industry, coupled with the popularity of China as an investment theme, the launch of his new investment trust attracted a record amount of money, more than £500m. Initially the shares, issued at £1 each, performed well, and before long were trading at a premium of more than 15% to net asset value – a classic example of a warning bell sounding. What happened next was that the Chinese stock market started to perform less well, and a couple of Mr Bolton's core stock selections turned out badly (one of his companies being accused of fraudulent accounting practices). Given his high profile, these problems inevitably hit the headlines in a big way.

The fund slipped from a premium to a discount and, worse still, the share price fell as far as 70p, well below the issue price of 100p. The media was full of stories that Mr Bolton was unable to transfer his skills from the UK to China. Some gave the impression that he was over the hill and had lost his way. Many private investors expressed their disappointment by selling their holdings at between 70p and 90p a share.

By the time Mr Bolton retired from running the fund three years later, the media was still largely hostile, some going so far as to imply that his time at the helm had been a failure. At that point the shares were still trading on a discount of 14% to net asset value. Yet the net asset value itself had risen 90%, and the trust had handsomely beaten the fund's Chinese benchmark while he was in charge. That hardly justifies being called a failure.

More to the point, he had already laid the seeds of a high-return stock portfolio. Since his retirement the portfolio has continued to blossom under Dale Nicholls, its new manager. Eight years after launch the net asset value had risen to a peak of 300p and the shares, while still trading at a discount, were nearly four times higher than they had been at the earlier low point. Since then, not unsurprisingly, they have fallen back again; any investment in a developing economy such as China will always be more volatile than most.

The point is that those who sold out after the initial disappointing performance missed out on a chance to make a superb gain. This neatly illustrates the fact that you shouldn't believe everything you read in the media. A little time spent in research would have suggested that the move to a big discount was actually a classic buying opportunity, not a sell signal. Given that any equity investment should be seen as a long-term project, it was a mistake for investors to sell after just two years of experience, however disappointing the ride had been.

The other point is that the Fidelity China Special Situations story illustrates how investing in investment trusts can be both more hazardous and more rewarding than investing in an equivalent unit trust, precisely because of the discount/premium cycle. It takes more work and more courage to invest this way – whether that is for you is a matter only you can decide.

Another important difference between investment trusts and unit trusts is that investment trusts can 'gear' their returns in a way that unit trusts cannot. What this means is that, if the board of directors agree, the trust can borrow money in order to boost the amount of capital that they have to invest. If the fund manager can make a greater return with this extra capital than it costs to borrow the money, the trust and its shareholders will be better off. (To continue the driving analogy, they have moved up a gear or two.) The scope for gearing is another factor that makes analysing investment trusts more complicated as the decision to gear or not can make a significant difference to investment performance. It also adds to the risk of share price volatility.

Each trust makes its own decision, adding to the diversity of returns. Some investment trusts never gear, believing that their portfolio is already risky enough. Gearing can work both ways. When interest rates were much higher than they are today, many trusts mistakenly geared up by borrowing at a fixed rate, in some cases locking into permanently high borrowing costs. With the march of time this problem has gradually unwound. In a world of very low interest rates, as we have today, gearing does appear to make more sense. The effect of gearing means that investment trusts in general outperform their unit trust equivalents when prices are rising in a bull market, but are certain to suffer disproportionately the next time the stock market takes a tumble. Care therefore needs to be taken when comparing unit trusts and investment trusts. In the main, the last few years have been good to investment trusts, as they have had the double benefit of narrowing discounts and gearing. It will not always be so.

Should you be put off by the greater complexity of investment trusts? I don't think so, although it does obviously depend on how much time for research you have at your disposal. Potentially investment trusts are a rich feeding ground for the self-directed investor. There are plenty of pricing anomalies you may be able to exploit. One reason is that professional investment institutions, which once were big buyers of investment trusts, have steadily divested their holdings over the years in favour of managing their investments directly. In a market dominated by individual investors, pricing anomalies do not always disappear as quickly as they would do in the professional institutional market.

In my view their complexity means that investment trusts will never be mass market investment vehicles in the same way as unit trusts were designed to be. That is actually a good thing. If they were to become more broadly owned, it would remove most of the advantages that private investors enjoy with them today. The very first investment trust, FOREIGN & COLONIAL, despite its long illustrious history, after more than 150 years is still only capitalised at £3.9bn. By contrast, in the few months after Neil Woodford launched his CF Woodford Equity Income unit trust in 2015, it had attracted more than £6bn of investors' money. The Fundsmith Equity fund, launched in 2010, now has nearly £14bn. Now that is what I call a mass-market product – simple, easy-to-own and simple to monitor. Investment trusts will never be that, but they do have other advantages instead.

You will see in the media that financial firms such as ours are often criticised for not recommending investment trusts more frequently. There is a simple reason for this. Many investment trusts are quite small and that makes it difficult for firms with large numbers of execution-only clients to suggest them. The reason is that buying and selling shares in many investment trusts in size is difficult. The top 20 largest trusts rarely trade more than £2m in a day. This won't matter to a DIY investor who is looking to buy or sell between £1,000 and £10,000 of trust shares, or to advisors who can spread client orders over a period of time. But for a firm like ours with more than a million clients, recommending an investment trust could suddenly swamp the market with buy orders, something that could never happen with a unit trust.

Just suppose we recommended an investment trust through our newsletter. What might happen? The market makers, the professional firms that take and implement buy and sell orders, would see the recommendation and mark up the price of the trust well before the orders came through. Buy orders on any significant scale could not all be fulfilled, leaving clients frustrated. Worse still, the clients might want compensation for failing to have their orders fulfilled, particularly if that price continues to move up. If our advice was to sell, then the problem would be even more acute.[*] This is why platforms offering execution-only services are wary of investment trusts and is why I also think they are generally unsuitable for the broadest mass market.

That does not mean they might not be right for you. If you can get to grips with understanding how investment trusts work, they can be an attractive way to invest. They can still help you even if most of your money is going into open-ended funds. I own shares in RIT CAPITAL, for example, in part because there is no open-ended alternative. The premium or discount at which investment trusts trade can also be extremely useful in seeing how investor sentiment is moving. It can be a good indicator of whether a particular sector or market is on the cheap or expensive side. If many more trusts are trading at premiums, it may be flagging up that we are near to a market top, while large discounts across a number of sectors suggest the opposite.

Having recently been appointed a non-executive director of two trusts, INVESCO INCOME GROWTH and JUPITER EMERGING AND FRONTIER INCOME, it has given me an opportunity to invest some more money in the trust sector. As a shareholder it is generally a good sign if directors of a trust have a significant personal holding in the shares. It means that their interests will be closely aligned with yours. If the investment manager is doing a poor job, the board has every incentive to try and improve the situation. Now that I am approaching retirement, I have a particular interest in generating income and I am keen to ensure that the trusts where I am on the board are making sufficiently good returns to sustain and ideally grow their dividend-generating capacity into the future.

Thirty years ago it was often said that the boards of many investment trusts were ineffectual – I recall that my boss, Peter Hargreaves, was fairly outspoken on that subject (as well as on many others). As a generalisation it had some merit. It is no accident that some of the oldest surviving trusts started life as investment vehicles for the wealth of successful merchants. They and their successors had every incentive to keep the management of their trusts on their toes, but that was far from being a universal situation, especially once the big investment management firms moved in on the action. Too often it was the external managers rather than the directors who called the shots.

Since then the quality and calibre of non-executive directors has improved by leaps and bounds. Of course, as one of the new breed of directors myself, you may be thinking: 'He would say that, wouldn't he?' and you would be right.

---

[*] See Peter Spiller's observation on page 177.

"INVESTMENT TRUSTS ARE A RICH FEEDING GROUND FOR THE SELF-DIRECTED INVESTOR. THERE ARE POTENTIALLY PLENTY OF PRICING ANOMALIES YOU MAY BE ABLE TO EXPLOIT."

But I genuinely believe that it is nevertheless true. I would not have dreamt of agreeing to do the job unless I thought that I could make a difference. Whether or not you agree, it can only be good that more private investors are now making the effort to understand how trusts operate and to understand which boards and managers are really doing their best for shareholders.

> MARK DAMPIER *has been head of research at Hargreaves Lansdown, the UK's largest independent stockbroking firm, since 1998. He has been in the financial services industry for more than 30 years, initially working as an advisor helping individual clients to invest their money. He has become one of the best-known and most widely quoted figures in the fund management industry. He wrote a regular column in the* Independent *on funds and markets for many years, and regularly comments in the national press and on broadcast media.* Effective Investing *(Harriman House, 2015) was his first book (and, he swears, definitely his last!).*

PRINCIPLES AND PORTFOLIO PICKS

Investment trust expert JOHN BARON *gives an insight as to the factors to be considered when harnessing the potential of investment trusts – starting with an overview of some key investment principles, before suggesting how best to capitalise on investment trusts' unique characteristics. The piece finishes with an example of a real portfolio – one of eight such portfolios run in real time by John's company on the website www.johnbaronportfolios.co.uk.*

KEY INVESTMENT PRINCIPLES

RECOGNISING WHEN SENTIMENT and fundamentals diverge is the prerequisite of a good investment decision. This is no easy task but it can be doubly rewarding when it comes to investment trusts. Their closed-ended structure, ability to gear and lower cost – all of which help to account for their superior performance over unit trusts – in combination present a wealth of opportunities to informed investors.

FIRST STEPS

The prerequisite for any successful investment journey is clarity regarding financial goals and risk tolerances.

Equities produce better returns than bonds and cash over the long term, which accounts for why most investment journeys should start with a bias in their favour. But the path is rarely a smooth one. Market corrections are part of the investment cycle, which is one reason it is important to adopt a long-term investment approach.

It is also why it is important, at the outset, to ensure that portfolio construction truly reflects financial objectives, risk tolerances and time horizons. Other factors to consider can include currency exposure and income requirements.

Choosing the appropriate benchmark and timescale to monitor a portfolio's performance can also help in attaining financial goals. However, never let benchmarks dictate how a portfolio is constructed – they cannot be beaten if they are simply copied.

Furthermore, in pursuing a long-term approach, it should be remembered any meaningful performance comparisons require a minimum five-year period. At best, over the short term, benchmarks should be seen as a reference point for monitoring a portfolio's progress.

TIME IN THE MARKET IS BETTER THAN MARKET TIMING

Clarity about those factors influencing portfolio construction can then be complemented by the application of tried-and-tested investment principles.

Once invested, it is important to remain so provided such an approach continues to reflect investment objectives and risk profiles. Many investors try to time the markets, and a few are successful. But for most long-term investors it is better to remain invested.

The evidence certainly suggests that the longer one is invested, the more likely a positive return will result. Recent research from Fidelity has shown that over the period 1980–2012, investing in global equities for 12 years or more produced no negative returns. By comparison, five-year periods produced a 16% chance of a negative return.

Furthermore, recent figures from Fidelity quantify the cost of missing good days. Over the ten years to 31 August 2018 (from 15 September 2008), the FTSE All-Share produced a total return of 121.85%. Had the ten best days been missed, the return would have fallen to 21.37%. Missing the best 20 days would have resulted in a negative return of -15.16%.

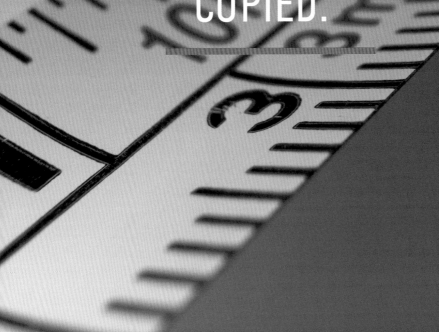

"NEVER LET BENCHMARKS DICTATE HOW A PORTFOLIO IS CONSTRUCTED – THEY CANNOT BE BEATEN IF THEY ARE SIMPLY COPIED."

In terms of pounds and pence, sticking with the market over this period would have resulted in an investment of £1,000 turning into £2,218.46. Missing the best ten days would have seen this return fall to £1,213.72, while missing the 20 days would have seen the return fall to £848.36 – both being significant differences.

Bad luck aside, evidence further suggests some investors have a tendency to buy after markets have risen, and to sell when they have fallen – and then to remain in cash for too long, and so exacerbate the original mistake at additional cost. This is easy to criticise with the benefit of hindsight, but difficult to counter at the time.

Yet it is precisely at such times that markets tend to bounce – when the bad news is in the price. The single best trading day during the past 10–15 years was on 24 November 2008 when, in the middle of the financial fallout from a ballooning credit crisis, the UK equity market rose 9.2%.

Barclays has also highlighted that investors who tried to time the market from 1992 to 2009 were down 20% compared to those who had simply stuck with it. So ignore the noise and chatter. The evidence suggests that time in the market is better than market timing.

DO NOT SPEND YOUR DIVIDENDS UNLESS YOU HAVE TO

There is another reason to stay invested – to enable the full harvesting of dividends, which account for the vast majority of market returns over time.

The Wharton professor Jeremy Siegel calculated in 2005 that, over the previous 130 years, 97% of the total return from stocks came from re-invested dividends. $1,000 invested in 1871 would have been worth $243,386 by 2003. Had dividends been reinvested, the figure rises to $7,947,930!

The message is clear: do not spend your dividends unless you have to. Re-investing dividends is the best way of growing wealth over time – and to fully access these dividends, investors must stay invested.

However, there is a downside to this rule: the longer in the market, the greater the chance of a market setback. This can be particularly galling if one is about to realise financial objectives – especially after a long investment journey. A couple of strategies, pursued together, can help to mitigate the effect of such an event: diversification and regular rebalancing.

DIVERSIFY TO REDUCE PORTFOLIO RISK

The aim of diversification during an investment journey is to reduce portfolio risk by investing in 'uncorrelated' assets – asset classes that tend not to move in the same direction over the same period.

Equities, bonds, commercial property, renewable energy, commodities, infrastructure, 'real assets' (such as gold, vintage cars, rare stamps or fine wine) and cash are, to varying degrees, examples. While few investments will escape a major market correction unscathed, adequate diversification away from equities will help to reduce losses.

This important investment discipline is often overlooked – especially in rising markets. There are no fixed rules as to the pace and extent of diversification. An investor's risk profile, time horizon, income requirement and investment objectives are key factors. But there are some general principles used by my company when seeking portfolio diversification.

When starting an investment journey, it makes sense to focus on equities because of their superior returns and because longer time horizons usually allow greater tolerance when it comes to volatility. However, as time passes, our portfolios become increasingly diversified.

One of the key asset classes we employ is bonds – mostly corporate, as we are wary of government debt. Bonds usually act as a good counterweight to equities. Each is driven by different economic forces – as such, when one rises in price, the other usually falls.

Other less-correlated assets also become increasingly evident as the investment journey unfolds including commercial property, renewable energy, infrastructure and commodities. The open 'Diversification' page on my company's website (www.johnbaronportfolios.co.uk) describes this journey in some detail.

How many asset classes should one employ? The answer, as with investment generally, is to keep it simple – five or six usually suffice. Too much diversification also increases costs.

Meanwhile, in addition to assisting with diversification, such asset classes can also help portfolios produce a higher and, importantly, still growing income – with the website's most diversified, and therefore defensive, portfolio yielding 5.5% at the time of writing.

REBALANCE – BUT NOT TOO FREQUENTLY

Rebalancing is one of the first principles of investing, and yet it is often overlooked. The concept is simple. A 60/40 equity/bond split may, because equities perform well, turn into a 70/30 split. Evidence suggests it pays to rebalance provided one's risk profile and investment objectives remain in sync.

Forbes has shown that $10,000 invested by way of a 60/40 split in the US in 1985, and rebalanced annually, would have been worth $97,000 in 2010 – whereas an unbalanced portfolio would have been worth $89,000. However, again, do not rebalance too frequently. Keep it simple and dealing costs low – for most investors, an annual rebalance is usually sufficient depending on how markets have performed.

Furthermore, it is sometimes forgotten that as much attention should be given to the process of liquidation, as investment timelines approach, as to the running of the portfolio. A gradual and balanced liquidation as the finishing line approaches is one method. There are others. Peace of mind should never be underestimated, particularly at the end of a long investment journey!

BE PREPARED TO BE A CONTRARIAN

In addition to tried-and-tested investment principles, insights borne of experience often assist when managing a portfolio. As touched on previously, in very large part, recognising when sentiment and fundamentals diverge is the prerequisite of a good investment decision.

Sir John Templeton once said: "It is impossible to produce superior performance unless you do something different from the majority." A successful investor must be prepared to be a contrarian.

A benchmark can only be beaten when deviating from it – and it should be remembered this may involve periods of underperformance. However, such an approach should be tempered with a commitment to an over-arching strategy otherwise portfolios can be unduly buffeted by prevailing winds.

While acknowledging that a portfolio can contain a blend of strategies and preferences at any point in time, the overall objective of the portfolios run on my company's website is to hold good quality companies, and to focus on what we know (the company and fund manager) rather than on what we have little regard for (market and economic forecasts).

SEIZE THE ADVANTAGE!

Some have suggested it can be difficult for private investors to compete with the professional fund managers – the pension funds, banks, investment houses and wealth managers. Yet the private investor has many advantages – the most important being time.

Many professional fund managers are trapped in a three-monthly cycle of trustee or actuary meetings, which encourages the shadowing of benchmarks. Private investors are free of this restraint. They can afford to take a longer-term view, and therefore stand a better chance of recognising mispricing and being able to capitalise from it.

To benefit from this natural advantage, patience is a virtue. Unloved assets can take time to come right, but then more than make up for lost time when they do. Warren Buffett once said: "The stock market is a device for transferring money from the impatient to the patient."

KEEP IT SIMPLE

Meanwhile, it is important investors remember that investment is best kept simple to succeed. Complexity usually adds cost, risks confusion and hinders performance. When diversifying a portfolio, do not use too many different asset classes – the simpler, the better. But perhaps more importantly, investors should avoid overly complicated investments – especially if they are difficult to understand.

Accordingly, the website portfolios avoid hedge funds, absolute return funds, structured products, multi-manager funds and any other investment vehicle or approach which has high costs and poor transparency. Many tend not to live up to expectations.

In keeping investment simple, investors are also keeping costs down. Picking complicated or expensive products can easily cost a further 1.5% a year in fees – this may not sound a lot, but it can materially affect the final sum achieved.

For example, a £100-a-month investment producing a 5% annual return will be worth £150,000 after 40 years. But if a further 1.5% in annual costs is deducted, the final portfolio value will fall to just £105,000. This is a significant difference.

BE SCEPTICAL OF 'EXPERT' FORECASTS

At the very least, question consensus forecasts. The renowned economist J. K. Galbraith once said: "Pundits forecast not because they know, but because they are asked." Successful investors tend to be sceptical – after all, one of the prerequisites of being a contrarian is to question the consensus.

In doing so, such investors are asking what could go wrong – their default position is not to own a stock. This contrasts with those fund managers who are more focused on short-term relative performance for fear of being left behind by their peers – scepticism takes a back seat as non-ownership is less of a possibility.

EMBRACE EINSTEIN'S EIGHTH WONDER

One should never ignore the magic of compounding – allegedly described by Einstein as the eighth wonder of the world. Compounding is the regular reinvesting of interest or dividends to the original sum invested, with the effect of creating higher total returns (capital plus income) over time. Time and a decent rate of return allow the concept to fully bloom.

£100 a month invested over 20 years and producing a 3% annual total return will produce a final portfolio value of £32,912. If the rate increases to 7.5% (the average long-term return for US equities) then the final figure rises to £135,587.

The challenge is to achieve the higher rate of return. Again, the message is clear – start early, be patient and try not to interrupt the magic of compounding.

HARNESSING THE POTENTIAL OF INVESTMENT TRUSTS

This section explains some of the key characteristics of investment trusts and the factors to consider when best harnessing their potential.

WHY INVESTMENT TRUSTS?

Having acknowledged the importance of some basic investment principles and insights, most portfolios would benefit from using investment trusts when seeking stock market gains. There are a host of reasons why they are superb investment vehicles, of which four are highlighted below.

1. Better performance

Despite not being well known or understood, investment trusts have in general a superior performance record when compared to their better-known cousins – unit trusts and OEICs. Furthermore, investment trusts have on average beaten most of the global investment benchmarks whether delineated by region or country – unlike unit trusts and OEICs.

Part of the reason is they charge lower fees. Another reason is that, like other public companies, trusts can borrow to buy more assets. Historically, this has benefitted their share prices in part because markets have risen and because of good fund management.

2. Better suited

Another reason is because of their structure. Unlike unit trusts or OEICs, investment trusts are 'closed-ended' – they have a fixed number of shares like other public companies such as M&S and BP. But instead of specialising in clothes or oil, they specialise in financial assets.

Accordingly, investment trusts can take a long-term view of their assets as they are not subject to the same relentless flow of monies, both in and out, as are open-ended funds. As such, they are better suited for certain types of investment – particularly those less liquid.

The closure of a number of high-profile property open-ended funds during the mistaken rush to the door following the EU referendum result reminded investors of the importance of this point. Investing in private equity or smaller companies requires a similar approach. Their very nature and therefore at times illiquidity requires the incubator effect best offered by the closed-ended structure of investment trusts.

3. Income friendly

One of the most attractive features of investment trusts is their ability to retain a percentage of their dividends and income received from holdings in the underlying portfolio, in any one year. This surplus cash is called the 'revenue reserve'.

This reserve can be used to supplement dividends going forward to ensure a smooth progression even if, within allowances, the underlying economy and/ or markets go through a rough patch and the underlying portfolio sees some dividend cuts.

Such a feature is important to those investors seeking income. Knowing the extent of reserves – the term usually expressed as the number of months it could independently maintain the existing dividend – is a key factor when selecting investment trusts.

There is a growing tendency for investment trusts to dip into their capital reserves in order to supplement or pay a dividend. Provided dividends are not over-promised, this is a welcome development as it better allows income investors to access hitherto low-yielding but high-growth sectors.

4. Corporate governance

Investment trusts tend to display greater transparency in the interests of shareholders. Like other public companies, investment trusts have an independent board of directors whose brief is to represent shareholders – and these directors have teeth!

Shareholders themselves have significant powers. They can vote on issues such as changes to investment policy and the appointment of directors. They can attend shareholder meetings and ask questions about the running of the trust – it is, after all, their company.

This leads to a much more transparent environment. It is difficult for investment trusts to hide in the shadows because of mediocre performance, certainly when compared to lacklustre unit trusts. They are on notice – reward shareholders or questions will be asked.

HARNESSING THE POTENTIAL

So how should an investor best harness their potential? There are various aspects to consider.

The discount

The most talked about is the level of discount. As with other public companies, the share price of an investment trust does not always reflect the value of its assets – and usually stands at a discount.

This allows investors to take advantage of movements in the discount, which is often influenced by swings in sentiment towards the investment and/or underlying portfolio, and by the extent of debt which can contribute to volatility. Such is the investor's opportunity.

As a first step to those new to investment trusts:

- The ideal purchase is when a trust, run by a fund manager with a good long-term track record, stands at a wider-than-average discount – possibly because of a market wobble or the sector and/or manager is out of favour.

- It is usually wise to ignore the short-term noise and focus on the long term. Should sentiment improve, the investor benefits from both the underlying assets rising in price and the discount narrowing.

- The ideal sale is when the discount has narrowed considerably and other factors may suggest caution, such as a change in manager or outlook for the underlying markets.

- Should a portfolio's assets fall in price, investors can further suffer from a widening of the discount.

Needless to say, there are many nuances to such trades.

Other factors

While the level of discount is important, so are many other factors when valuing an investment trust, including:

- the reputation of the manager AND investment house

- the underlying strategy

- the outlook for the sector, region or theme

- the valuation of the trust relative to its peer group *and* the underlying portfolio relative to its universe

- the level of management and any performance fees

- the effect on the NAV of the level, cost and duration of any debt

- the extent of dividend cover and revenue reserves (particularly if investing for income)

- the capital structure of the company

- the nature of any discount control mechanism.

"IT IS DIFFICULT FOR INVESTMENT TRUSTS TO HIDE IN THE SHADOWS BECAUSE OF MEDIOCRE PERFORMANCE, CERTAINLY WHEN COMPARED TO LACKLUSTRE UNIT TRUSTS. THEY ARE ON NOTICE – REWARD SHAREHOLDERS OR QUESTIONS WILL BE ASKED."

Some are particularly important. The outlook for the asset class in question, together with the manager's long-term record, underlying strategy and due diligence processes, are key. Meanwhile, net asset values can be materially affected by the extent and cost of debt – something which is not always picked up by discount calculations.

The valuation of the underlying portfolio relative to its universe is a further key determinant which is also often underestimated – again, the attractions of a seemingly wide discount can be somewhat negated if the portfolio is expensive without good reason.

Conversations and long-term holdings

Some of these factors are best explored through conversations with the trusts' managers themselves. When it comes to the website's portfolios, we rarely make an initial investment without first speaking to the manager – whether they be located in Tokyo, California or elsewhere.

Changes regarding most of the above factors can, to varying degrees, influence swings in sentiment and thereby the discount and prices. Capitalising on such swings can be profitable in the short term.

However, it should be remembered that such an approach is best employed when initiating a long-term holding. Choosing and sticking with a trust which has a good track record often results in better long-term performance than constantly dealing in an attempt to capture short-term price movements.

A 'REAL' PORTFOLIO – BY WAY OF ILLUSTRATION

Words and theories are best illustrated when put into action. The rest of the chapter introduces and sets in context a 'real' portfolio by way of example.

THE WEBSITE WWW.JOHNBARONPORTFOLIOS.CO.UK

By way of background, the above website is owned by my company Equi Ltd. It reports on the progress of eight 'real' investment trust portfolios (i.e. they exist in fact), including same-day details of trades, new portfolio weightings and yields. Members are informed by email whenever the website is updated.

The portfolios pursue a range of strategies, risk and income profiles – with yields of up to 5.5%. And while never complacent, they have performed well relative to their respective benchmarks – the website's Performance page has more details.

Meanwhile, the website's other open pages (Rationale, Diversification and FAQs) provide an indication of the 'rhythm' of the website, and the Subscription page gives details of our seven-day free trial allowing access to the closed pages.

INTRODUCING THE SUMMER PORTFOLIO

Background

By way of illustrating some of the investment principles and insights touched upon earlier in the chapter, it may be helpful to highlight some of the salient characteristics of the website's Summer portfolio.

I have also been reporting on this portfolio in my monthly column to readers of the *Investors Chronicle* since 2009, where it is called the 'Growth' portfolio. While briefly explaining portfolio changes over the previous month, the column very much focuses on specific investment themes and principles.

Within this context, it is important to understand the portfolio's remit. Five of the website's eight portfolios pursue an investment journey over time and, to reflect their position in the journey, four are named after the seasons.

Spring's objective is capital growth courtesy of a portfolio comprised almost entirely of equities. As time passes, the bond and 'other' less-correlated assets increase both to generate a higher income and to help diversify holdings away from equities and so protect past gains. The Winter portfolio finishes with a yield of 5.5% at the time of writing.

Subsequent to the establishment of these four portfolios, the government introduced the Lifetime ISA (LISA). The website's LISA portfolio helps smaller portfolios capitalise on these proposals – and therefore, because of its equity bias but smaller number of holdings, could be seen as a precursor to the Spring portfolio.

The website's Diversification page provides an overview as to the pace and extent to which these five portfolios' exposure to various asset classes builds over time. The page also highlights the nature of the 'other' asset types used by the portfolios in their quest to diversify away from equities, including cash weightings.

Breakdown

Below is a breakdown of the portfolio at the time of writing. All holdings and weightings are rounded to the nearest 0.5%, and are updated on the day a portfolio change is made (as detailed on the website's Dealing page) and at the end of each month. The relevant stock market 'ticker' code is also given next to each holding.

Breakdown of Summer portfolio to 11 October 2018

BONDS	
New City High Yield (NCYF)	6.0%
UK SHARES	
Finsbury Growth & Income Trust (FGT)	5.5%
BlackRock Throgmorton Trust (THRG)	5.0%
Standard Life Equity Inc Trust (SLET)	4.5%
Henderson Smaller Companies (HSL)	4.5%
Standard Life Smaller Cos (SLS)	4.0%
Oryx International Growth Fund (OIG)	3.5%
Montanaro UK Smaller Cos (MTU)	3.0%
INTERNATIONAL SHARES	
JPMorgan Japan Smaller Cos (JPS)	5.5%
North American Income Trust (NAIT)	4.0%
Henderson Far East Income (HFEL)	4.0%
Edinburgh Worldwide (EWI)	3.5%
Templeton Emerging Markets (TEM)	3.0%
Atlantis Japan Growth Fund (AJG)	2.0%
THEMES	
Herald (HRI)	4.5%
HICL Infrastructure Company (HICL)	4.0%
Allianz Technology Trust (ATT)	4.0%

International Biotechnology Trust (IBT)	4.0%
Bluefield Solar Income Fund (BSIF)	3.5%
Standard Life Private Equity Tst (SLPE)	3.0%
BlackRock Commodities Income (BRCI)	3.0%
COMMERCIAL PROPERTY	
Standard Life Property Income (SLI)	4.5%
TR Property (TRY)	3.0%
CASH	**8.5%**
TOTAL	**100%**

Performance record of the Summer portfolio to 30 September 2018

	2018	2017	2016	2015	2014	2015	2012	2011	2010	2009
SUMMER	4.3	19.7	9.0	13.9	8.0	27.6	20.1	-12.2	28.4	32.5
MSCI WMA GROWTH	3.8	11.3	19.3	3.0	6.5	17.0	10.0	-2.3	13.4	19.8

Equities

As seen from the portfolio breakdown, the Summer portfolio is predominantly invested in equities. This reflects its position in the investment journey. Having progressed through the early stages of that journey courtesy of the equity-focused LISA and Spring portfolios, which contain a small but growing number of holdings, this portfolio has a larger number of holdings still to help further reduce individual company risk while also allowing a modicum of diversification.

Within this exposure, the portfolio's remit allows it to continue with the LISA and Spring's focus on smaller companies – particularly at home, but also abroad. The sector's long-term record is impressive. Indeed, it is generally accepted that a small-cap focus is one of the more reliable investment strategies in generating higher returns than the wider market over time.

And smaller companies should continue to do well given the present environment of low interest rates and moderate, if rising, inflation; an economy that continues to defy the sceptics; the sector's attractive rating relative to earnings outlook; and favourable long-term trends including the advance of technology – which is disproportionately helping many of these companies disrupt established markets. The future is indeed small.

However, it is important to remember the importance of maintaining portfolio balance relative to objectives. While positive about smaller companies, the Summer portfolio also maintains exposure to trusts which focus on larger companies and which have a good track record regarding dividend growth – again, both at home and abroad.

This balance changes as the investment journey progresses, with larger companies assuming greater importance in part because they usually exhibit less volatility in extreme market conditions. In such conditions, investment trust discounts can also widen more. Such is the importance of taking the long view, which the Summer portfolio is well able to do.

Like most portfolios, this one has its geographical preferences. At the time of writing, it favours the UK and Japan.

Brexit has once again cast a long shadow over the UK market. International comparisons suggest valuations are at the bottom end of a range of metrics – and not having been this cheap for a number of decades. Just as the portfolios benefited from defying consensus and increasing their domestic exposure over the referendum period, they are hoping to again benefit from the sceptics presently holding sway.

Meanwhile, Japan's economy is in a sweet spot and the equity market's rating looks attractive. In addition, the government is encouraging companies to be more shareholder-friendly and domestic institutions to reverse their traditional underweighting of domestic equities. Improving fundamentals, cautious sentiment and attractive market valuations usually furnish healthy returns for the patient investor.

The website's portfolios have also benefited from exposure to individual themes – the Summer portfolio is a particular example, given its place in the investment journey and therefore latitude regarding the number of holdings.

In this increasingly globalised and fast-developing world, it is of value to maintain exposure to sectors at the cutting edge of such progress via fund managers who specialise in these areas. Technology and biotechnology are two examples.

Investment opportunities abound when it comes to the technology sector. This is a golden age of innovation, in which the frontier of what was thought possible is advancing all the time. Advances are introducing more and more solutions to problems and/or are lowering costs on a sustainable basis – and this is helping to create sector cycles which are more independent of the general economy.

Our confidence in these developments is illustrated by the extent to which the website's portfolios have benefited from pursuing these themes. We should also not underestimate the potential of smaller companies within the sector addressing key challenges, such as cyber security. Technology is one of the few sectors which continues to grow its share of the global economy as businesses and consumers continue to invest and spend.

It is a similar story with biotechnology. The DNA discoveries of Watson and Crick in 1953, the sequencing of the human genome, and the falling cost yet increased power of computer technology, has transformed the potential and efficacy of biotech companies. Visits to the Francis Crick Institute confirm one's faith in the potential of science.

Indeed, an emphasis on innovation and the reinvestment of cash flow into R&D has created a virtuous circle. No wonder the large pharmaceutical companies are circling. And because the sector keeps delivering strong earnings growth, at the time of writing it is still attractively rated relative to the S&P 500 despite growing at a faster pace.

Diversification and income

The expansion in the number of the Summer portfolio's holdings also allows us to start introducing other asset classes both to help protect past gains and to generate a higher income – a process which is continued in a meaningful way by the Autumn and Winter portfolios. The introduction of these other asset classes, though modest, should not detract from the fact that this is very much a 'growth' portfolio.

Just as 'income' portfolios should, where requirements allow, contain 'growth' investments to help maintain a balanced approach (the Autumn portfolio is an example), so should growth portfolios contain some exposure to income-producing assets other than direct equities. This acknowledges that the majority of total returns over time come from re-invested dividends, as highlighted previously in the chapter.

Such an approach also acknowledges that, while one of the key investment principles pursued by the eight portfolios is to remain invested, equity market setbacks will occur. A modicum of cash and exposure to less-correlated assets better enables volatility to become a friend to those with a long-term strategy – particularly growth investors.

Therefore, bonds, infrastructure, renewable energy, commodities and commercial property all make an appearance – together with a reasonable emphasis on cash, the best 'diversifier' of all. In combination, and while accepting few investments will totally escape a major market setback, such investments should help to cushion the blow whenever they occur. They also provide a resource when taking advantage of weaker equity prices.

Meanwhile, such investments can also help portfolios achieve higher income levels, which are often welcome during the latter stages of an investment journey. What is more, they can help portfolios keep up with inflation when generating that income. And there is currently some concern that economies globally may be seeing the early stages of an inflationary pick-up.

History suggests this alone should not cause equities too much trouble. However, the market is also aware that too much inflation or a sudden pick-up (notwithstanding a possible inverted yield-curve) could provide a headwind for equities.

Where appropriate, therefore, portfolios should have some exposure to asset classes where underlying prices have a near-defined correlation with inflation – such as infrastructure and renewable energy. They should also include other asset classes where the correlation is less-defined but inflation nevertheless has usually provided a tailwind – including commodities and commercial property.

The extent of this exposure will depend on the portfolio remit – minimal during the early stages of an investment journey, increasing measurably as that journey unfolds. The website portfolios, including the Summer portfolio, recognise Warren Buffett's suggestion that wide diversification is only used when investors do not understand what they are doing. The portfolios employ five to six asset classes. Too many would also increase costs.

AN HOLISTIC APPROACH

It is hoped this section of the chapter has allowed an insight as to the thinking behind the portfolio's construction. The portfolio embraces a number of theme and sector preferences, but is very cognisant of the need to pursue an overarching strategy over the long-term which reflects its position in the wider investment journey.

However, it is worth repeating that enthusiasm for any particular investment should always be tempered with the need to maintain portfolio balance. No matter how compelling the investment case, an overly aggressive tilt towards a particular holding or theme not only raises the portfolio's risk profile but can unduly affect long-term performance should it go wrong. Resisting temptation is just as important as backing conviction – within balance!

It should also be remembered that the portfolio's preferences, and indeed changes, should not be seen in isolation. An 'holistic' view is taken of each of the eight portfolios. Changes need to be judged as part of the whole, rather than simply a list of individual trades, as their management reflects a range of factors and metrics – some in competition, and some not.

For example, in addition to attributing great store to our conversations with the individual investment trust fund managers – particularly when initiating a position – the Summer portfolio also balances a range of financial metrics between holdings when deciding on the final combination.

These include the extent of revenue reserves to ensure sound foundations when it comes to the portfolio's overall capacity for income growth, a comparison of company debt levels and the 'see-through' effect on discounts on a fair value basis to maintain an element of robustness should markets turn down, and ensuring a balance when it comes to both company discounts and underlying portfolio valuations to reduce portfolio vulnerability should prevailing market investment approaches change.

JOHN BARON *is one of the UK's leading experts on investment trusts, a regular columnist and speaker at investment seminars, and author of* The Financial Times Guide to Investment Trusts *(a further edition is due shortly). He is a director of Equi Ltd which owns the website www.johnbaronportfolios.co.uk.*

The website reports on the progress of eight real investment trust portfolios, including same-day details of trades, new portfolio weightings and yields. The portfolios pursue a range of strategies and income objectives, and enjoy an enviable track record relative to their benchmarks.

John has used investment trusts in a private and professional capacity for over 35 years. After university and the Army, he ran a broad range of investment portfolios as a director of both Henderson Private Clients and then Rothschild Asset Management. Since leaving the City, he has also helped charities monitor their fund managers.

INVESTING IN ALTERNATIVES

Investment trust expert MAX KING *provides an introduction to the fast-growing alternative assets sector.*

A CCORDING TO SIMON Elliott of brokers Winterflood, only 55% of the investment funds sector is accounted for by funds investing in equities. The remaining 45% – and the fastest-growing part of the sector – is accounted for by funds investing in 'alternatives' to equities. This growth has been fuelled by an insatiable demand for high-yielding funds. Charles Cade of brokers Numis estimates that alternatives accounted for 65% of issuance in the sector in the first half of 2018, after 76% in 2017 and 85% in 2016.

Lumping all these investment companies into a single category risks masking the diversity of where and how they look to make money. The alternatives sector comprises a number of quite different vehicles. The main sub-sectors are property, debt instruments, infrastructure, private equity and renewable energy. In addition, there are specialised companies that invest in niche areas such as aircraft leasing and music rights.

There is clearly no lack of choice – and, if this rate of expansion continues, alternatives will soon be dominating the whole investment funds sector. Some caution is advisable. History shows that issuance of new trusts is often the result of investment fashion as much as of soberly-judged opportunity, and fashions tend not to last. None of the Lloyds insurance vehicles launched in the 1990s, for example, now survive; they turned into insurance companies before being taken over. The listed hedge funds or funds-of-funds which were popular a decade ago are steadily disappearing as a result of disappointing returns. A number of the income funds launched in the last ten years have recently hit pockets of turbulence or worse.

Nor are alternatives a new phenomenon. Many of the UK's oldest investment trusts, including FOREIGN & COLONIAL (dating back 150 years) and SCOTTISH MORTGAGE, were not founded to invest in equities but in fixed-interest securities. They switched from 'alternatives' to equities along the way and would probably not have survived if they hadn't. Living up to the promises and projections in terms of investor returns made at launch has always been a challenge, especially as the world changes.

There is little doubt what has powered growth in recent years: it is the search for income. Negligible interest rates and very low bond yields have compelled investors to look elsewhere for income to live off. Equity income has been popular, but investors have also sought assets which have a low correlation to equities (which are assumed to be volatile and risky). The one thing you can rely on is that whatever investors want at any one time, the eggheads in the City will always provide.

The core problem for investors is that when interest rates and bond yields are low, a fund that pays a yield of 5, 6 or 7% without drawing on capital has to be taking a lot more risk. Its investment return before costs will be even higher unless returns are leveraged up with debt, which is risky in itself. Unfortunately, there appears to be a behavioural flaw in the thinking of many investors; they assume that the yield, if not its upward progression, is guaranteed. This is certainly the belief of a fund's managers and sponsors, but it doesn't always work out that way. If things go wrong, or the rules and regulations change, the danger is that a promised payout will be cut.

Investors also forget the old adage that 'a bird in the hand is worth two in the bush'. Turned around, it means that income now will be coming at the expense of rather more capital growth in the future. Ideally, investors would maximise total return (income plus capital gain) and be happy to draw on capital to supplement income, or to invest in funds that do that. But the Victorian belief that spending capital is a sure path to the poorhouse persists.

The reality is that income certainly matters, but so does income growth – and it is the latter which is the driver of future capital gains. With capital gains subject to taxation only on sale, and even then only outside SIPPs and ISAs, investors should logically be happy to sacrifice some income for capital growth. But that is not the way fund flows into the trust sector have been running. So before investing in an alternative asset fund paying a generous yield in a world of 2% inflation, it is important to understand where the yield is coming from and how sustainable it is.

Gauging the risk of a particular trust is not always easy. Be extra careful when there is an assurance, implicit or explicit, that a trust is somehow 'low risk'. Don't automatically assume that those managing or promoting a fund fully understand the risks behind their business models.

At the top end of the risk spectrum sit listed **private equity funds**. Many of these funds came a cropper in the financial crisis due to leverage and excess commitments to new investment. Some were panicked into distress fund-raisings, some went into wind-ups and some ploughed on. Since then, they have, with one or two exceptions, prospered, benefiting from good underlying performance and narrowing discounts to asset value. In some cases, returns have been spectacular. Although the private equity cycle is now well advanced, there could well be more to go for. According to the *Financial Times*, the private equity industry worldwide has $2trn of uncommitted funds to invest, meaning it's a better time to sell assets than to acquire, but managers have learned their lesson and become more cautious than in previous cycles.

The sector divides into direct investors and funds which invest in a range of unlisted private equity funds. The higher visibility of the investments of the former generally results in lower discounts to net asset value. Asset values are usually conservative and out of date so value is often better than it appears. Funds such as 3I, HG CAPITAL and (until Edward Bramson seized control) ELECTRA, which consistently sold assets at large premiums to book value, demonstrated this. They have been the ones to own, while those that sold at poor prices or failed to sell, such as CANDOVER and BETTER CAPITAL, have been poor investments despite being available on enticingly wide discounts.

Funds-of-funds suffer from an extra layer of fees, but they provide a diversity of managers and access to funds otherwise not available to most private investors. An average return of 75% over five years is impressive and suggests that the double-digit discounts at which all five of them have been recently trading may be unwarranted.

The private equity sector is shrinking with seven funds in 'managed wind-up' and one (Candover) already gone, compared with just one recent arrival – APAX GLOBAL ALPHA in 2015 – with the highest yield in the sector at over 6%. The trusts in managed wind-up offer a guarantee that their discounts will disappear as the date of wind-up approaches, but they cannot guarantee how well their investments will perform, not least because the remnants of their portfolios – the 'orphan assets' they have not so far managed to sell – are likely to be among their least successful investments.

Also investing in private equity are a few specialist funds such as RIVERSTONE ENERGY and SYNCONA. Riverstone invests in oil and gas fracking prospects and projects in North America; given how strong oil prices have been in 2018, the flat performance of its shares and the persistent double-digit discount to net asset value must count as disappointing. That could not be said of Syncona, which is transitioning from what was an innovative investment fund-of-funds to a UK-focused investor in early-stage life-science companies. Its shares have risen 50% in a year.

One of the most remarkable fund issues of 2017 was the raising of over $500m of new money by CATCO, which uses its capital for catastrophe reinsurance. This was in the wake of a disastrous sequence of hurricanes and fires which halved its share price. Presumably, investors who subscribed for the new shares blamed the weather rather than the managers. Catco has always been open about the risks in its business, but investors may have been lulled by the high yield paid in good times.

Possibly less risky but also promising high yields are the £720m BIOPHARMA CREDIT fund, which is investing in the debt, secured on royalties, of life sciences companies, and HIPGNOSIS SONGS, which recently raised £200m to buy catalogues of old songs. Whether either fund has secured the right deals to deliver the promised returns over time remains to be seen.

Infrastructure funds have come in for considerable criticism not so much for taking excess risks as for being overpaid for the supposedly low risks of privately-financed investment in the UK public sector. The high returns have largely been the result of falling bond yields which made the income streams from these projects, secured for up to 30 years, especially attractive, but the politicians who were once desperate for this investment don't like being made fools of. Dire retribution is threatened, regardless of signed contracts.

This type of project accounts for a diminishing proportion of the infrastructure funds, who are busily diversifying into private sector and international projects while showing much less interest in dealing with the UK's public sector. The long-term consequence will be a drying up of private capital for public investment in the UK but that is not a concern for investors. The recent bid for JOHN LAING INFRASTRUCTURE suggests that all the political scare did was create a long-term buying opportunity.

Less controversial are the infrastructure funds which focus on renewable energy. Investors have steadily overcome their initial suspicion of these new vehicles, meaning that they all now trade at premiums to asset value. The suspicion

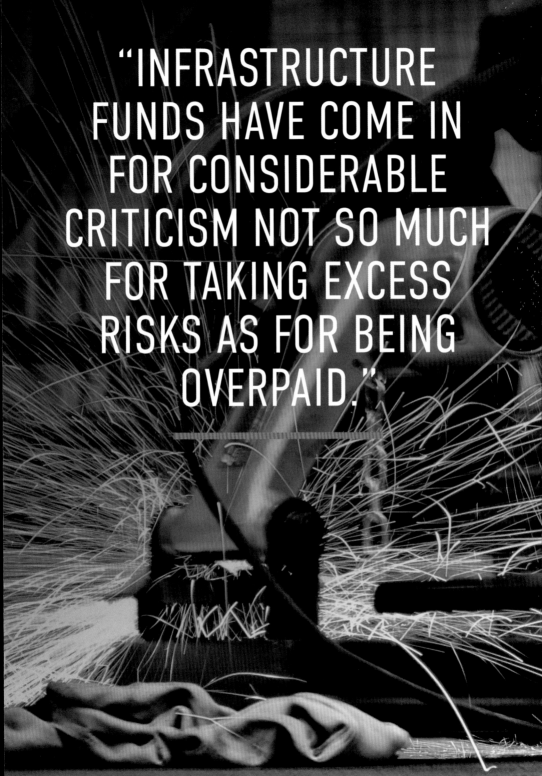

was based on the large subsidies that solar and wind power have needed to be economic, the cost of which is passed on to consumers in higher prices. But so long as the consumers haven't noticed, or aren't bothered by this hidden tax, then the politicians, hungry for green credentials, don't seem to care. Anyway, the subsidies on new projects are falling as efficiency improves.

The **funds investing in debt** are returning to the roots of the investment trust sector. Some funds invest in fixed-rate debt, some in floating, some in long-dated income streams, some in short-dated. There are funds investing in high-yield bonds, distressed debt, unlisted loans and regulatory capital for banks. There is no emerging market debt fund, but that is probably not for want of trying. The diversity reflects the ebb and flow of sentiment towards fixed-interest securities and trends within the market rather than a campaign to cover all bases.

They all offer attractive yields but the opportunity for income growth and hence capital gains comes largely from retained earnings, which in turn depends on the skill of the managers. Yields are higher when the income is secured on specified assets rather than on the company as a whole, justified by the struggles of some funds whose security turned out to be faulty. Is the 6.9% yield on UK MORTGAGES too good to be true or a bargain? Its manager, TWENTYFOUR ASSET MANAGEMENT, is well regarded and manages two other listed income funds but the security of residential property could prove illusory in a recession.

The financial crisis and subsequent restrictions on banks led to a surge of interest in peer-to-peer lending. The result, inevitably, was the launch of six funds with £2.5bn of capital, appealing to those who prefer a collective vehicle to direct lending. Unfortunately, we will not know how good their credit control is until we have the next economic downturn. One fund has already had to make material provisions for credit losses, but it could be a mistake to be too cynical. The quality of credit control in commercial banks has always been low, particularly for smaller commercial and personal loans handled out of bank branches. These funds, helped by more modern IT, may be able to do it better.

Once upon a time, you had to be really rich to invest in **hedge funds**. These funds, discreetly boasting stellar returns, were famous for their exorbitant fees (a 2% annual management charge, plus 20% of all returns) and the doors were firmly closed to latecomers. Their managers billed themselves as the cleverest whizz-kids on earth, enjoyed rock-star status and even greater riches. Then the exclusive clubs opened their doors to everyone, the mystique vanished and it was downhill all the way in terms of performance. Some managers were too rich to bother to come into work anymore, some lost their 'magic' touch, some failed to recognise that market conditions no longer favoured the strategies they had followed.

As a result the ranks of the investment trusts following hedge fund strategies grow thinner every year, but it may be too soon to write the sector off. After several years of dull returns, BREVAN HOWARD posted a 9% return in the second quarter for its macro fund and 5% for its global fund, as some big bets on bond spreads in the eurozone paid off. Bill Ackman's PERSHING SQUARE, whose fortunes peaked when it listed in Amsterdam in 2014, appears to have returned to earlier form after three down years. It still trades at a 23% discount to asset value.

The final segment of the alternative funds sector is **property**. Confusingly, many property companies are structured and taxed as 'real estate investment trusts' (REITs) but are not included in the investment trust sector. As a generalisation, property funds seeking to harvest the income from property ownership are in, while development companies which focus on adding value to their holdings are out – but this is not a hard-and-fast rule. SEGRO (out) has owned the Slough Trading Estate for 100 years, while F&C COMMERCIAL PROPERTY TRUST (in) has been a fairly active developer. Many conventional property companies also pay generous dividends and trade on large discounts to net asset value. They may prove a better investment than some of the property investment companies with high yields, which have less potential for added value and trade above net asset value.

Among the specialist funds, PHP (not in the sector), MEDICX (in) and ASSURA (not in) all own doctors' surgeries on long-term leases which have been guaranteed by the NHS, making them comparable to infrastructure funds. IMPACT and TARGET HEALTHCARE do the same with care homes, but without the guarantee. EMPIRIC and GCP STUDENT LIVING own and rent out student accommodation, supported by partner universities but so does UNITE, the first operator in the area, which is a company rather than a fund. There are funds owning and leasing supermarkets, logistics warehouses and social housing; all of them promise a high and rising income, but with very different risks. The NHS will always pay for doctors' surgeries, but care home operators can (and do) go broke. Well-located logistics warehouses may be irreplaceable, but student accommodation may not be. Housing associations should have access to cheaper finance than they can get through a listed fund.

Other property funds invest more broadly, focusing on generating an attractive and rising income from higher-yielding properties, plus an element of added value. Five funds invest in Europe of which two are focused on logistics warehouses and one on flats in Berlin, but the best exposure to Europe (62% with the rest in the UK) comes from TR PROPERTY, the only investment trust which invests in property company equities (93% of the portfolio) rather than directly into bricks and mortar (7%).

In conclusion, alternative funds are a disparate lot and investors need to tread carefully, thinking objectively about the sources of income and risk. High income does not come without risk and income growth is important for capital returns. Issuance is often a reverse indicator of future performance, so it is usually better to wait until they have proven themselves before investing. But alternative funds can also provide excellent opportunities. The shares of private equity fund-of-funds PANTHEON INTERNATIONAL, which sunk low in 2008, have since multiplied tenfold in value. There may be hidden jewels in what investors throw out, but all that sparkles is not gold.

MAX KING *was an investment manager and strategist at Finsbury Asset Management, J O Hambro and Investec Asset Management. He is now an independent writer, with a regular column in* MoneyWeek, *and an adviser with a special interest in investment companies. He is a non-executive director of two trusts.*

USING TRUSTS TO DIVERSIFY

||||||||||||||||||||||||||||||||||||||||||||||||||||||||||||||||||||||||

Industry expert ALEX DENNY *explains how using investment trust with different styles and objectives can reduce the risk of investing in financial markets.*

W HEN IT COMES to investing, the benefits of diversification are clearly significant. Most investors will be familiar with how spreading your investments across a range of areas can reduce your exposure to single-asset risk. Putting all your investment eggs in one basket can offer extraordinary returns (think Apple in 2003 or Tencent in 2017), but it can also lead to catastrophic losses (Northern Rock in 2008 or Volkswagen in 2015).

Indeed, some investment fads can be so volatile that they can produce incredible returns and losses in quick succession. Bitcoin returned over 1,000% in 2017 and peaked at around $19,000 in December that year but is down more than 50% since then at the time of writing.

Everyone likes to see their money grow, but there is no risk-free way of guaranteeing these enormous returns. Turning £20 into £10,000 is the kind of gamble you might be willing to take. Turning £10,000 at the time of investment into just £5,000 at the time of redemption is exactly the kind of mistake we all like to avoid.

As a general rule, the majority of investors will therefore look to build a core portfolio of diversified mainstream investments and savings, split across the three broad areas: cash, bonds and equities. This core portfolio will be held through bank accounts and, probably, funds.

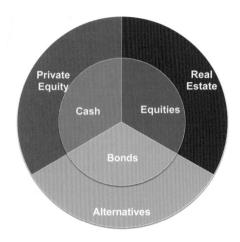

Source: Fidelity International, 31 August 2018 – indicative chart only.

The allocation or balance between these different assets will vary between different people and are clearly dependent on individual objectives and circumstances – what you are saving for, your age, appetite for risk and capacity for loss.

These core asset classes are exactly that – core. They form a central component of how our financial systems and markets work, but as such they may all suffer from related setbacks. For example, an equity investor may feel confident that holding a range of index trackers provides sufficient diversification. However, in today's global economy, major inflexion points can occur simultaneously across all markets – just see returns over the second half of 2008 or mid-2015 for a painful reminder.

"SOME INVESTMENT FADS CAN BE SO VOLATILE THAT THEY PRODUCE INCREDIBLE RETURNS AND LOSSES IN QUICK SUCCESSION."

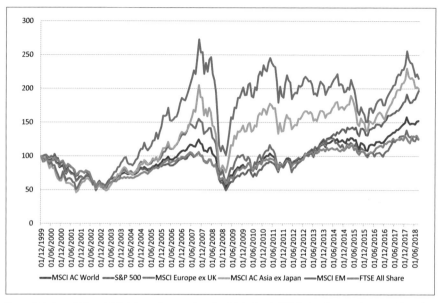

Source: Datasteam, 31 August 2018. Index performance based on total return in GBP. Past performance is not a guide to the future.

INVESTMENT TRUSTS AND AVOIDING SYSTEMATIC RISK

There are lots of reasons why global equity markets can follow each other; markets are not rational in the short term. Driven by sentiment, a sell-off in one market can often trigger a downturn in another. The trick to avoiding this sort of risk – and achieve genuine diversification – is to access parts of the market which are not well-covered or represented in an existing core portfolio.

Investment trusts are nearly all actively managed and have structural advantages which allow them to avoid these systemic risk pitfalls. Their capital structure – with a fixed number of shares and no flows of cash in or out from investors – allows them to invest in much smaller, illiquid companies which fall outside of mainstream indices (or have negligible correlation to them).

They also have the ability to invest in companies before they are even listed, as well as alternative areas like real estate or long-term infrastructure projects which aren't well represented in mainstream funds due to liquidity issues.

There are investment trusts which specialise and focus on investing in these kinds of areas – smaller companies trusts, private equity and venture capital trusts, real estate investment trusts – as well as trusts which follow relatively mainstream markets from the core of your portfolio while adding these non-core elements as well.

Take FIDELITY ASIAN VALUES PLC as an example. It is an actively managed investment trust whose manager, Nitin Bajaj, focuses on buying good, well-run businesses, which are undervalued by much of the market. This often entails buying companies that operate in sectors which are very unfashionable – but can still be very profitable and therefore create good investment returns. This contrarian investment style, by its nature, leads the manager towards industries and companies that do not make up a significant proportion of the regional market index.

In fact, at the time of writing, the company has 99.5% its portfolio held in stocks and assets which do not form part of the MSCI AC Asia ex Japan Index, which is most commonly used as a comparator for funds investing in the region. This figure is called 'active money' and gives an indication of how much, or how little, a fund or company's portfolio differs from a typical benchmark tracker.

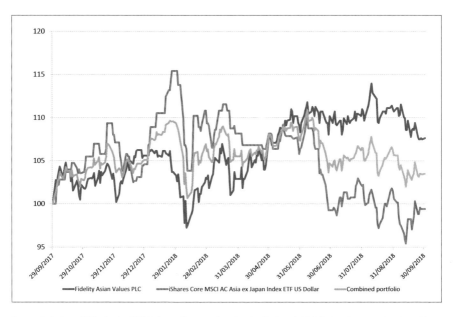

Source: Datasteam, 30 September 2018. Index performance based on total return in GBP. Past performance is not a guide to the future.

With a near total lack of stock overlap, it stands to reason that a holding in the company is not closely correlated with the index over the shorter term – though it still benefits from the long-term structural tailwinds which support the region's growth. It is therefore possible to complement a mainstream equity portfolio with this type of investment to take out the impacts of short-term trends, smoothing returns and improving risk-adjusted returns at a portfolio level (although diluting out some of the additional absolute returns that may be added by active management).

Another example, in developed markets, is the recent launch of BAILLIE GIFFORD US GROWTH TRUST which eschews simple index returns by having authority to invest up to 50% of its portfolio in companies which are not listed at all. Whether you're looking to gain exposure to specific alternative asset classes or you are attracted to the ability to invest in small or unlisted companies, these examples highlight to good effect the benefits that investment trusts can offer when held as part of a well-diversified portfolio.

ALEX DENNY is the head of investment trusts at Fidelity International. This article does not constitute investment advice and should not be used as the basis of any investment decision. Past performance is not a reliable indicator of future results.

———————————————

GOOD DIRECTORS ARE ESSENTIAL

GEORGE KERSHAW, *partner of the headhunting firm Trust Associates, which specialises in recruiting investment trust directors, explains what makes a good board member and why it matters so much.*

What makes a good trust director?

George Kershaw: When trust boards approach us to help them identify new non-executive directors, they will usually have a formal or informal skills matrix. This will show us which specialist skills they would like to find in successful candidates to complement the existing skill base.

In addition, there are two important overlays.

The first is the character of candidates. Specialist skills can be hired in to cover particular issues. The non-executive director is expected to be able to put areas of specialisation into the broader context of the governance of the trust. To do this, he or she must be blessed with a wide breadth of view as well as good judgement and the charm to put across ideas and suggestions constructively. It is important that they are easy to work with.

We also observe that many successful candidates have impressive academic credentials. Sweeping generalities have many exceptions but it is probably fair to say that investment company directors require more cerebral excellence than entrepreneurial talent.

The second important overlay is diversity, in particular, gender diversity. When we started in 2002, only 6% of non-executive directors were women and a significant proportion of trusts had male-only boards. It happens that 30% of successful candidates appointed through ourselves have been women. That figure has been constant over many years, as well as more recent periods. The installed base of directors is indeed now rising towards that figure and has reached 22% as of July 2018.

Has the process by which they are chosen changed in recent years?

GK: Considerably more care and time is required of boards in appointing new non-executive directors than in years gone by. Much of this increase has followed from the introduction and refinement of governance codes. The Code of Corporate Governance (the Code) is advisory and relies on the principle of 'comply or explain', meaning that boards must give an explanation if they fail to follow the code's guidelines. (This is in contrast to the Listing Rules that trusts agree to when they list their shares on the stock exchange, which are compulsory.)

Many boards have tended to opt for 'explain' rather than 'comply' to justify the continuation of their previous practices, but the increased focus on governance has meant that boards feel under increasing pressure to comply. The relevance of this to the process of new appointments is that the code enjoins boards to recruit new directors through open advertising or the use of search consultants (principle number 20 in the 2018 Code).

This has now been in place for several years and there are now very few boards which ignore this principle. In practice, very few boards opt to advertise new non-executive director searches as they do not have an HR department to process applications. One of the more obvious changes to the recruitment process has therefore been that search consultants are involved in the vast majority of appointments.

Many boards are more clear about which set of skills are required in the successful candidate as a result of two other governance-oriented practices which are increasingly commonplace: an 'away day', when all the directors can meet to discuss the progress of the trust without the distraction of normal board business, and a formal process of board evaluation which is now required at least once a year.

As the use of search consultants has increased, we notice that most boards now require more than one firm to pitch for the business. In the early days, it was much less common for consultants to be appointed through a competitive tender process.

Is the quality of directors higher than it was?

GK: The make up of boards has changed significantly in the 21st century, largely as a result of changes to the Code – in particular, the requirement to use headhunters and the encouragement to limit the terms of non-executive director to nine years. Shareholders, and their voting agencies, also more frequently vote against the reappointment of directors. Boards were accused, before these changes, of being 'pale, male and stale' and 'clubby'.

There was a certain amount of justification to this comment. 'Pale' is still an accusation with some validity, although that is beginning to change as more non-gender diversity feeds into the areas from which candidates are selected. 'Male' is much less of an issue in even quite recent history as the installed base of women directors rises towards 30%. For search consultants, it remains quite a challenge as the percentage of women who have achieved senior positions is lagging so far behind the percentage of women appointed to boards.

Successful candidates have mostly achieved very senior status by the time they are likely to be considered for board positions. However, the percentage of women who occupy the senior roles in fund management, for example, is still only about 7%. In consequence, successful women can be in strong demand and some individuals can receive a large number of approaches. One impressive woman, who we were fortunate to put onto a board shortly after she retired from her executive career, subsequently received no fewer than 40 invitations to join boards as a non-executive director.

'Stale' is also much less of an issue now, largely because of the Code. The 2018 version of the Code, due to take effect in 2019, has clear language discouraging chairmen in particular from serving more than nine years.

The use of headhunters has significantly increased the pool of potential candidates and reduced clubbiness. The average number of directorships per director has now fallen to 1.3. Interestingly, the figure for women is 1.6.

The use of search consultants has also tended to reduce the influence of their investment managers, who were frequently previously invited to act as search consultants. This, together with the more strongly worded Code and the increased propensity of shareholders (and their voting agencies) to vote against director re-appointments, has resulted in increased director independence from the investment manager.

Most observers would agree that these changes have resulted in higher quality directors who are paid more than they used to be and take their duties more seriously. It is also fair to point out that some investment managers have not welcomed these changes and accuse boards of focusing too much on corporate governance and not enough on encouraging, and assisting, the managers to produce good returns.

What in practice are the board's most important functions?

GK: The role of directors of investment companies has changed over the years. If you travel back far enough in time, investment company boards met monthly to make changes to the trust's portfolio as they thought fit. The role of the manager was to implement the changes which the board had decided upon and to deal with the administration of the company. The key skill of the directors was therefore experience of fund management. These trusts were almost all 'self-managed'. Over several decades, this has changed markedly in both respects.

There are only a small number of self-managed investment trusts where the investment management company is owned by the shareholders of the investment trust. Alliance Trust is the largest such example today. The board of such a trust is therefore responsible for the running of the company through the executives of that company. The board is ultimately responsible for all issues such as the remuneration of the senior executives and corporate acquisitions and disposals.

The vast majority of trusts, however, have no employees and deal only with third-party organisations. The role of the boards of such companies is to represent the interests of their shareholders who also are their customers (unlike most PLCs). Most directors of investment trusts would agree that the most important function of the boards of these companies is to check that the portfolio of the trust is run in accordance with the mandate which has been explained to shareholders and that it is run as well and as cost effectively as is possible.

Where the performance of any of the third-party suppliers is deficient, it is the board's role to assess the alternatives and, if necessary, to cancel their existing contract and to select an alternative supplier.

Many boards nowadays will have an 'away day' to address these high-level responsibilities as well to consider any significant changes that they should consider in terms of mandate or investment manager or, indeed, whether they should consider winding up the trust and returning the proceeds to shareholders.

If we look at the board's functions through the eyes of a search consultant, we can focus on the skills criteria that we are instructed to use. In each case, boards are after individuals who know which questions to ask and are able to understand whether the answers are satisfactory. The criterion which arises most is experience of fund management; not perhaps surprising as these are investment trusts. Boards are after an understanding of what the selected fund manager is trying to achieve and, ultimately, whether they are doing it well enough. Should the board need to interview alternative managers, experience of fund management is essential.

The next criterion which arises frequently is a requirement for an accounting qualification, normally in the case of a search for an audit chair. While not a Code requirement, most boards do now require the chair of audit to have such a qualification. This might easily be added to one of the other skillsets which the board has identified as being desirable, such as investment management as per above.

Less frequent, but still quite common, is some experience of marketing. One of the ways of minimising the discount of share price to net asset value is to ensure that the shares of the trust are being well marketed.

An understanding of the technical aspects of investment trusts is also quite a frequent criterion. This has become more valued as the range of tools available to trust boards has increased.

For example, boards now have considerable powers to influence the level of discount at which the share price stands to the NAV. Discount control mechanisms (DCMs) are now commonplace and varied.

Where can boards go wrong?

GK: Unfortunately there are many examples of boards which have failed to use these powers wisely. A typical example is of one trust which invested globally. It had had a share buyback programme in place which had kept the discount at less than 10%. The chairmanship changed as a matter of course and after his departure the board lacked both technical investment trust knowledge and anyone with marketing experience. The buyback program was abandoned without putting anything else in its place.

Predictably the discount widened and that prompted a hedge fund to pick up a significant holding in the shares at a discount of 15%. The board then reversed its decision and brought back the hedge fund's holding at a discount of 5%. The hedge fund consequently made a profit at the expense of shareholders and questions were rightly asked about the quality of corporate governance. Other international trusts have made similar mistakes, which all stem from a failure to understand why the discount was so large and how to address the problem in a way which benefited the current shareholders.

There are many examples of boards which have made unwise decisions because they did not have appropriate experience. One notable example occurred when the board of an investment trust with a mandate to invest in Japan, despairing of the Japanese market's continual weakness, switched the investment manager and gave the mandate to a company running hedge funds.

This might have been a smart move, but for two factors. The first was that the switch was made just as the Japanese market rose by nearly 10%. The new manager had hedged the portfolio against further falls. Shareholders therefore were both sorely disappointed and surprised that they had gained nothing from the rise in the market.

The second was a serious lapse of good governance by the board. They had failed to canvass the views of shareholders. Had they done so, they would have known that most shareholders held the shares because they wanted some limited exposure to the Japanese market. It was not the role of the board in this instance to take a view about whether Japan was a good place to invest without asking shareholders and explaining very clearly how they had changed the mandate of the trust.

It is not surprising that the consequence was that the board was replaced on a shareholder vote and the trust was liquidated. These examples are now quite rare because directors take their duties more seriously and the standard of corporate governance has significantly improved across the board. Investors who buy shares in investment trusts are entitled to think that the board is acting in their interest and should rightly be held to account if they are not, as increasingly they are.

GEORGE KERSHAW co-founded Trust Associates in 2002 and focuses principally on finding non-executive directors for investment companies, as well as a variety of other projects, including research into shareholder attitudes, share buybacks and corporate governance. He led the CSFB investment trust team from 1996 to 2000.

HOW TO
RATE A TRUST

TONY YOUSEFIAN, *investment trust research analyst at FundCalibre, explains what he and his colleagues are looking for when assigning a rating to an investment trust.*

I NVESTMENT COMPANIES HAVE been around for 150 years. Having survived a number of world wars and stock market crashes, the longevity of many surviving trusts is impressive. A key advantage is that the closed-ended structure of investment trusts lends itself to taking a long-term view on investment opportunities.

According to the Association of Investment Companies (AIC), more than half of investment companies have had the same fund manager at their helm for more than a decade.[*] Almost a quarter (23%) have had at least one of their managers in charge for 20 years or more. Considering how many of us in other roles change jobs far more regularly, this is a surprisingly large percentage.

Another important factor is that investment companies have a board of independent directors who oversee the management of the investment company and provide continuity. With 400 trusts from which to choose, selecting the right one for your portfolio can be daunting, especially if you are also looking at the 3,000 rival open-ended funds on offer. But there is help at hand. Fund researchers have the job of narrowing down the choices on offer to a more manageable number of funds they think are the best. It is notable, however, that only a few conduct research into investment trusts. FundCalibre is one.

---

[*]   The Association of Investment Companies, 19 June 2018.

THE WAY WE ANALYSE INVESTMENT TRUSTS

For us the longevity of the manager is vitally important. This is because we like fund managers, whether they run open-ended or closed-ended vehicles, with long-term track records. It means they have experience of investing through all the different stages of a stock market and economic cycle, not just the good times. You should never confuse a bull market with investment genius, as the old saying goes.

The longer the track record, the more effectively we can analyse the value they add. To do this we use a proprietary screening tool, AlphaQuest, that we have developed ourselves. AlphaQuest is the first stage in our fund-rating process. It is a quantitative screening system that analyses the past performance of a trust. We do this by stripping out the impact of market movements to identify the returns which can be directly attributable to its fund manager. It then measures the consistency of the returns that the fund manager produces, to help us determine whether they are genuinely skilled or merely have been lucky.

While many screening systems that analyse past performance exist, we think ours is unique because we attempt to calculate the probability of future performance as well. Our process is designed to produce an estimate of how likely a manager is to continue to deliver superior returns over the next 12 months. Managers must have a track record of at least three years to be considered and a trust must pass this screen before we will proceed further with our research. The best trusts on our analysis are then eligible to be given an 'Elite Rating'.

Our process has three steps:

1. We start by running the AlphaQuest screen, as outlined previously. Only trusts that pass this screen and whose managers we think show a high probability of continuing to deliver over the next 12 months will proceed to the next step of our process.

2. Those fund managers who pass the AlphaQuest test are then subjected to further detailed qualitative analysis. Our experienced research team will interview the fund manager face-to-face, on at least one occasion, to better understand and assess how their investment process and style gives them an edge over other managers.

3. Once this analysis has been completed, the research will be subject to peer group review within our team. Only then will those trusts, whose managers we believe to be the most skilful, be awarded our Elite Rating.

Only a minority of trusts – about 30% of the total – survive the initial screening. To qualify we need to be able to assign at least a 60% probability to a trust's next-year outperformance. Those trusts which qualify typically register between a 60% and 90% probability of achieving that; we have never found a fund that has more than a 90% probability of success, underlining that there are no sure things in investment. Since we launched the process three years ago, the open-ended funds we have given a top rating to have subsequently outperformed. We don't yet have similar figures for the investment trust process, so it is too early to demonstrate a similar result.

We do want the Elite Rating to be a badge you can believe in. Unlike some agencies, we don't run a tiered system of funds rated 1 to 5, or gold, silver and bronze. Our philosophy is simple: a fund is either good enough to qualify for a rating or it's not. This means that we rate far fewer funds than our competitors (around 150 compared with more than 400), leaving investors with a much more manageable number from which to choose.

OTHER FACTORS TO CONSIDER

While the aim of an investment trust is the same as an open-ended fund, they do have other elements which we also need to analyse when considering them for a rating. From the perspective of a buy-and-hold investor, perhaps the biggest difference is that inflows and outflows of money do not affect the investment strategy of a trust. If a lot of investors all want to redeem their money from an open-ended fund all at once, it can result in the manager being forced to sell positions he still likes purely in order to meet those redemptions.

This is not the case for investment trusts. That is what makes the closed-ended structure particularly suitable for specialist trusts holding assets that cannot be easily or swiftly bought and sold (such as property, private equity or very small companies). Trust managers don't have to sell their holdings in order to release money back to investors looking to liquidate their investments.

(a) Discounts and premiums

Because an investment trust has a limited number of shares, the price of its shares is affected not only by the performance of the underlying investments, but by investor sentiment towards the trust itself. Sometimes in life, the more popular something is, the more expensive it is, and vice versa. The same is true for investment trusts. The price you pay for a share is based on the value of the investments held in the trust, but also on how popular the shares are.

If the shares are seen as desirable, their price may rise to a premium to its net asset value (NAV). If they are not so appealing, their price may fall to a discount. This means you are sometimes paying a bit more for a share in a trust or could be getting a 'bargain'.

In theory, a discount allows you to buy into a trust for less than the value of the assets, but it is important to think about why it is trading at a discount. Is it a function of short-term negative sentiment or has the market identified a fundamental flaw with the investment strategy or fund manager? It isn't a given that the discount will narrow or become a premium. Some trusts trade perpetually below NAV. You have to look at the history of the premium and discount.

Likewise, while you need to be wary of paying more for the value of the assets than you need to, some sectors have a long history of trading at a premium. Infrastructure trusts are a good example. This sector has traded on a premium, as high as 20% on occasion, for the best part of a decade or more. You need to look at a trust's historic pricing to understand whether or not it is offering good value or not.

(b) Gearing

Another key element of an investment trust is gearing. This is the mechanism by which an investment trust borrows money in order to make extra investments, with the aim of achieving a return greater than the cost of the borrowing. For example, take an investment trust with a value of £100m. If the stock market is rising, the fund manager may see lots of potential opportunities. But to take maximum advantage, he or she might want to invest an extra £20m. Having borrowed the money to do this, the investment trust is now '20% geared'.

In the right hands and benign market conditions, having the flexibility to allocate more capital to favoured assets can pay off. When the market gathers momentum, an investment trust with gearing gets an extra boost. In 2012, for example, when Shinzo Abe became prime minister of Japan promising wholesale reform, the Japanese stock market was seen as attractive by many investors. Abe's reforms (later coined 'Abenomics') held out the promise that he could finally lift the Japanese economy out of its longstanding deflation. Investors who were convinced that, after many years of false dawns, the reforms would have the desired effect were highly rewarded if they invested in a geared Japanese equity trust, such as the BAILLIE GIFFORD JAPAN TRUST. While the average open-ended Japanese equity fund returned 130.23% from 5 December 2012 to 1 October 2018, and the average

Japanese equity investment trust returned 233%, Baillie Gifford Japan Trust (which is Elite Rated by FundCalibre) returned 332%.* On the flip side, of course, gearing can also exacerbate losses and volatility during times of market stress.

So investors need to look closely at how much gearing is permitted in an individual trust (a matter for the board to approve), how much gearing the manager tends to use and how and when they use it. This will differ from trust to trust. Investors need to be comfortable with the level of gearing, as it can increase the risk significantly.

(c) Dividend capacity

Saving for a rainy day is an idiom we all know well. Investment trusts can do this too, via a 'revenue reserve'. When an economy is strong, dividend payments from companies can be a great source of regular income for investors, but how reliable they are can be anyone's guess. As we have seen in the past, companies can cut their dividend payments or stop them altogether if times are bad and they don't have the spare cash to return to their shareholders.

During the good times, investment trusts can retain up to 15% of the dividends they receive in a pot called the revenue reserve. The more dividends the fund manager generates from a trust's investments, the more money can be put aside for the future. During the bad times, when dividends become scarce, the fund manager can tap into the reserve and boost what might otherwise be a lacklustre dividend to produce a more steady return for the trust's shareholders.

This stability of income can be especially attractive to investors who need a consistent income, such as those who need the income from their investments to help pay monthly bills. The AIC has a list of investment company 'dividend heroes (see page 260) – trusts that have increased their dividends for at least 20 consecutive years. The dividend hero with the longest history, CITY OF LONDON INVESTMENT TRUST, managed by Job Curtis from Janus Henderson for the past 26 years, is one of our Elite Rated trusts. It has increased its dividend in each of the past 52 years. During that time Job has dipped into his revenue reserve on seven occasions to maintain its income-paying track record.

(d) The independence of the board

Last, but by no means least, accountability is becoming increasingly important to investors. Having an independent board is one way of ensuring this accountability. An independent board will be made up of a group of experienced professionals whose job is to support the fund manager, but also have a responsibility to identify if

---

* Source: FE Analytics, total returns in sterling, for the IA Japan sector, IT Japan sector and Baillie Gifford Japan Trust, 5 December 2012 to 1 October 2018.

the fund manager is going off track and the authority to question how performance may be improved. They also act as a fair and objective earpiece for investors.

The quality of the board will depend on the quality of its members. We would also suggest that investors carefully examine the qualifications and track record of an investment trust's board. How active have they been in looking after shareholders' interests? Is there a discount control mechanism in place? Are they willing to issue shares when demand is high to avoid the investment trust moving to a high premium and to buy shares when demand is low and a discount has got too wide?

CONCLUSION

There is a lot to consider when choosing an investment trust but, with the right guidance, it is possible to make more reasoned choices and the outcome can be rewarding. We currently have assigned an Elite Rating to just 12 trusts. You can find more details of the trusts which have qualified from our website. The regulators rightly require us to say that past performance is not a reliable guide to future returns. When you buy shares in an investment trust you may not get back the amount originally invested and tax rules can change over time. However the knowledge that professional analysts have analysed a trust in depth before assigning them a rating can be a valuable additional filter for anyone looking to have more confidence in making their own decisions.

12 Elite-Rated funds

Baillie Gifford Japan	Baillie Gifford Shin Nippon
F&C Global Smaller Companies	Fidelity China Special Situations
Fidelity Special Values	Jupiter European Opportunities
Lowland Investment Company	Murray International
Schroder Oriental Income	Scottish Mortgage
The City of London	TR Property

Source: www.fundcalibre.com.

TONY YOUSEFIAN *has been involved in discretionary investment management for both private client portfolios and funds, as an analyst and fund manager, since 1987. He joined FundCalibre as a research analyst in 2016. Tony's views are his own and should not be regarded as constituting financial advice.*

AN IN-DEPTH LOOK AT VCTS

GEOFFREY CHALLINOR *of wealth management firm Saunderson House explains the pros and cons of investing in venture capital trusts.*

INTRODUCTION

IGH EARNERS AND wealthy individuals can be subject to high income tax and capital gains tax liabilities. There are a number of government-backed investment initiatives which enable individuals to save tax efficiently but are often overlooked. Venture capital trusts (VCTs) are an important feature in this landscape.

The UK government has made a number of tax reforms in recent years to increase tax revenue and reduce the fiscal deficit. Most notable among these are changes to pension legislation, with people earning more than £150,000 a year (including their employer pension contribution) seeing their pension annual allowance drop to £10,000 per year and, unless they hold one of the forms of Lifetime Allowance Protection, their lifetime allowance fall to £1m. ISAs remain an attractive investment vehicle, although with annual contributions restricted to £20,000 they only provide a limited tax shelter.

Buy-to-let investing has been a successful strategy for some, providing a steady level of income in retirement and, in many areas, strong capital growth too. However, increases in stamp duty on buy-to-let properties (and second homes) and restrictions to landlords' mortgage interest relief now make this less appealing. Finally, with asset prices having risen sharply since the 'nil rate band' was fixed at £325,000 in April 2009 (where it will remain until at least 2020/21), family members and beneficiaries are increasingly left with inheritance tax bills to pay.

This changing landscape is driving investors to look at other tax-efficient investment schemes, namely venture capital trusts (VCTs), enterprise investment schemes (EISs) and business property relief (BPR). An overview of the tax reliefs for each scheme is shown in the following table. Here we cover the different types of VCT and their performance over the last ten years, before commenting on VCT fund raising and related considerations for investors. We then list some of the risks and drawbacks of investing in a VCT and, finally, present a case study of a generic VCT investor. It is important to note that VCTs will not suit everyone and they are not substitutes to more conventional tax shelters such as pensions, ISAs, CGT allowances and dividend allowances. However, they can be effective when used appropriately and, for high earners and wealthy individuals, should be included in wider financial planning discussions.

Overview of tax reliefs

	MAX INVESTMENT	INCOME TAX RELIEF	CGT RELIEF / DEFERRAL	TAX-FREE DIVIDENDS	TAX-FREE GROWTH	IHT FREE	LOSS RELIEF
VCT	£200,000	30%	No	Yes	Yes	No	No
EIS	£1,000,000*	30% + carry back	Deferral	No	Yes	2 years	Yes
BPR	Unlimited	No	No	If in ISA	If in ISA	2 years	No

*£2,000,000 for "knowledge-intensive" companies.
Source: HMRC.

VENTURE CAPITAL TRUSTS

VCTs were introduced in 1995 to encourage investment into small UK companies. They are closed-ended investment companies listed on the London Stock Exchange. They pool investors' money and employ a professional manager to make investments in unquoted companies or companies whose shares are traded on the AIM and PLUS Markets. These companies must carry out a qualifying trade and, at the point of investment, be less than seven years old (with certain exceptions), have fewer than 250 employees (or fewer than 500 for a 'knowledge-intensive' company) and have no more than £15m in assets. To retain government approval as a VCT, it must invest a minimum 70% of its assets in qualifying holdings, rising to 80% for accounting periods beginning on or after 6 April 2019. The balance can remain in non-qualifying investments.

Overview of VCTs

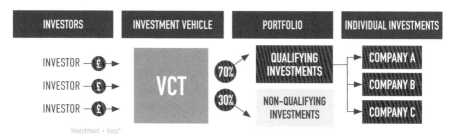

* The investment will be subject to initial fees and annual management charges, while performance fees are common.

VCTs may raise money for new share pools or existing ones. Established VCTs will typically raise money for an existing share pool, providing access to a portfolio of maturing investments which has the benefit of immediate diversification and, in most instances, is already paying dividends.

As of 5 April 2018, at least 30% of all new funds raised must be invested in qualifying holdings within 12 months of the accounting period in which the VCT issues shares, with the remaining funds invested by the end of year three.

VCT TAX BENEFITS

There are three main tax benefits available on investments of up to £200,000 per tax year:

- **Income tax relief at 30%** on the purchase of newly issued VCT shares[*] (received upfront), allowing investors to reduce their income tax liability in that tax year.

- **Tax-free dividends,** providing the potential for a regular stream of tax-free income.

- **Tax-free capital gains,** meaning investors have no tax to pay on gains when shares are sold.

---

[*] Under the latest VCT rules (since 5 April 2018), income tax relief is restricted where an investor sells shares in a VCT and subscribes for new shares in the same VCT within a six-month period.

VCTs are therefore among the most tax-efficient investment vehicles available and can be a useful option for investors looking to complement their pension plans or other long-term investments, such as ISAs. It is worth adding that investing in small UK businesses offers the potential for significant long-term growth if the companies in the VCT are successful. They may also bring extra diversification to an investor's portfolio.

TYPES OF VCT

While all VCT managers must follow the same qualifying investment criteria, each has a slightly different objective and investment focus and will employ a different investment strategy in order to achieve their goals. The different types of VCT fall into one of three broad categories:

- **Generalist VCTs** invest in a wide range of (predominantly) unquoted companies across different sectors. They are 'evergreen' in nature – i.e. they don't have predetermined wind-up dates – and tend to focus on high-growth, high-risk investments. They aim to deliver tax-free income and/or capital growth, with the bulk of an investor's return likely to come from the former (paid from the sale of portfolio holdings as well as income produced within the portfolio).

- **AIM VCTs** invest in companies whose shares are traded on AIM. Like generalist VCTs, they are diversified across different sectors, focus on rapidly growing businesses, are evergreen in nature and aim to deliver tax-free income and/or capital growth.

- **Specialist VCTs** concentrate on just one sector, such as media or technology. Their risk profile is determined by the sector that they invest in and, related to this, the business models of investee companies. Those at the lower-risk end are often branded 'planned exit' or 'limited life' VCTs, both sharing the same objective of returning the invested capital at a modest profit at a predetermined date, typically as soon as possible after the company has passed its five-year qualifying period. However, with the introduction of a 'capital at risk' condition to the VCT rules in the 2018 Finance Act, these lower-risk strategies are no longer viable.

The VCT market has total assets of £4.3bn,[*] which is spread across 85 VCTs (including different share pools) and 27 different managers (note that some managers run more than one type of VCT). Generalist VCTs are the most

---

[*] Figures from the Association of Investment Companies as at 31 August 2018.

common type, representing 77% of assets across 54 VCTs and 16 managers. AIM VCTs represent 17% of assets across 8 VCTs and six managers, while specialist VCTs represent 6% of assets across 23 VCTs and nine managers. The largest VCT, with £613m of assets, is OCTOPUS TITAN VCT (generalist).

VCT PERFORMANCE

The track records of VCTs vary widely, with some performing very well and others very badly. Of course, the year in which an investor purchases VCT shares will influence the returns that they experience, although more important for long-term investors is the manager that they select. Investors should undertake (or seek an adviser that undertakes) thorough due diligence to understand the manager's investment strategy and evaluate the likelihood of them successfully executing it.

According to figures from Financial Express Analytics, over the ten years to 31 August 2018 the VCT sector as a whole is up 120% on a share price total-return basis. This does not include tax reliefs. By comparison, the FTSE All-Share index of companies listed on the UK's main market is up 106% (on a total-return basis). The figures show that the top-20-performing VCTs are up an average 191% over the period, which includes average dividend payments of 71p per share. Looking at the performance of different strategies, 16 out of the top 20 are generalist, three are AIM and one is specialist. It is important to note that the data only considers VCTs that are open, and thus does not capture the worst-performing VCTs, which have closed.

VCT FUND RAISING

VCTs have traditionally launched share offers shortly before the tax year-end, with fund raisings in recent years filling up quickly as demand for the strongest-performing VCTs has outstripped supply.

For the 2017/18 tax year, the VCT sector raised £728m, the second-highest amount on record and the highest at the current level of 30% income tax relief. The highest ever fund raising was £779m in the 2005/06 tax year, when upfront tax relief was 40%.

For the 2018/19 tax year, we expect to see a fall in the amount raised, as although demand is likely to remain strong (given current pension limits), we anticipate less supply across the sector. The changes to VCT rules announced in the 2018

Finance Act mean that, with certain 'specialist' strategies no longer viable, these VCTs will no longer be raising capital. Further, even for those VCTs whose strategies have not been impacted by the new rules (in the same manner at least), given the large sums raised last year, there is a meaningful amount of capital to deploy and therefore limited need for new money. We suspect that a figure closer to the £542m raised in 2016/17 is more likely than a repeat of the 2017/18 fund raising. As such, interested investors should be prepared to act promptly to subscribe in this year's most in-demand offerings.

RISKS AND DRAWBACKS

VCTs have a higher-risk profile than an investment in larger companies. Businesses in the early stages of their development have a higher failure rate than more established businesses and can change value more quickly and more significantly than larger companies. Investors therefore have a greater risk of losing their capital and dividends can be reduced or suspended altogether.

Although VCTs are listed on the London Stock Exchange and in theory can be bought and sold at any time, as only newly issued shares qualify for income tax relief, the secondary market is illiquid. This means that even if a buyer can be found, many VCT shares trade at substantial discounts to their respective NAVs. Further, as the price of shares bought on the secondary market is determined by supply and demand, should these not align (as is often the case), the difference between the buying and selling price (the spread) may be wide. Disposing of a VCT holding in the secondary market may therefore only be possible at a price significantly below the NAV of the shares. A large number of VCT managers do, however, offer share buyback schemes, which they typically undertake at a 5–15% discount to NAV.

It is important to note that income tax relief is clawed back if the shares are not held for at least five years. Investors should be prepared to invest for at least this long and a longer time frame is advisable. It is worth adding that how much an individual benefits from the tax reliefs will depend on their particular circumstances and HMRC may change the rules at any time. Investors should also note that the ongoing charges associated with VCTs are typically higher than those for mainstream collective investments, while it is common for them to have a performance fee.

WHO MIGHT CONSIDER BUYING VCT SHARES?

VCTs are most suitable for individuals with a balanced or adventurous attitude to risk, with surplus cash available to invest for the long term and a large income tax liability. Pension and ISA allowances should already have been fully utilised, as well as any tax-free growth available using dividends allowances and annual capital gains tax exemptions.

CASE STUDY

David is a high earner and comfortable taking a higher level of investment risk. He makes full pension and ISA contributions, although is looking at other tax-efficient ways to supplement his income in retirement. He plans to work for another five years and will have considerable surplus income over that period.

After meeting with his financial adviser, David agrees to invest £50,000 per year for the next five years into a range of generalist and AIM VCTs. For this example, for the sake of simplicity it is assumed that the VCTs have an average target dividend yield of 5%, which is achieved every year in perpetuity, and there is no movement in capital values.

When David enters his first year of retirement, he has a VCT portfolio of £250,000 at a net cost of £175,000 (after 30% income tax relief). He has received £37,500 in tax-free dividends (5% on the sum invested over five years) and stands to receive a further £12,500 in tax-free dividends each year thereafter. The tax-equivalent yield of £12,500 in dividends to an additional rate taxpayer on a net investment of £175,000 is 13.0%. David must remain invested for five years into retirement to keep all of the tax breaks provided (as the income tax for each contribution invested for fewer than five years would otherwise be repayable), so this should be seen as part of a long-term holding and capital to which he does not need access. The VCT holdings could be sold if required, although David understands that this would be at a discount to NAV.

For a well-managed generalist or AIM VCT, a 5% dividend yield together with some uplift in capital value over the long term is a reasonable expectation. However, dividends may be higher or lower in any single year depending on market conditions and the level of realisations, while portfolio values are also likely to fluctuate.

CONCLUSION

In recent years it has become more difficult for high earners and wealthy people to shelter their income and capital from the taxman. VCTs help investors to mitigate future tax liabilities and receive tax-free income and gains by making long-term investments in risky start-up and growing businesses. The scheme is well-established and we anticipate growth in this area as investors look for additional financial planning options given restrictions to more conventional tax shelters. However, it should be noted that HMRC has changed the rules governing the schemes in the past and may do so again in the future.

It is important to recognise that VCTs are not suitable for all individuals and investors must understand and be comfortable with the level of investment risk inherent in the offerings. Their high-risk nature should not automatically be viewed as a negative, since the track records of some managers show strong investment returns even before the tax reliefs are factored in. We recommend that interested investors seek information and advice from specialist financial professionals before making a subscription.

GEOFFREY CHALLINOR *CFA is an investment analyst at Saunderson House.*

PROFESSIONAL PERSPECTIVES

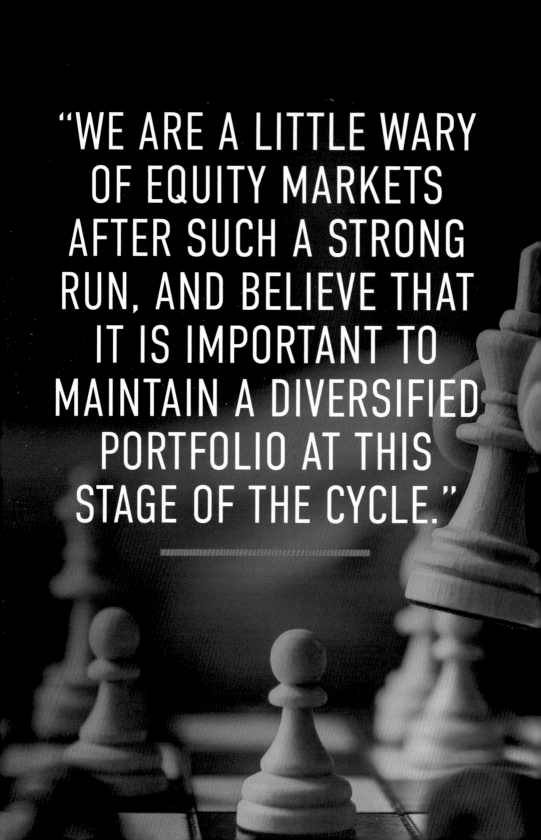

"WE ARE A LITTLE WARY OF EQUITY MARKETS AFTER SUCH A STRONG RUN, AND BELIEVE THAT IT IS IMPORTANT TO MAINTAIN A DIVERSIFIED PORTFOLIO AT THIS STAGE OF THE CYCLE."

THE HEALTH OF THE INDUSTRY

Top-rated trust analyst CHARLES CADE, *head of investment company research at Numis Securities, answers a series of topical questions about the state of the investment trust sector (interview at the end of September 2018).*

How do you see the health of the IT sector as we go into 2019?

Charles Cade: The sector is in very good health, with net assets of over £180bn. There has been record levels of new and secondary issuance in recent years (e.g. £11.9bn raised in 2017 via IPOs and secondary issues). The sector's assets grew by 13.7% per annum from 2012–17, outpacing the 11.6% growth in the assets of unit trusts/OEICs. Much of this has been driven by the strong demand for alternative income mandates given the low returns on cash or corporate bonds. However, there has also been significant growth in demand from UK retail investors via platforms such as Hargreaves Lansdown. These investors have typically focused on companies with an equity mandate, such as SCOTTISH MORTGAGE and FINSBURY GROWTH & INCOME.

What is the biggest threat to the industry at the moment?

CC: The industry faces a number of threats. One of these is the growing focus on costs, partly driven by regulation. Historically investment trusts were regarded as low-cost savings vehicles compared to open-ended funds, the fees of which typically included commission for intermediaries. However, this has changed since RDR (the Retail Distribution Review) and there has been growing pressure on investment company fees. Mifid II, the latest chapter in EU financial services regulation, has increased this focus on fees by forcing firms to show the underlying costs of fund investments.

While we welcome greater transparency of costs, we do not believe that investors should focus on fees alone. For instance, many investment companies typically focus on specialist mandates, such as property, infrastructure or private equity, where the costs of management are inevitably higher than for a mainstream equity fund.

Discounts have narrowed to record lows – is there any way but down from here?

CC: At present equity funds are trading at a discount of around 5%, while alternative asset investment companies are trading at around asset value on average (albeit this disguises a wide spread). Discounts tend to follow market movements and they could well widen if there is a significant correction in equity markets. However, we do not see discounts returning to the level of 2008 when there was distressed selling of some funds (particularly property, private equity and hedge funds). This is partly because the profile of investors has changed, with a greater emphasis now being placed on long-term returns rather than exploiting short-term discount movements. In addition, balance sheets are now in much better shape than before the global financial crisis and discount control mechanisms are far better structured, designed to suit the liquidity of the underlying portfolio. Indeed we believe that many of the listed private equity funds currently offer significant value, trading on discounts to NAV in the high teens.

Is governance really better than it was? What would you like to see more boards doing?

CC: Yes, the standard of governance is far better than it was in the 1990s. Most boards are now fully independent from the manager and are clearly focused on looking after shareholders' interests. In addition the make-up of boards is far more diverse, which brings in a greater range of skills, and boards are refreshed more frequently. Some boards need to be more proactive if a fund is too small to appeal to investors, has a wide discount, and/or is performing poorly. We accept that they should take a long-term view and that funds can fall out of favour because of a turn in market sentiment towards an asset class or investment style. However, mergers remain extremely rare and are typically seen as a last resort as an alternative to a wind-up.

Alternative assets have delivered a valuable new source of returns to investors, but is the sector peaking (too much supply, style drift, etc.)?

CC: There has been huge growth in alternative income funds, and most typically have a yield of more than 5%. Investment companies are well suited to these asset classes as the underlying investments are often relatively illiquid. In general these funds have performed well, but some of the debt funds (notably P2P GLOBAL INVESTMENTS and RANGER DIRECT LENDING) have failed to meet investor expectations. We believe some have been overly aggressive in raising capital; for instance, CIVITAS SOCIAL HOUSING raised a C share before the ordinary share was fully invested. Others have sought to broaden their mandates to maintain their growth. For example, several renewable energy funds have started investing overseas, while infrastructure funds have moved into demand-based and regulated assets, which may have a somewhat higher risk profile than their original offerings.

What have been the most interesting launches of the past 12 months in your view (excluding your own, of course)?

CC: Our focus at Numis has primarily been on secondary issues, while our recent IPOs have been very specialist, such as the £270m we helped raise for TRIAN INVESTORS. Elsewhere I would nominate a couple of funds launched since the start of 2017.

The first is BIOPHARMA CREDIT. This is a good example of a specialist alternative income fund that is well-suited to the closed-end structure. The fund is managed by Pharmakon Advisors, based in New York, and seeks to pay a yield of 7% per annum, with a total return target of 8–9% per annum. It invests in a portfolio of loans issued by life sciences companies or secured on life sciences assets. At IPO in March 2017, the fund raised $762m, including $339m issued in exchange for a seed portfolio, and the company's net assets have already grown to $1.08bn through secondary issuance.

The second is MOBIUS INVESTMENT TRUST. This fund has just raised £100m versus a target of more than £200m. This was a disappointing outcome which partly reflects tough market conditions for emerging markets over the past year. However, we believe that funds launched at a difficult time in the cycle often tend to be the best performers over the long term. Mobius IT will invest in 20–30 small to mid-cap companies in emerging and frontier markets with an absolute return focus. The fund benefits from a strong management team, including Mark Mobius and Carlos Hardenberg, who were formerly responsible for managing

TEMPLETON EMERGING MARKET IT (£1.9bn market cap). We believe that Mobius IT has a differentiated mandate, as well as a competitive fee structure and an effective discount control policy (via an exit at close to NAV after four years). If the fund gets off to a solid start in terms of performance, we would expect it to be able to grow through secondary tap issuance.

What has been the biggest disappointment over the same period?

CC: Listed private equity funds have performed very strongly in recent years, significantly outperforming market indices. However, most of these funds continue to languish on wide discounts and the sector's assets have shrunk through corporate action, with several funds, such as SVG CAPITAL and ABERDEEN PRIVATE EQUITY, winding up – and others (for example, ELECTRA PRIVATE EQUITY) returning capital. The listed sector includes a number of leading private equity managers such as Hg, Pantheon or HarbourVest that it would be extremely difficult for most investors to access directly. We believe these remain well-placed to deliver attractive returns over the medium/long term. Unfortunately, however, persistent discounts mean that the listed private equity sector has struggled to grow its assets, with investors focused on alternative income mandates.

Are investment trust fees now competitive enough against passive and open-ended alternatives?

CC: Numerous investment companies have reduced fees in the past few years and many of the large equity trusts are extremely competitive versus open-ended funds. For example, CITY OF LONDON has an ongoing charges figure of 0.41%. Many investment companies have also removed performance fees in recent years, although we believe that the combination of a low base fee and a well-structured performance fee should be an attractive proposition for investors as mangers will only get paid if they deliver strong returns. This is similar to the variable fee structure, adopted by three of Fidelity's investment trusts, including FIDELITY CHINA SPECIAL SITUATIONS, whereby the management fee moves up or down by +/-0.2% pa depending on the fund's performance relative to its benchmark. ICs should not seek to compete solely on fees, as the key is for them to use the structural advantages to deliver better long-term risk-adjusted returns (on a net basis after fees).

Are you expecting a trend to higher bond yields – and what will the impact be on valuations and discounts?

CC: Short-term interest rates have risen in the US and to a lesser degree in the UK. However, long bond yields remain low by historic standards, with UK 10-year treasuries yielding 1.5%. That is significantly less than the yield on the FTSE All-Share of 3.8%. At the start of the year, a synchronised pick-up in global economic growth was expected to lead to higher long-dated bond yields. However, the picture is now less clear as there are numerous political concerns, including an escalation of the trade war between the US and China, and the threat of a hard Brexit.

We do not expect an imminent shift to a higher interest rate environment. However, if UK interest rates were to rise significantly, this could well start to impact demand for some of the alternative income funds with exposure to long-term fixed cash flows. Many of these funds, however, have cash flows linked to floating-rate assets – TWENTY-FOUR INCOME is an example – meaning that their yield should rise in-line with interest rates. Many infrastructure funds have returns that are linked to inflation. In theory the discount rates used to value infrastructure funds should rise in parallel with treasury yields, but we believe that there is a buffer incorporated in the valuation methodology as the spreads between discount rates and gilts are wider than they were when interest rates were higher. So the impact of higher yields might not be as great as it appears.

Are there more or fewer discount opportunities to exploit than there were?

CC: There are far fewer discount opportunities at present, partly because of the benign market conditions we have experienced for several years, but also because of share buybacks and other discount control mechanisms. There are also a number of value investors, such as Wells Capital or 1607, which are out there waiting to buy funds which are trading on attractive discounts. Funds which survive despite having very wide discounts tend to be very small (and off the radars of most investors) and/or invest in a specialist asset class where the published NAV may not be a true reflection of the portfolio value. Development property is an example.

Are boards doing too much or little by way of gearing?

CC: We believe that boards should be responsible for setting the parameters for a fund's gearing, but the actual level of gearing should be determined by the manager. Most equity funds have gearing of less than 20% of net assets, which is relatively modest. We believe that this is sensible, although we believe that boards should be willing to encourage managers to employ more gearing following a market correction. The gearing of funds investing in property is far lower than in the run up to 2008 and private equity funds have a far lower level of outstanding commitments. In our view this focus on maintaining a strong balance sheet is sensible.

Is it true that dividends are being paid increasingly from capital? If so should we be concerned?

CC: The ability to smooth a fund's dividend over the cycle by using revenue reserves is a key advantage that investment companies enjoy over open-ended funds. However, we believe it is vital that an investor buying a fund for yield should seek to understand how this is being generated. Most equity investment companies charge a proportion of management and finance costs (typically c.60–65% for an income-oriented fund) to the revenue account. However, some funds, such as EUROPEAN ASSETS (yield 7.3%) or INVESCO PERPETUAL UK SMALLER COMPANIES (3.9%) pay an enhanced yield financed primarily from capital. This policy has helped to generate investor buying given the strong demand for income, but it will exacerbate capital losses if we enter a bear market. In addition, equity income funds have traditionally been regarded as relatively low risk, with a beta (sensitivity to overall market movements) of less than 1.0×. However, some investment companies paying an enhanced yield (e.g. JPMORGAN GLOBAL GROWTH & INCOME, 4.8% yield) have a focus on growth stocks and may therefore perform differently from their peers in a market correction.

Are you expecting more or less issuance in the next 12 months and if so where?

CC: We expect equity investment companies trading on premiums to continue to issue shares to meet investor demand. Growth-oriented funds are in favour following a strong run; most of the Baillie Gifford funds for example are trading at premiums. Funds with a focus on capital preservation, such as PERSONAL ASSETS and CAPITAL GEARING, are also popular. The IPO market has, however, been more difficult in 2018 to date, partly because of more volatile market conditions. We are aware of several IPOs currently being marketed and there are several others at the test-marketing stage. Most of these have specialist income mandates, typically with a yield of 5–7% and a total return target of up to 10%.

It is hard to get critical mass for an IPO of a new equity investment company due to the nature of the typical buyer (retail and private wealth managers).

For instance, Stuart Widdowson raised £88m for ODYSSEAN IT to invest in UK smaller companies and Mobius IT raised £100m. However, there is potential for these funds to grow in the secondary market if they perform well. To be successful we believe that an equity trust needs to have a manager with a strong track record and to be differentiated from existing open or closed-end funds. For instance, BAILLIE GIFFORD US raised £173m in March 2018 and has since grown to £267m through a combination of asset growth and secondary issuance. It is differentiated by investing up to 50% of its portfolio in unquoted securities.

How big do you need to be to have a viable launch these days (given the prospect of secondary issues also)?

CC: There are costs involved with a launch which mean that it is rarely viable below £100m. In addition, many investors are reluctant to buy small funds and institutional investors often have a limit on the size of stake that they can hold (e.g. 5–10%). On the other hand, it is important that a fund does not raise too much capital as excess cash will lead it a drag on its performance.

Where are the biggest gaps in the investment company universe from your perspective?

CC: The key advantages of ICs relative to open-ended funds are probably the ability to smooth income and to provide exposure to less-liquid asset classes. In our view multi-asset income funds combine both features and these have the potential to be very attractive long-term savings vehicles for ISAs and pensions. However, the universe is currently small (ABERDEEN DIVERSIFIED INCOME & GROWTH, SENECA GLOBAL INCOME & GROWTH, and the recently launched JPMORGAN MULTI-ASSET). Unfortunately, these vehicles are very difficult to launch at IPO because they are targeting a highly diverse retail market. The core buyers of ICs, such as private wealth managers and institutional investors, are typically reluctant to buy multi-asset vehicles as they prefer to maintain control of their own asset allocation.

What is the biggest change that you would like to see to grow the sector?

CC: I would like to see a greater commitment to the sector from some of the platforms in terms of research and recommendations, rather than just offering the ability to execute transactions. In addition, it would be good if investment companies could find a way to access the defined contribution savings market more effectively. You would think that the large private equity and infrastructure funds should be well-placed to provide exposure to alternatives in a liquid investment for that market.

Which sectors do you see having the best outlook for returns over say the next two to three years?

CC: We are a little wary of equity markets after such a strong run, and believe that it is important to maintain a diversified portfolio at this stage of the cycle, possibly reducing exposure to riskier assets and retaining some cash to be able to take advantage of opportunities if there is a market correction. That said, it is extremely difficult to time markets correctly, and we believe that ICs are still well-placed to deliver attractive returns for investors over the medium to long term. We favour backing experienced management teams who have been through previous market cycles.

Any advice for DIY investors looking to go into the sector for the first time?

CC: There is now a huge amount of information available on ICs. A good place to start is the AIC's website and most funds have good websites, including factsheets and commentary from the managers. We would be wary of relying on information in the Key Investor Information Document as we believe many of the figures are misleading and/or not directly comparable to other funds. The key is to try to understand a fund's risk/return profile and match this with your objectives in terms of investment time frame and capacity to take short-term losses. We would be wary of simply buying funds based on historic performance or those with the highest yield. For a novice investor, a diversified global equity fund would probably be a good starting point.

CHARLES CADE joined Numis from Winterflood Securities in 2008 to head up their investment companies team. Numis has around 50 corporate clients and regularly scores highly in annual quality-of-broker-research surveys.

———————————

USING TRUSTS FOR INCOME

RICHARD CURLING, *manager of the Jupiter Monthly Income fund, discusses the pros and cons of using investment trusts to generate an income.*

What is the objective of the monthly income fund?

Richard Curling: The objective is to pay an annual income of 4.5%. That is paid in regular monthly instalments. What we're trying to do, in practice, is find investments with high-quality long-dated cash flows from which we will pay a secure monthly dividend over the long term, while trying to preserve and hopefully grow the value of the capital.

How much of the portfolio is represented by investment trusts?

RC: The monthly income fund has 90% in investment companies of one sort or another. Broadly speaking, about half of it is in traditional equities, some of which are UK equities and some of which are overseas equities. (The Asian funds have always been quite good at producing income, for example.) The other half is in so-called alternatives. That includes infrastructure funds, various kinds of real estate trusts, plus other more esoteric ways that investment companies now produce income.

Why is there such a high proportion of investment trusts in the portfolio – what are the advantages for a professional income investor?

RC: Investment trusts have some clear advantages over unit trusts and other types of investment vehicle. The most obvious advantages are the ability to borrow (gear up) – though that obviously works both ways – and the ability to smooth income, which is really important and something unit trusts don't have.

Connected with the ability to smooth income is the very long track record of paying – and growing – dividends that some trusts have. If you are the board of a trust that has been paying a dividend for 50 years, as some of them have, you don't want it to be you who decides to cut it. So I think you can have more reassurance that dividends are going to be sustained in some investment trusts than others.

The third benefit of a closed-ended vehicle is to do with investment flows. The fact is that unit trust investors, as a matter of human nature, have a tendency to put their money in at the top of the market cycle, when things are expensive, and take it out at the bottom, when they are cheap. That accentuates movements in the market and has a negative impact on the performance of open-ended vehicles.

Some recent work by Cass Business School showed that investment trusts have outperformed unit trusts or open-ended vehicles over time. That's a useful bit of empirical research to support what we intuitively feel.

Does that mean you are able to pay your 4.5% yield (after fees) without having to draw on capital?

RC: Yes. Of course, unless you're running an income fund, it is the total return that you should be looking at. Whether that return derives from income or capital doesn't really matter, but the ability to convert capital into income in an investment trust is a trick that seems to be increasingly widely used and you obviously have to be aware of that when it happens. An increasing number of investment trusts are choosing to pay fixed dividends, regardless of whether that is covered by the trust's income. I happen to think that paying uncovered dividends is legitimate when income is very expensive, which it is at the moment.

The main reason so much of the fund is invested in investment trusts today is that it opens up the universe of opportunities to lots of illiquid types of investment that are not so suitable for unit trusts. Good examples are the environmental infrastructure trusts (wind farms, solar farms etcetera), and property. Long leasehold property in particular offers a very interesting income stream for long-term income pursuers, particularly some of the ones that have inflation-linked rents.

In an income-scarce world, it's very difficult to find income from the traditional sources – bonds, cash and equities – and when you can, the yields are low, so it is very expensive. And it can also be very concentrated. Half of the dividend income from the UK stock market comes from just five companies. You need a broader range of opportunities to be properly diversified.

Another important factor, as I have mentioned, is taking insurance against future inflation, which is very damaging to income investors. The investment trust universe is very helpful here. A lot of the newer trusts have underlying cash flows and revenue streams which are in some way linked to inflation. For example, you can invest in some long leasehold REITs that have 100% inflation protection. They have upward only, inflation-linked rents with an expired term on their lease of 25 years. Effectively it's a 25-year index-linked investment. You get a yield of between 4% and 5% on those, whereas for an equivalent-dated index-linked bond – well, you're lucky if it's positive.

People who want a regular income tend also to be the ones who are most vulnerable to inflation.

RC: Yes, and I think unexpected inflation is one of the big hidden risks in markets at the moment. Nobody's really talking about it. We've been living in a world where all the attention has been on trying to avoid deflation. It is true that there's very little sign of inflation at the moment. There have been such strong forces counteracting inflation, like globalisation and ever cheaper manufactured goods from China, that inflation hasn't appeared on people's list of things to worry about. But I do think it's a significant risk out there which you can protect yourself against while still getting a good income.

Even though we haven't seen the evidence yet?

RC: Yes, inflation fear hasn't yet broken out in any significant way. The factors supressing it have been quite powerful so far. The big risk, though, is that if inflation does take off, the traditional response to dealing with inflation is to raise interest rates, and given the level of indebtedness around the world, it's going to be difficult to do that without doing an awful lot of damage to the economy. So it may not be a very big risk, but the impact would be big, if it was to happen.

So you are not finding any difficulty at the moment in finding things that allow you to pay the 4.5%?

RC: No. There are quite a lot of opportunities now in some interesting new areas that are relatively new, ones where traditional investment trusts haven't played before. In this space I would put housing, and in particular social and rental housing. In the healthcare space, GP surgeries and nursing homes; and then there are some very esoteric ones, like buying music rights, where an IPO (the HIPGNOSIS SONGS fund) happened recently.

Did you put money into that one?

RC: Yes, I took some of that, though not very much. I think we need to see the model prove itself. But I think the investment thesis may be right. Then you've also got the new lending companies which are essentially banks, but not deposit takers, so lenders to small and medium enterprises. They are interesting because the risks are likely to be less correlated to the normal stock market cycle – another benefit.

When we were talking earlier about converting capital to income, it is interesting that a number of private equity companies, which fall into the alternative space, are now agreeing to make distributions to shareholders as a way of returning some capital. Traditionally that hasn't happened, as it's more difficult for private equity companies to do, given their structure and their future funding commitments to companies they have invested in.

An example of that is NB PRIVATE EQUITY which recently confirmed that it was going to pay a 4%-a-year dividend. PRINCESS PRIVATE EQUITY, which is part of PARTNERS GROUP, also pays a fixed percentage of its NAV as a distribution. F&C PRIVATE EQUITY has done that for years. It pays 4% of NAV once a year. That meets a demand for shareholders to give something back and it seems a sensible way of doing it.

Where then is the downside in using trusts for income?

RC: My main worry is the levels of gearing that some of these new investment companies are adopting in order to achieve the target yield. It seems to me that the temptation is to say, 'In order to get this issue away, we've got to have a 5% yield. How are we going to get there? We have to account for our fees. So given that the underlying yield from the assets is x%, let's knock off our fees and then gear it up until we get to the required yield number.'

That's one thing I'm watching carefully. You need to make sure that the income isn't there simply because it's over-geared investment. The other thing that I think we have to be aware of is style drift – trusts going into new areas because they have run out of opportunities in their chosen area of operation. That has happened a bit with the traditional PPI/PFI infrastructure stocks.

Because they are not making any more PFI deals in the UK, they have started buying PFI assets overseas. They may turn out to be good, but it gives you a different risk profile and it's different from what they started off doing. Likewise, in the green

"THERE ARE QUITE A LOT OF OPPORTUNITIES NOW IN SOME INTERESTING NEW AREAS – INCLUDING SOME VERY ESOTERIC ONES, LIKE BUYING MUSIC RIGHTS."

infrastructure space, they've been investing overseas too, because the opportunities just aren't available in the UK. I think we have to be very careful about that.

With the renewables, the generous initial subsidies are being wound down...

RC: Yes, subsidies have stopped so, people aren't constructing the assets. There are some interesting opportunities as tax vehicles such as Enterprise Investment Schemes reach maturity; they are a good source of acquisitions for the listed companies. But in general they're not making them any more. Underlying all of this is the fact that many of these companies are externally managed funds. As a fund manager their incentive, if this isn't too cynical, is to increase the assets they are managing, even if it means reducing the quality of the portfolio. I wish there were more internally managed investment opportunities in this area, because that arrangement prouduces a much better alignment of interests.

In some cases the management fees are quite hefty.

RC: Yes, they are. That is also something that concerns me. I'm surprised at how high the management fees are on some of these investments. I know that lots of them have introduced scaling, so that the fees reduce as funds under management increase, but that doesn't really resolve the underlying issue. The trusts have raised a lot of money and they're charging big fees on it, certainly big sums in absolute terms.

In some cases I think they are difficult to justify. As investors maybe we need to put more pressure on fees and maybe become more imaginative about how these fees are structured. So, maybe you would have a structure where they'd earn a higher fee for the first three years, while they are making the investments, and then a lower fee when it moves into what I call 'reading the meter' mode.

What is clear that the way you are investing the monthly income fund has changed a lot since the great financial crisis.

RC: Yes, ten years ago we had a lot of bonds. We basically just had bonds and equities. There were virtually no alternatives. It's been very much a recent development, mainly in response to low interest rates.

So the obvious question is how are these type of investments going to perform if and when interest rates start to rise, as they have begun to do?

RC: The risk for any income-generating asset must be rises in underlying interest rates. That basically means the US bond yield, which underpins the whole financial system. I'm well aware of that, and so the things that I'm looking at particularly is having fewer bond-like assets – that is, those which offer a fixed rate of return over a fixed period of time. What I want now is a greater proportion of floating rate returns – and inflation-linking is also helpful, certainly if interest rates go up because of higher inflation.

It is also important to look for opportunities where the income can grow, rather than just pay a fixed amount. That's becoming an increasingly important part of what I do because I'm very aware that the bond cycle is turning, and interest rates are likely to go up. I don't know when and I don't know how much and I don't think it will be very much, but that is a threat to any income-generating investment.

Have you been able to make capital gains as well as paying out your target income yield?

RC: Yes. So far, that's been the outcome. But my priority is to ensure that we can pay that income month in, month out, and that there's a reasonable cushion there to do that, and that it's reasonably protected from events that are likely to happen. Preserving capital is important, but if we can grow it too, then that's good.

Why don't you own any of the big five UK dividend payers directly in the fund? Surely you might as well buy them yourself rather than pay someone else to buy them?

RC: There's nothing that would stop us doing that. It's just that the mandate has always been to do it through investment companies. Under half of the fund is now in equity funds, and relatively little of that is in the UK. We don't want to have to rely on the big five equity investments that everyone else is forced to buy. For example, we own the multi-cap DIVERSE INCOME TRUST as a way of spreading that income across a wider base. As it happens, the way the fund has evolved, it has become a useful vehicle for taking advantage of the growth in alternatives in the investment trust sector, where all the issuance has been in the last few years.

Is it your policy to buy the trusts at IPO or at a later stage, when the price has settled down?

RC: Both. But one of the things that I have found is that because of the scarcity of income, a lot of the alternative trusts have become quite popular and so trade at premiums. I don't like buying assets at a premium to NAV. So I've tried to be a patient investor, waiting for secondary issuance as the opportunity to buy more shares in some of the things that I particularly like. So, buying both at IPO – and then, if there's something we really like, buying it in secondary issuance; but not buying it in the market, purely because the premiums tend to be too high. I guess that's one advantage of doing it through a fund like this, rather than as a private individual, as individuals mostly can't do that.

Do you worry that it is getting harder to launch a new investment trust because of the minimum size wealth managers say they need to see a new trust reach to justify supporting in an IPO?

RC: Everyone is concerned about how easy it is to buy and sell shares in trusts they invest in. The big wealth managers certainly want to see the size of the trust they invest in increase because of these liquidity issues. We have the same problem because we're an open-ended vehicle investing in closed-ended vehicles or illiquid assets. We have to keep a close eye on liquidity too. We never want to be a forced seller of something. That is why I tend to run cash balances in the fund of between 5 and 10%. It also gives me ammunition for secondary issuances or opportunistic purchases when they come along. But you are right that some companies struggle with this chicken-and-egg situation; investors won't invest in you until you're bigger, and you can't get bigger until they invest in you.

One obvious question: why don't you create a closed-end version of the monthly income fund?

RC: I think that is a very good idea and we should, precisely because the main issue with investing in the alternative space – which is where the really interesting income opportunities are – is the liquidity. Some of them are frankly not suitable for being held in an open-ended vehicle. A closed-ended vehicle to take advantage of this whole new area of alternatives would be very interesting. They are all very different and it takes a lot of research to pick out the best ones. I suspect that the opportunity to buy a portfolio of the best opportunities would be an attractive proposition.

Is there a lot of crossover between the monthly income fund and the other one you run, the fund of investment trusts?

RC: No, there isn't. The fund of investment trusts doesn't have an income requirement, whereas the monthly income fund clearly does. The fund of investment trusts tends not to have alternatives in it, just equity exposure. But there are one or two that overlap – private equity funds is one example – and some common themes. I quite like the small and mid-cap space in both, for example, but for different reasons. I like it in the fund of investment trusts because it's growth, and I like it in the monthly income fund because it is a more diversified approach to income, rather than the big five.

What's your thinking about discounts – how much of what you do is about finding attractive discount opportunities?

RC: I think it's down the list of priorities. It's a 'nice to have' rather than an 'essential to have'. If you can add some value by buying at a discount, so much the better. If you look at the ranges that these trusts have traded in over time, there are, within the subsectors, clearly times to buy them and times not to buy them. So, infrastructure is the classic example. Everybody got very over-excited about it, it became very popular, infrastructure trusts traded at a very high premium, and apparently nothing could go wrong.

Then John McDonnell, the shadow chancellor, stood up at the Labour Party Conference and threatened to nationalise them – and suddenly political risk entered into the whole equation. That knocked back the share prices quite a bit. In practice, there are a number of ways the political risk could happen. It wouldn't necessarily just be nationalisation. It could be special taxation. There are lots of ways of skinning that cat.

And then Carillion went bust and that introduced some operational risk into the equation as well. The effect of this was the premiums on infrastructure trusts evaporated. The two big trusts, JOHN LAING INFRASTRUCTURE and HICL, started trading at a discount. That to me was a good buying opportunity because the markets often overreact. They overreacted on the upside, put them on too high premiums, and then overreacted on the downside, putting them on too big discounts.

Since then the share prices have rallied and the discounts have reduced again?

RC: Yes. A number of things have happened. We saw a bid for John Laing Infrastructure which was at 20% premium to NAV. That was quite reassuring, although slightly surprisingly it was a bid from another fund manager rather than a bid from a pension fund bid, which would have been more reassuring. But to my mind it did underpin the asset value and the central case. And then HICL sold an asset for at a 20% premium to what they had it in the books for. That was reassuring that the secondary market for PFI assets was good.

So, sometimes there is an opportunity to buy these things when something happens. Look at social housing. A housing association went bust and that provided a reality check for that sub-sector and provided a good buying opportunity. Unlike conventional investment trusts, where you try to buy at a bigger discount, with alternatives it's about avoiding buying at a big premium and then taking advantage when there's further issuance at NAV, or something happens and there's an overreaction in the share prices.

What is the most important lesson you have learnt about investing in investment trusts?

RC: The mistake that I have made on occasions has been topslicing and selling too early. With funds even more than companies, you want to stick with your winners, particularly if you feel that you've found a really good manager. That is more important than whether a sector is in or out of favour. For example, I really like HENDERSON SMALLER COMPANIES. The manager, Neil Hermon, has outperformed in 15 of the last 16 years. That is up markets, down markets, flat markets. SCOTTISH MORTGAGE has also worried me a bit for ages, but it's continued to perform extremely well. I've sold an awful lot of shares over the years, which has been completely the wrong thing to do!

RICHARD CURLING *joined Jupiter Asset Management in 2006 and is a fund manager in the UK Growth team. He manages the Jupiter Fund of Investment Trusts, the Jupiter Monthly Income Fund and the Jupiter UK Alpha Fund.*

PERSPECTIVES OF A WEALTH MANAGER

JAMES BURNS, *a partner at Smith & Williamson, explains why investment trusts are favoured by firms that manage private client portfolios.*

Why are investment trusts popular with wealth managers?

James Burns: Investment trusts have always been popular with wealth managers, and have become more so in recent years as more and more asset classes have opened up as options in the investment company space. As the sector has morphed from consisting mainly of conventional UK-registered companies into a much broader investment universe, we have become even bigger supporters. We are always among the first to get an early call for brokers promoting new launches.

The sector has changed a lot since the financial crisis. Up until then it was primarily equity trusts. There was a very small fixed income sector and we had a big boom in property investment companies leading up to the financial crisis. Hedge funds also came in for a while. But since the financial crisis there has been a massive explosion in different asset classes to access. The easy explanation is that the banks have come out, or at least had to retreat, from many parts of the market. So now we have things like commercial property lending, aircraft leasing and more specialist property sectors, such as student and healthcare property. There have been a few more private equity launches too.

Overall there are far more different asset classes to play with now. The financial crisis has been good for the sector in that respect because the investment company structure is an absolutely ideal vehicle for these less-liquid pools of capital. At the same time, the investment company sector has really benefited from wealth managers looking to build diversified multi-asset class portfolios, an approach which is becoming much more common.

How do you use investment trusts within the firm?

JB: One is as a core building block for a portfolio. Conventional equity investment trusts such as MONKS and SCOTTISH MORTGAGE have good management teams and are very attractively priced these days. The sector also offers good income vehicles with revenue reserves and good historic payout ratios. With trusts whose managers have the ability to invest in smaller and less-liquid shares than they are allowed to do in their open-ended funds, you are hopefully getting their best ideas as they can afford to take a longer-term view.

The second attraction is the ability to access multi-asset trusts which give you diversification away from conventional equity and bonds, whether that is in the form of commercial property lending, renewable energy or whatever. I always look at the sector in these two ways. The key thing for me is that natural selection works in the investment company sector. If you are not performing, or the management house is not performing, shareholders and boards are much more active now. Poorly performing vehicles will die out. Dead wood gets kicked out relatively quickly.

Do you expect fees to continue coming down?

JB: Yes. There is certainly a long list of funds that have cut performance fees in the last few years. I think that boards of trusts now realise that they are able to assert their strength in negotiations with management houses over fees. Their argument is that as investment companies have the advantage of permanent or semi-permanent capital, so their fees should be coming down. Trusts like the ones I mentioned, Monks and Scottish Mortgage, are now charging incredibly attractive fees for active management.

Are trusts doing too much or too little by way of using gearing?

JB: On the whole I think the use of gearing has been pretty good. There are different approaches. Some boards are involved in every gearing decision. Others give managers leeway up to a certain level. Some trusts say that as we have a long-term view, we are going to be geared pretty much all of the time. Other managers look to reduce gearing when they think that valuations are looking potentially stretched. We have seen very few increasing their gearing recently.

"NATURAL SELECTION WORKS IN THE INVESTMENT COMPANY SECTOR. POORLY PERFORMING VEHICLES DIE OUT. DEAD WOOD GETS KICKED OUT RELATIVELY QUICKLY."

What about the added volatility that shares in investment companies have?

JB: You can't dispute that trusts will be more volatile than open-ended funds in terms of price because of the supply-and-demand dynamic and also potentially because of gearing. We always say that, if it is part of a sensibly constructed portfolio and if you are happy with the level of volatility, then investment companies make absolute sense. A lot of people use the sector for income and as long as that income is being paid, that is the key thing. In 2008 in the equity income sector, only one trust cut its dividend. Every other trust in the sector held its dividend while open-ended funds were cutting. That is important for clients because they want to know that their income will keep on growing and they can afford to hold for the longer time.

Are the regulators doing enough to promote investment companies as an alternative?

JB: The Financial Conduct Authority has probably been showing a bit more interest lately. The AIC lobbied hard to make sure that investment companies are not classified as complex investments under the latest European legislation. The truth is that investment companies are slightly more complicated investments, but it is really just a case of having a few more moving parts to look at. You have to do a bit more research. The good thing about investment companies that needs to be emphasised is that in this post-RDR, governance-driven world there is a board of directors there to protect shareholders' interest, which is a big positive.

But has the quality of investment trust boards improved? They were the butt of many jokes not so long ago…

JB: Over the last decade boards have been showing far more independence over fees and moving management contracts around. We have seen more examples of directors taking their responsibilities more seriously than they were. There is definitely still room for more improvement. I can think of a couple of cases recently where boards have failed to bite the bullet and move the management contract when they should have done.

Are you in favour of more boards introducing discount controls?

JB: I am actually quite relaxed about that. I am still of the view that there are few things more fun than buying a really good investment trust that is trading on a discount because of some short-term wobble in the market. What I don't like to see are boards turning to cash registers at the wrong time, purely because they have put a line in the sand. The risk is that they end up shrinking the trust to a point which may not be in the interest of everyone. That said, what you don't want are no controls at all and boards adopting a laissez-faire approach, with a discount staying at 20% forever. I quite like the idea of trusts with a fixed life, giving us as investors the ability to get out after a few years. While the discount may move out a bit in the short term, you know that on a three- or four-year view you can exit at NAV.

Is there a limit on how large a trust has to be for you to invest in at IPO?

JB: Ideally we are looking for investment companies with £100m in assets, but we won't say no if it is less than that, particularly if we think it has the potential to grow, and will be able to raise more money with secondary issues. There is no one absolute limit. £100m is our unofficial limit. At some other houses it is £250m. I can understand why they do it, but it also means that there are trusts in the area that they don't consider at all, so they are missing out on some very good vehicles. While we monitor our holdings, we do allow exceptions. We think our approach is more flexible.

What has been the driving force behind the wave of recent launches?

JB: Yield has been a big driver of new issues and that makes sense. Things like REAL ESTATE CREDIT INVESTMENTS we really like because you are getting attractive income yields from the lending and still have an equity cushion above you. If you buy Land Securities, by comparison, you are just taking the equity risk, so if you can get 6% yield on real estate lending, that is attractive. The search for income has been a particularly big factor behind all the new issues in the alternative asset space. In 2017 nearly all IPOs had an income story behind them. PERSHING SQUARE, one that wasn't, was a big launch that has not been particularly successful. This year, however, we have seen some interesting new issues in the conventional equity sectors.

Are you not worried that income-based IPOs are becoming too much of a fashion thing?

JB: Yes. I am becoming a little concerned. The investment company market does have a tendency to get quite excited about certain asset classes. Some of the issues recently have become very niche-specific, particularly in the REIT space.

Has the alternative asset sector grown too far too fast? Some of them seem to be running out of opportunities…

JB: I have some concerns on that score, but there have been further bright spots too. The bid for JOHN LAING INFRASTRUCTURE earlier this year at a 20% premium showed that there is still interest in the assets among large institutional players in the market. Some trusts like CARADOR are winding up, and there are others which have not quite done what they were meant to have done, but the positives still outweigh the negatives in my view. As income sources they have mostly been great for private clients.

How has your view of the outlook changed over the past 12 months?

JB: The whole investment trust sector has done incredibly well since the financial crisis. It has grown in size, there have been lots of success stories and the alternative asset trusts have introduced some great new choices for investors. It is probably only natural that we should have turned a bit more cautious now. Both the sector and the markets would probably benefit from a pause for breath.

In general we still think the outlook is positive for both bonds and equities. Interest rates are rising, but slowly. Of course the markets are vulnerable if we get an inflation shock, particularly in the United States. I am probably a bit more cautious than some of my colleagues, but for now the outlook appears to be relatively benign. Let's hope that it stays that way.

What changes have you made to your portfolios over the last year?

JB: We have not made a huge number of changes. We have taken a bit of profit on our private equity trusts. SYNCONA has been a terrific performer for us and so we have sold that down a bit. We first bought in at the launch price of 100p and it has more than doubled since then. We never expected it to do as well as it has so quickly. It has still got exciting long-term prospects, but we won't be chasing it at this price. We have also added a holding in DIVERSE INCOME TRUST on the view that it will provide some portfolio protection as a diversifier. In general we have become slightly more defensive.

With the markets being quite richly valued, and discounts tight by historical standards, it has been hard to get too excited. We have mostly been looking out for specific opportunities rather than adding to existing positions in the market leaders. For example we added a holding in RIVERSTONE ENERGY earlier in the year, on the view that the oil markets were likely to be stronger than most people had thought, and the discount had gone out a lot. The UK income trusts have taken a bit of a beating, too, which could become interesting.

And you have been sticking with Mark Barnett's trusts, which have underperformed for some time now?

JB: Yes we have. I have probably had more grief about that from my colleagues than anything else! However, I don't believe that Mark has lost the ability to run money. There is always a danger of overreacting to a run of poor performance. His value style of investing has gone massively out of favour but I hope – and expect – that the performance will come back, although it may take a change in the market environment before it happens. [*Editor's note:* Barnett is the manager of both the EDINBURGH INVESTMENT TRUST and PERPETUAL INCOME AND GROWTH, which together have assets of more than £1.1bn.]

Have you been taking stock in this year's IPOs?

JB: We have done a few. We supported Baillie Gifford's new American trust, for example, which has already done remarkably well, given how tough it is to outperform in the US market. They are in a bit of a sweet spot at the moment; everything they touch is doing well. Mostly, though, we have concentrated on secondary issues. We are going to be seeing Mark Mobius to talk about his new emerging markets investment trust and there is also a new Japanese trust that Asset Value Investors are hoping to launch which looks interesting.

What do you think will happen to discounts if the market does have a significant downturn?

JB: If the tide does turn, then discounts will obviously come back off current levels, but by how much is an interesting question. We have been looking for opportunities to add some further portfolio protection, as I mentioned. It is not that easy. Trusts that have a fixed life offer some protection, as you know that you can get out when the wind-up date comes round. Of course, if discounts do widen a lot, that could be a good buying opportunity, and I would hope that we could profit from that. Nothing is ever black and white in this business!

James Burns's top ten holdings at 30 Sept 2018

FUND	WEIGHTING	BENCHMARK -/+
Temple Bar	4.5%	--
Henderson Alternative Strategies	4.3%	--
Real Estate Credit Investments	4.2%	--
RIT Capital Partners	4.2%	--
Schroder Asian Total Return IC	4.1%	--
Edinburgh IT	4.1%	--
Pantheon International	3.8%	--
Riverstone Energy	3.5%	--
Henderson European Focus Trust	3.4%	--
Utilico Emerging Markets	3.3%	--

JAMES BURNS *is a partner in Smith & Williamson and responsible for leading the firm's research into investment trusts. He also manages three multi-manager funds that invest in investment trusts and a number of private client and discretionary management portfolios, and co-manages the firm's Managed Portfolio Service.*

THE CASE FOR ACTIVE MANAGEMENT

SANDY CROSS, *of Edinburgh discretionary investment management firm Rossie House Investment Management, explains the central role that Scotland has played in the development of the investment trust sector and the key role that active investment management plays in constructing client portfolios.*

I AM HAPPY TO nail my colours to the mast as a firm believer in the benefits of active management. Passive investing has its place – if you want a low-risk way to have your savings return slightly less than a market index over time it works brilliantly (or at least has done up to now). However, my colleagues and I are pretty sure that if you want your assets to be not just managed, but stewarded for the long term, you will find that a skilled and thoughtful human will do you rather better than a robot. Our aim, then, is to identify talented managers who can produce very good returns over long periods without exposing our clients' assets to excessive risks. There is a view that these managers do not exist. We disagree. They do exist. They just aren't easy to find. On the plus side we find there is one part of the asset management market where they are easier to spot than usual – and that is in the investment trust sector.

A CONSTANTLY INNOVATIVE STRUCTURE

The concept of a listed company, the purpose of which is to invest in other companies, was pioneered by London lawyer, Philip Rose, creator of the FOREIGN & COLONIAL INVESTMENT TRUST in 1868. His intention was to allow those with 'moderate means' the opportunity to access types of investment (for example, overseas bonds and shares) and a level of diversification that was out of reach to all but the wealthy. This was an enormously creative (and egalitarian!) thing to do at the time. But the really interesting thing is the way in which the sector has hung on to that sense of striving for innovation. Rossie House has its head office in Edinburgh, a city that is also home to a disproportionate number of well-known investment trusts. On the face of it they are leftovers from the huge fortunes made in Dundee in the jute industry (the material was much in demand for sacking material as international trade expanded and – famously – to make sandbags in the American Civil War).

This money needed to be invested somewhere, and investment trusts provided a very neat vehicle for securing and growing the wealth generated in the jute industry. Robert Fleming, who founded the eponymous bank and was grandfather to the James Bond author Ian Fleming, launched the first Scottish investment trust in 1873 and it is still active today. But these funds are more than leftovers. They are hugely modern wealth-creating machines.

Take the largest investment trust in the UK (at the time of writing), the FTSE 100 member SCOTTISH MORTGAGE INVESTMENT TRUST, which is managed by Edinburgh-based Baillie Gifford. It launched in 1909 with a plan to provide loans to fund the rubber plantations that supplied the emerging automotive industry with the raw material for tyres. That was exciting stuff at the time. But look at the Scottish Mortgage portfolios now and you will see that, while it isn't for everyone, the trust is as brave and exciting (adventurous?) today as it was 100 years ago. That, we think, tells you a lot about the adaptive and long-term nature of the investment trust structure.

EVOLVE, ADAPT, ENDURE

So what has made the trust industry so successful? Where has this remarkable ability not just to hang on but to thrive through centuries of war, crisis and financial upheaval come from? A key part of the answer lies in the fact that the pool of capital inside a trust is fixed, something that encourages a patient, long-term approach from those who are managing it. Sure, investors can sell their shares – but, however much they might want to, they can't pull their capital out of the fund itself. Top investment managers love this. It means they can invest for the long term without the constant admin distraction of inflows and outflows of capital. Better still, they can also hold small company positions or unusual specialist assets, which, while they may be less liquid than large equities or bonds, can still offer excellent long-term opportunities. The result? A really skilled and

"BETTER, WE THINK, TO WORK WITH PEOPLE WHO FOCUS ON WHAT IS USEFUL AND POSSIBLE THAN WHAT IS USUALLY IMPOSSIBLE AND NOT NECESSARILY USEFUL."

properly interested manager will naturally gravitate towards investment trusts, where we will hope to find and support them!

TODAY'S INNOVATORS

When Philip Rose set up his investment trust he opened a whole new world of investment to ordinary people. Today's trusts are doing the same thing – just with different assets. Twenty years ago it was, thanks in part to Rose, perfectly simple for anyone who wanted a standard equity or bond portfolio to get into one. But a variety of other assets – private equity, commercial property and unlisted companies, for example – remained the preserve of the rich.

No more. The ability of trusts to invest in the less liquid assets that mainstream open-ended funds find too risky has led to the most significant recent development for investment trusts – the large-scale growth in alternative asset trusts. Think about property. Hold it in an open-ended fund and you may find that come a crisis you get a wave of redemptions; have to sell it in a hurry; and have to take a crisis price. Hold it in a closed-ended fund and that will never happen. The trust might move to a nasty-looking discount but the assets can stay intact. That's a hugely valuable feature – and the reason why there are now funds investing in areas ranging from aircraft leasing, healthcare facilities and social housing to litigation finance.

HARNESSING THAT INNOVATION FOR CLIENTS

We aren't militant about out what vehicle we use for investing our clients' money. We will take the best wherever we find it. However, we do find that many of the managers we consider to be superior are drawn to managing equity investment trusts and may also include some of their best, but liquidity constrained, ideas in their investment trust portfolios rather than similar open-ended funds they manage.

We are particularly keen on using trusts in specialist areas. We hold a number of high-quality Asian investment trusts for regional exposure and also like to buy alternative asset funds for diversification purposes. Listed private equity is one area we have been invested, for example – although, as with all investments, we like to keep a firm eye on costs. At the other end of the trust spectrum, we like a number of the big global funds. Investment trusts started out with global mandates and it remains an area in which they excel. Very often, too, you can buy in at a highly competitive price. The MID WYND INTERNATIONAL INVESTMENT TRUST, for example, has a management fee of 0.5% per annum. In the world of asset management that represents genuine value.

KEEPING A CRITICAL EYE

Nothing is ever settled. The past is no guide to the future. And we are not set in our ways. Reasonable fees, the appeal of the structure to able managers with a long-term perspective and – in some cases – effective use of borrowing have meant investment trust returns have fared well compared to open-ended returns in many studies. But we should never forget that a trust is just a structure and, as with all funds, it will only ever be as good as its managers and the assets they choose. So we keep as close an eye on the negative trends in the sector as the positive.

We are watching the fairly high fees in alternative asset funds and also noting the practice, in certain cases, of constantly issuing new equity, which arguably undermines the fixed-pool-of-capital argument in favour of trusts. Among more conventional equity trusts we are watching the way boards manage discounts and premiums. We love the idea that when you buy a trust you get an independent board to steward your interests. But we won't invest in trusts where the board isn't doing that well.

FOUR THINGS TO THINK ABOUT WHEN YOU CHOOSE AN INVESTMENT TRUST

1. Find managers who focus on companies rather than macro stories

Macroeconomic forecasting is hard to get right, as the fact the US Federal Reserve did not forecast any of the last eight recessions would testify. It therefore follows that investment stories based too emphatically on exciting-sounding macro themes have a tendency to disappoint, as many a macro hedge fund return would suggest. Fortunately, investing isn't really about macro trends. It is primarily about companies – their products, their cash flows, their profits, their management's expertise and their cultures. And while identifying the trends in these isn't easy, it comes with many fewer variables than forecasting the direction of global interest rates. Better, we think, to work with people who focus on what is useful and possible than what is usually impossible and not necessarily useful.

2. Find managers with some sense of stock market history

We cannot predict the future using the past, but we can learn useful lessons and minimise the future mistakes. A visit to Edinburgh's Library of Mistakes, a splendid financial history resource, can be most instructive on this front. There, and in numerous business school libraries, shelves groan with research that comes to one key conclusion: about three quarters of M&A is a complete failure for shareholders. I can therefore tell you with some certainty that shares in companies engaged in M&A, other than small infill acquisitions, are less likely to be good investments than those that stick to organic growth. If your manager loves an acquisitive company, acquire holdings in someone else's fund.

History teaches us similar lessons about leverage. We always want to be ready for a crisis (there is almost always one on the way). We know that it is the companies with the most debt that come a cropper the fastest in a crisis. Having debt to pay back and banks to keep happy reduces flexibility and autonomy, which are both things that managers need most when the chips are down. Long-term investors are far better off accepting lower annual returns in return for a greater degree of financial resilience and a greater chance of long-term survival. So check your managers' top ten holdings list. If there are too many highly leveraged firms you may be better off avoiding the fund.

3. Find managers who back themselves

You want to see a manager investing in their own fund. If it isn't good enough for his own money, why should it be good enough for yours? There are all sorts of definitions of risk around in the financial world. The only one that should matter to most investors is the risk of permanent loss of capital. If a manager isn't investing in his own fund you might wonder why he reckons his own capital isn't safe there and take yours elsewhere.

4. Find managers who think more than they trade

Very often the biggest difference between a successful asset manager and an unsuccessful one is turnover. Low turnover means lower costs (which are a helpful predictor of long-term performance). But it also suggests a higher level of conviction. You want a manager who has a clear strategy which brings him good ideas and who then gives those ideas time to play out. All too many managers get swayed by the short-term direction of the market: it takes only the smallest of worries that their own strategy might mean they underperform the market in the short term for them to adopt someone else's. We're looking for the small number of managers in the market who can demonstrate more stamina than most. The ones who have a (good) plan and stick to it regardless of what everyone else is up to.

SANDY CROSS *is an investment director at Rossie House Investment Management.*

_____

ADVANTAGES OF CONCENTRATION

Kepler Trust Intelligence analyst WILLIAM SOBCZAK *explains how trusts that have the courage to opt for a highly concentrated portfolio can succeed in achieving above-average performance.*

S INCE THE LAUNCH of the first index fund in 1976, passive investing has proven to be a successful investment strategy for both institutional and retail investors. The first of its kind, the Vanguard 500 Index fund, has delivered an annualised rate of return of 10.01%, totalling to a return of over 1,500% since 1989. While good in absolute terms, in relative terms because of fees it has underperformed the index, with the S&P 500 delivering an annualised return of 10.12% over the same period. Although there is only a small difference between the two annually, we calculate that over the 42 years this equates to underperformance of about 53%.*

On the other hand, active management hasn't, if one looks at the performance of the average fund, covered itself with glory either in terms of outperforming benchmarks. According to the most recent S&P Indices vs Active Management (SPIVA) report, which offers information on the passive vs active debate in the US over the course of 2017, 63.1% of large-cap managers, 44.4% of mid-cap managers, and 47.7% of small-cap managers underperformed the S&P 500, the S&P MidCap 400, and the S&P SmallCap 600 respectively. Over a five-year period, the numbers look even worse for supporters of active management: 84.23% of large-cap managers, 85.06% of mid-cap managers, and 91.17% of small-cap managers lagged their respective benchmarks.

---

*   These and all other calculations in this article were correct as at 9 July 2018.

So while outperformance of a benchmark is possible, the numbers above suggest that active managers are mediocre, and that those who can achieve outperformance over the long term are therefore difficult to identify. The interesting question, then, is what marks this small sub-set out from the great majority? What are the small minority of active managers who are outperforming their benchmarks doing differently?

GO BIG OR GO HOME

The overwhelming evidence is that fund managers who are willing to back their convictions with punchy bets are the ones that tend to outperform by the highest margin. There have been numerous studies looking at the different attributes that contribute to manager outperformance, ranging from simplistic momentum strategies (Jegadeesh and Timan, 1993) to the quality of the managers' education (Chevalier and Ellison, 1999). A growing body of more recent work suggests that the concentration of a manager's portfolio has a significant effect on the relative performance delivered by the manager.

Using active share and tracking error, Antti Petajisto (2013) uncovered the evidence that the most active managers were the ones most likely to outperform their benchmarks, even after taking account of fees. It was in his previous work with Martijn Cremers in 2006 that the term 'closet' tracker/indexing was popularised, and as can be seen below, four types of active management were examined.

We can take away two conclusions from the study. Firstly, that the most active stock pickers were able to add the most value for investors, beating their benchmark on average by about 1.26% a year (after fees) and secondly, that while 'closet' indexers essentially matched their benchmark index performance before fees, that inevitably meant that they consistently underperformed after fees.

Despite these findings, closet indexing is a relatively common strategy in both bull and bear markets. More recently Cremers has suggested that fund managers should aim for an active share above 80% if a large-cap manager and above 90% if a small-cap manager. However, he estimated in 2016 that only 30% of US mutual fund assets are held in funds with an active share of at least 80%, and only about 10% of funds with an active share of at least 90%.

Supporting the work of Petajisto (2013) and Cremers (2006), Cohen, Polk, and Silli (2009) examined the performance of stocks that represent the managers 'best ideas'. They discovered that the most bullish ideas were the ones that consistently delivered the greatest returns. Yet, because of the way that the investment industry works, and in particular how managers are incentivised, they believe that having a highly concentrated portfolio is not the 'optimal' course for many managers to pursue. The tendency in practice is for them to introduce stocks into their portfolio about which they have much less conviction.

Cohen, Polk, and Silli summarise four key reasons that managers may over-diversify in this way:

1. Regulations can often make it difficult for investment funds to be highly concentrated.

2. Following the work of Berk and Green (2004), manager compensation is often tied to the size of the fund. Managers are therefore incentivised to continue broadening their investment portfolio even if they do not have alpha-generating ideas.

3. Since the performance of the portfolio is such an important determinant for the manager's wealth, large investments in a small number of holdings could, in the wrong circumstances, put a manager's job security at risk.

4. Investors tend to judge investment decisions in irrational ways. For example, Morningstar's well-known rating system makes it difficult for a highly concentrated fund to secure a top rating, however good its return. Morningstar's methodology heavily penalizes idiosyncratic risk.

Following the research from Petajisto, in 2015 Martijn Cremers took a slightly different approach to understanding the relationship between concentrated portfolios and performance. This time he assessed only high active share portfolios and looked at how important investment holding periods were in determining performance.

Fascinatingly, he found that it was only the investment managers who had a patient perspective, defined as a holding duration of more than two years, who outperformed, to the tune of more than 2% per year. In comparison, funds which traded frequently generally underperformed, whether or not they had a high active share. Cremers found that both closet indexers and low active share funds underperformed on average even if they adopted a patient strategy.

INVESTMENT TRUSTS: THE THEORY IN ACTION

The findings from these studies are particularly relevant for investment trusts, where there is a well-known argument that the capital structure of a closed-end vehicle gives managers the ability to take a longer-term view on available investment opportunities. Being able to build up a revenue reserve also allows the manager of an investment trust to deliver smooth and consistent income, not having to make short-term decisions as a result of fund flows, and to plan for the future from a longer-term perspective.

Finally, and some would say most importantly, since investment trusts have independent boards, the manager is answering to people who should, at least in theory, have investors' long-term goals in mind rather than the short-term swings in sentiment that open-ended fund managers are open to. It follows that investment trusts whose managers adopt a patient investment strategy and hold highly concentrated portfolios should – if these academic theories are correct – be more likely to deliver superior performance over time.

According to our analysis, theory certainly seems to be filtering down into practice. Within the equity investment trust universe, the average number of holdings has steadily reduced over the past five years, with the average trust having 82 holdings, compared to 91 in 2013. This represents a decrease of over 10%, which we think is significant.

Indeed, this matches with the anecdotal evidence we pick up from meeting managers and boards of an increasing desire for a more concentrated approach. Several managers we have met recently have told us that they expect to run more concentrated portfolios than they have in the past. Examples include JPMORGAN AMERICAN, HENDERSON EUROTRUST, JPMORGAN CLAVERHOUSE, and JUPITER UK GROWTH (formerly Jupiter Primadona).

While overall it seems that investment trust portfolios are becoming more concentrated, one can see significant variations between constituents of the various sectors. For example, the UK equity income and flexible investment sectors have seen the average number of holdings over the past five years decline by at least ten stocks, whereas, in the UK equity and bond income sector and European sectors, the average number of holdings has increased by more than 20 stocks.

As the academic literature illustrates, alongside greater portfolio concentration, lower turnover portfolios also tend to outperform. Over the past four years, we can clearly observe a shift towards more patient investment strategies in investment trusts, with the mean turnover of portfolios reducing by about 20%.

Just as with the portfolio concentration statistics, turnover rates vary greatly among sectors. The sector with the lowest portfolio turnover over the past year was the Japanese sector (including smaller companies) at 16.37%. By contrast the greatest turnover was in the global equity income sector, which on average had a turnover of over 40%.

Average number of holdings: changes over five years by sector

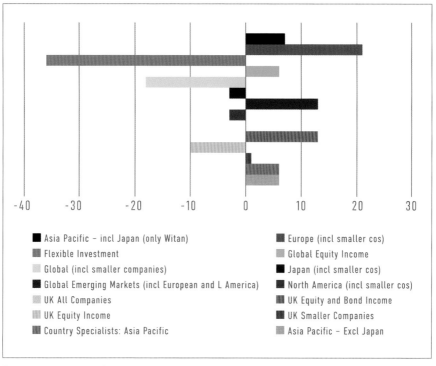

Source: Morningstar, Kepler Partners.

APPLYING THE THEORY

Having examined the investment trust universe, we have composed a list of trusts that can be defined as concentrated in terms of either the total number of holdings or the proportion of their assets which is invested in their largest holdings. We have also included trusts which pursue an explicitly 'concentrated' approach, even though the total number of holdings may seem anything but.

Concentration in the key sectors

SECTOR	AVG	MOST CONCENTRATED	NO OF HOLDINGS	LEAST CONCENTRATED	NO OF HOLDINGS
Asia Pacific – Excl Japan	72	Martin Currie Asia Unconstrained	37	Fidelity Asian Values	156
Country Specialists: Asia Specific	59	Weiss Korea Opportunity	15	Fidelity China Special	167
UK Smaller Companies	72	Strategic Equity Capital	12	BlackRock Throgmorton	166
UK Equity Income	61	Value and Income	40	Lowland	128
UK Equity & Bond Income	101	Henderson High Income	100	Acorn Income Fund	127
UK All Companies	97	Aurora	15	Mercantile	108
North America (incl smaller cos)	72	North Atlantic Smaller Cos	24	JPMorgan American	189
Global Emerging Markets (incl European and L America)	84	Fundsmith Emerging Equities	48	Genesis Emerging Markets	145
Japan (incl smaller cos)	79	CC Japan Income & Growth	42	Fidelity Japan Trust & JPMorgan Japan Smaller Cos	101

SECTOR	AVG	MOST CONCENTRATED	NO OF HOLDINGS	LEAST CONCENTRATED	NO OF HOLDINGS
Global (incl smaller cos)	94	Lindsell Train	18	Foreign & Colonial Investment Trust	509
Global Equity Income	76	IP Select Global Equity Income	54	JPMorgan Global Growth & Income	144
Flexible Investment	63	Personal Assets	36	Capital Gearing	180
Europe (incl smaller cos)	99	BlackRock Greater Europe	38	JPMorgan European Smaller Comp Ord	145

Source: Morningstar, Kepler partners.
Baillie Gifford, Jupiter European Opportunities plc and Alliance Trust plc are clients of Kepler Trust Intelligence.

Managing two trusts with fewer than 30 holdings, Nick Train, co-founder of fund management boutique Lindsell Train, has the most overtly concentrated approach. Over the past ten years FINSBURY GROWTH & INCOME has delivered returns of 297.4% in comparison to the 96.6% returns from the FTSE All-Share. Train believes that the Lindsell Train business model encourages patient investing. A small and compact team ensures that employees aren't compelled to continually offer new ideas in the hope of gaining greater recognition.

Among trusts that don't necessarily have the lowest concentration or turnover in absolute terms, some stand out as having a high-conviction approach for different reasons. This is in the sense that the top ten holdings amount to a large proportion of the portfolio. For example, JUPITER EUROPEAN OPPORTUNITIES has just 42 holdings, which is barely half the sector average of 70, and of these the top holdings account for over 70% of net asset value. The manager, Alexander Darwall, has an enviable long-term track. Over ten years this trust has tripled the returns of the benchmark, the FTSE World Europe.

Within the global sector, SCOTTISH MORTGAGE, while having 95 holdings, is heavily concentrated in terms of its top ten holdings representing 53.6% of NAV. Run by James Anderson and Tom Slater, the portfolio revolves around investing in innovative companies that the managers believe can revolutionise established industries. This has led the trust to become the largest UK listed equity investment trust with assets of more than £6bn.

Although at first sight one might not think that it fits the bill, ALLIANCE TRUST offers, despite having more than 190 individual holdings, what Willis Tower Watson calls "concentrated diversification". The trust utilises the best ideas of eight different managers. Each portfolio usually has only 20 names and a very high active share, effectively making the main portfolio an aggregate of a number of more-or-less independent concentrated portfolios. A similar mandate for institutions has demonstrated significant outperformance since it was launched in 2015. By putting eight such portfolios together, shareholders in Alliance Trust benefit from all the advantages of concentrated portfolios, but with the benefit of some additional diversification.

Another concentrated trust in the AIC global sector is the INDEPENDENT INVESTMENT TRUST (IIT). With a portfolio of 23 stocks relative to the peer group average of 80, IIT has performed well over both the short and long term. The company aims to provide strong returns over extended periods through investing in UK and international securities and, on occasions, futures. This allows the manager an unusually high degree of freedom. Over one, three and five years the trust has generated double the returns of the MSCI World index.

WILLIAM SOBCZAK joined Kepler Partners in February 2018 as an investment trust analyst. He is a graduate of the University of Western Australia with a BSc in Psychology. Kepler Trust Intelligence offers investors a library of high-quality, up-to-date investment strategy articles and fund analysis all written in-house by experienced analysts, on two separate retail and professional investor sites.

KEEP AN EYE OUT FOR ANOMALIES

NICK GREENWOOD, *manager of the Miton Global Opportunities fund, explains some of the new dynamics shaping the investment trust market and why sudden share price movements may not be all that they seem.*

T HE INVESTMENT TRUST sector continues to evolve. A key driver remains the rapid consolidation of the wealth management industry. Until recently wealth managers had been the key owners of closed-ended funds. Last year there was an aborted merger between Rathbones and Smith & Williamson. This would have created a business managing £52bn. In any walk of life, when an organisation becomes truly vast, staff at the sharp end are no longer allowed to use their initiative. Otherwise, someone somewhere will abuse that freedom.

The sheer size of funds now managed by a small number of houses makes it difficult for investment trusts to figure within these portfolios. Those trusts which continue to find favour are likely to be the very largest where the major chains feel comfortable that they will be able to source sufficient shares in the open market. A number of quite well-known funds are beginning to find that they need to grow if they are to retain their place on buy lists; a message we were getting some years ago. In the meantime, it is likely that some medium-sized trusts derate. At that point, they will be of interest to us, increasing our pool of opportunity.

Closed-end funds are a natural structure for alternative asset classes which are less liquid than equities. Examples include property, peer-to-peer lending and forestry. Until relatively recently the vast majority of trusts were equity funds.

The calculation of the stated net asset value for a portfolio of stocks and shares is straightforward. They are daily traded and the resultant figure gives a fair representation of the true value of the portfolio. Calculating a net asset value for an alternative portfolio is a far more subjective exercise.

The adopted methodology can over time fail to replicate the asset's real-world value or may purely have become stale, not incorporating recent developments. Nevertheless, past experience of only handling equity trusts has left investors tending to treat stated net asset values as verbatim. An extreme example within our portfolio has been residential property in Berlin; our estimates of true value have on occasions been in excess of 50% higher than the official figure.

While the bulk of opportunities continue to come from the disruption of supply and demand and alternatives, recent additions have come from new sources. These trends may well prove to be enduring. There has been increased volatility due to the heightened ownership of the sector by self-directed investors, who typically trade through platforms such as Hargreaves Lansdown, AJ Bell and Alliance Trust Savings. As a result, a greater proportion of trades are now smaller and electronic.

In the past market makers could effectively close the market in medium and smaller trusts by posting bids and offers only valid in modest size. Electronic trades are typically smaller than the minimum size the market must make. Therefore a market maker remaining on the bid will quickly find themselves on the receiving end of multiple sell orders. They will soon find themselves with more inventory than they would like. This soaks up the limited capital they commit under current business models. As a result prices will quickly fall. Competitors will follow suit, as they also do not want to receive multiple sale orders. Thereby a Dutch auction ensues and trust share prices can now fall suddenly and sharply. Once buyers are attracted or the market rallies, this process rapidly reverses.

There were two market declines in the first half of 2018. At the end of January, there was a global sell-off where a number of trusts popular with private investors quickly fell. In March, trusts where individuals had unrealised gains were hard hit by a flurry of capital gains tax selling. This triggered significant falls as it coincided with a market wobble when buyers were delaying purchases. A number of trusts fell more sharply in the March sell-off despite the general fall in markets being more modest than in January. These declines occurred in the absence of much movement in underlying portfolios.

INDIA CAPITAL GROWTH saw its discount widen from 4.7% in January to 19.9% on 3 April, much of the widening coming in March. This decline bottomed out hours before the tax deadline. India Capital Growth's discount had rapidly narrowed to 8.3% by 18 April. PHOENIX SPREE saw its shares oscillate between 337p and 380p during April despite its estimated NAV remaining static around 355p. Meanwhile we saw our own shares move from a 2% premium on 14 March to a 5% discount on 4 April. This discount had narrowed to less than 1% by 18 April and at the time of writing is trading at a premium. Given the significant increase, over recent years, of our shares held via platforms, it should not have been a surprise that we have become a textbook example of the new trading pattern.

The other development is that a number of closed-ended funds listed overseas are moving to London. In the United Kingdom we have a vibrant market in trusts which does not exist elsewhere. Funds that trade on a wide discount locally can list in London where, if they have a good story to tell, there are investors that will listen. The resultant demand should allow their discounts to narrow. Two recent entrants to our portfolio fit this theme.

STENPROP moved to London this summer. We accumulated a position via its existing listing in Johannesburg at a substantial discount to the latest NAV of 135p, despite an indicated 6.5p-a-share dividend which the company hopes to grow. The other new entrant that has recently transferred to London is LIFE SETTLEMENT ASSETS (LSAA). Funds that specialise in secondhand life policies have tended to be disappointing in recent years. This is largely because life expectancy has until recently been steadily increasing. This means that investors not only have to wait longer than expected for the policies to mature but also that they have to keep paying premiums for a longer period than anticipated. We acquired our initial stake in LSAA at 140¢ a share at a time when NAV was 210¢. At that price we believe that most concerns are reflected in the price.

The trust is refocusing its portfolio on UK mixed light industrial properties. These are located in unfashionable urban locations such as Mytholmroyd and Huddersfield. There is little new supply as new builds would be worth less than the cost of construction. Furthermore, incentives to turn these sites into housing reduces the availability further. Demand is increasing, the arrival of the internet means some business models no longer need to locate close to customers. Some activities can now be performed using cheaper provincial properties.

We undertake a significant number of meetings with managers of closed-ended funds. Many of these look uninspiring on paper and indeed the vast majority prove to be just that. Nevertheless, despite initial appearances, some prove to be gems. Our holdings in TALIESIN and DUNEDIN ENTERPRISE started with just those types of meetings. It would be nice to think that recent entrants such as Stenprop and Life Settlement Assets will pick up the baton and drive future returns.

OUTLOOK

It is ten years since the global financial crisis. It is a sobering thought that somebody who joined the City in the immediate aftermath would now have a decade's experience but have barely seen an interest rate rise let alone a cycle. Therefore, complacency abounds within the financial community and any change of scenario is likely to cause upheaval. Inflated asset prices are predicated on exceptionally low interest rates. Investors have few ready alternatives. This scenario may continue for a while yet. Looking forward, the biggest risk to the atmosphere of calm is rising interest and bond rates.

Since the end of March the US ten-year bond yield has risen from 2.7% to 3.2%. If this trend continues and investors find they can source a measurable yield from conventional sources of income, they will return to them. This would trigger volatility within the trust sector where 'income manufacturers' have been extraordinarily successful in raising capital. The combined market capitalisation of infrastructure and renewables alone is many billions. Such a figure dwarfs the clearing mechanism for trust shares. A modest decline in appetite for this type of fund would dramatically alter the short-term balance of supply and demand. Should the market in these trusts be overwhelmed, this would represent an opportunity.

NICK GREENWOOD *is a former private client stockbroker who has been managing the Miton Global Opportunities trust since 2004, joining Miton after its merger with Exeter Fund Managers. Miton Global Opportunities invests primarily in other investment trusts.*

DIVIDING RESPONSIBILITIES

ROBIN ANGUS, *executive director of Personal Assets Trust, describes how the board of the trust divides its work with its investment adviser, and dispenses with some other popular misconceptions.*

STRANGE BELIEFS

PEOPLE SOMETIMES BELIEVE the oddest things. I'm not referring here to 'fake news' and all the weird and wonderful tales circulated on social media about everyone from the Pope and Donald Trump to the casts of *Love Island* or *Celebrity Big Brother*, but to the straightforward misconceptions that take hold about everyday matters. Here's one example. Recently a shareholder wrote to share with me his fears that an outside predator might launch a bid for PERSONAL ASSETS.

I was able to reply that, while bids have taken place in the investment trust sector and will probably continue to do so as long as trusts exist, the idea that this might happen to Personal Assets worried me not in the slightest. Why would anyone want to bid for us? The usual justification for taking over an investment trust is to acquire cheap assets.

This would indeed be worrying for the board if Personal Assets' shares sold at a material discount, but they haven't done so since Discount Freedom Day in November 1999[*] and will never do so again. While buying £1 of assets for 90p

---

[*] The date when investment trusts were allowed to repurchase their own shares and reissue them from Treasury, two essential ingredients in a discount control mechanism.

makes good sense, buying the very same assets at 102p plus costs would make no sense at all.

It's true that sometimes an investment trust will be bid for not so much to acquire cheap assets as to put an indifferently managed pool of assets to better use. This, however, would again typically be mirrored in the existence of a discount and the mutterings of shareholder discontent, neither of which apply to Personal Assets today. I'm not one for making rash statements, but taking all these things together I feel I can say with confidence that Personal Assets is about as bid-proof as an investment trust can be.

'IT'S ALL ABOUT PERFORMANCE'

A common misconception concerns what an investment trust should aim to be doing for its shareholders. A very eminent trust chairman once remarked to me, as if it were blindingly obvious: "It's all about performance." Up to a point he was right, but there's a lot more to performance than how much you can get the net asset value per share to rise, which was what the trust chairman had been talking about.

The success or failure of an investment trust is no more limited to its NAV performance than the choice of a car has to do only with the speed at which it can be driven. While a Bugatti Chiron or a Lamborghini Aventador may go faster than other cars, they wouldn't be the obvious choice for the school run or pottering about town, to say nothing of their petrol consumption or the cost of insuring them.

Similarly, there are lots of things other than straightforward NAV performance that potential buyers of shares in an investment trust may want to consider:

*   How much risk is being taken to achieve the NAV performance?

*   Is possible extra performance a fair exchange for any extra risk?

*   How volatile have the returns historically been?

*   Does the share price properly reflect the NAV, or is there a persistent discount (or premium)?

*   How great is the yield and how safe is the dividend?

*   How hard is the portfolio being ridden to earn this dividend?

*   How efficiently is the company run in terms of its ongoing charges ratio (OCR)?

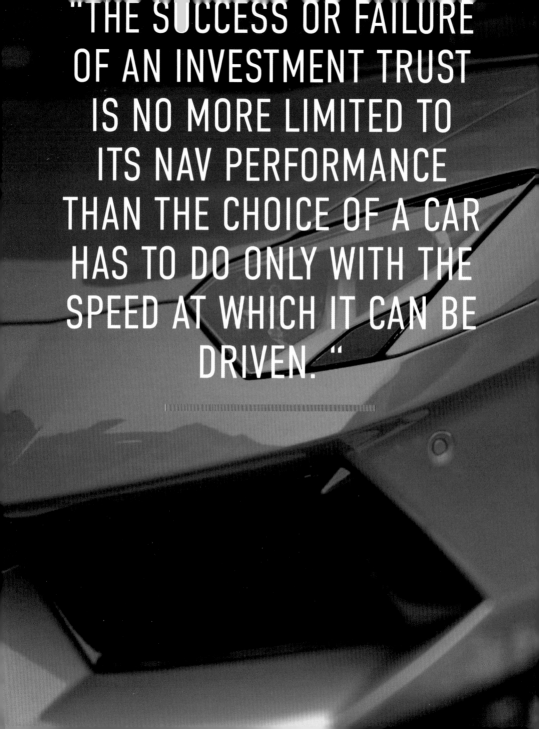

"THE SUCCESS OR FAILURE OF AN INVESTMENT TRUST IS NO MORE LIMITED TO ITS NAV PERFORMANCE THAN THE CHOICE OF A CAR HAS TO DO ONLY WITH THE SPEED AT WHICH IT CAN BE DRIVEN. "

- Does the way the company is managed meet the buyer's requirements on environmental, social and governance (ESG) matters, or on equality and diversity?

There are many other criteria I could mention here, but these should be sufficient to demonstrate that, while NAV performance pure and simple is a large part of the story, it's by no means all of it.

'IT'S ALL ABOUT STOCKPICKING'

The fallacies and misconceptions about investment and, more particularly, about investment management are legion, but a common fallacy I'd like to dispose of here is that successful investment is all about picking the right stocks and then hanging on to them. *'Don't put all your eggs in one basket,'* is a common piece of investment advice, as is *'OK, put all your eggs in one basket, but watch the basket.'*

But neither suggestion tells the whole story. One of my favourite books about investment is *The Money Game*, by 'Adam Smith' (the pseudonym of the talented and perceptive US economic commentator and journalist George J. W. Goodman). Its 'Chapter Nine, Mr Smith Admits His Biases', is the culmination of the first (and arguably most important) section of the book.

In it, Smith writes:

> "One of my biases is so strong that I have to mention it immediately, because it runs counter to an idea that is very common, i.e., that if you buy good stocks and put them away, in the long run you can't go wrong. Well, as Keynes once remarked, 'In the long run we are all dead.'"

Smith then introduces us to a certain Mr Bancroft, whose belief was that the best strategy for a conservative, long-term investor (like we all are, since very few of us will admit to being a short-term spiv) is "locking up [stocks] and putting [them] away". And Mr Bancroft chose his stocks carefully.

> "[But where] Mr Bancroft erred was in the locking up and putting away, for by the time his descendants managed to get their fingers on the portfolio, Mr Bancroft's Southern Zinc, Gold Belt Mining, Carrell Company of New Hampshire and American Alarm Clock Company were all worth 0, and in fact, so was the estate."*

---

* *The Money Game*, 'Adam Smith', Random House New York, 1968.

It's easy to laugh at poor Mr Bancroft. But 'buy and hold' is in fashion just now, and can be dangerous. I often think that if, back in 2000, I had taken a sabbatical and gone on my travels far from the markets (and if, of course, I had never heard of investment trusts), I might have put all my money into two ultimate blue chips of the time, which simply couldn't go wrong: GEC and Royal Bank of Scotland.

Reader, I held both of them – and lost at least some of my money. And just as business cases can change, cheapness isn't everything either. Stocks can be, and often are, cheap for good reasons. To quote a recent comment by Sebastian Lyon, our investment adviser:

> "There are many companies that we would not buy at any price. Avoiding the dross is more than half the battle when it comes to investment survival. While there may be plenty of superficially tempting opportunities in the stock market, we prefer to remain discerning. Choosing companies with attractive returns on capital, financial strength and earnings growth (usually in that order) is a more effective way to deliver steady returns than bottom-fishing across the stock market's detritus. These lessons have been learned from painful experience."

WHAT THE BOARD DOESN'T DO

One thing that is almost universally true of investment trust boards (the board of Personal Assets here being no exception) is that they are not involved in stock selection. It's not their job, any more than it is the job of the board of a football club to pick the squad for each match or of a bishop to pick the hymns for every Sunday service in every church in his diocese.

Indeed, I dread to think what a portfolio chosen by a board of half a dozen highly opinionated individuals might look like. A meeting to review it would all too easily become a cross between the voting at the Eurovision Song Contest and picking teams in a school playground. Ian Rushbrook [the former investment director of Personal Assets] used to refer to the famously argumentative board of the Independent Investment Company, which was founded in 1924 with three idiosyncratic investment titans as directors – John Maynard Keynes, Thomas Johnstone Carlyle Gifford (the founder of Baillie, Gifford & Co) and Oswald

"JUST AS BUSINESS CASES CAN CHANGE, CHEAPNESS ISN'T EVERYTHING EITHER. STOCKS CAN BE, AND OFTEN ARE, CHEAP FOR GOOD REASONS."

'Foxy' Falk of the stockbrokers Buckmaster & Moore. They rarely agreed on anything. It was not a formula for success.[*]

WHAT THE BOARD DOES DO

With all investment trusts, there is a distinction to be drawn between running the company (the responsibility of the board) and running the portfolio (the responsibility of the investment manager or investment adviser). The board naturally has a watching brief to ensure that stock selection remains consistent with the trust's investment approach as articulated over the years. But the danger of stock selection per se by the directors would be that the board might function like an international football team, full of prima donnas unable to work productively together.

A less obvious area where the board of an investment trust comes into its own is where the trust runs into a sticky patch such as Personal Assets suffered in 2014, when we suffered in investment terms a 'perfect storm' as our NAV actually fell when our comparator rose. In such circumstances the board's job is first and foremost to support and encourage the investment adviser.

GREEN, AMBER AND RED

Now let's look at the details of how responsibilities are allocated. Under the terms of the contract with our investment adviser there are four areas which have been reserved specifically to the board but as regards which the board is required to engage in active dialogue with the investment adviser:

- the level and form of liquidity within the portfolio

- asset allocation in the portfolio

- matters relating to shareholder communication

- hedging.

In addition to these, three matters are described as having been reserved to the board alone:

---

[*]   For a description of this fascinating company (which was no relation to today's much more successful Independent Investment Trust, chaired by Douglas McDougall and managed by Max Ward), see Nigel Edward Morecroft, *The Origins of Asset Management from 1700 to 1966: Towering Investors*, Palgrave Studies in the History of Finance, 2017.

- the company's gearing levels

- matters relating to the buying back and issuance of the company's shares

- investment in new asset classes.

In practice, however, the board and the investment adviser consult on these matters too, and as regards the first and third of them it would be strange if they did not. (For instance, neither the board nor the investment adviser could decide unilaterally to invest in the Turkish Lira or Argentinian equities!)

The company has no predetermined maximum or minimum levels of exposure to asset classes, currencies or geographic areas, but these exposures are reported to, and monitored by, the board in order to ensure that adequate diversification is achieved.

The resulting matrix is the distillation of years of experience. We set maximum and minimum percentages for each asset class and currency, and operate a 'traffic light' system for investment classes:

- **green** for core investments such as large-cap stocks in the UK, US and Europe

- amber for areas in which we are unlikely to invest and where doing so would require the investment adviser to seek board approval, such as Japan and corporate bonds

- **red** for investments not currently permitted, such as direct property and private equity.

All these parameters are reviewed at each board meeting.

Not every board will have the same division of responsibilities, but what is important is that the division is clear and preferably written down, so that nobody is in any doubt where the buck stops in each case.

ROBIN ANGUS, *a former stockbroking analyst, has been a director of Personal Assets Trust since 1984.*

———————————

BEHIND THE GROWTH OF VCTS

VCT specialist ALEX DAVIES *explains how the market for VCTs has changed, but continues to set new records.*

L AST TAX YEAR £728m was invested in venture capital trusts (VCTs), the second-highest amount ever. The largest VCT raised £200m, another record. The evidence suggests that VCTs are becoming more mainstream. Why is that?

The main reason is that VCTs are one of the last decent and relatively simple options left for wealthier investors to invest in a tax-efficient manner. Those investors have been directly in the taxman's line of sight for the past few years. The amount of tax they pay has gone up year after year. At the same time, many of the traditional ways to mitigate tax have been heavily restricted.

Ten years ago, before the recession:

- the highest rate of income tax was 40%

- the highest effective rate of dividend tax was 30.56%

- investors could contribute £225,000 to their pension in one tax year and the lifetime allowance was £1.6 million

- buy-to-let landlords could offset all their mortgage interest against their profits.

Compare that to today's rules and a much bleaker picture emerges:

- the highest rate of income tax is 45% and some people pay an effective rate of 60%

- the highest rate of dividend tax is 38.1%

- some investors are restricted to an annual pension contribution of as little as £10,000 and the lifetime allowance is just over £1m

- buy-to-let landlords can offset only 25% of their mortgage interest against profits and this will drop to zero in 2020.

To put this in context, our calculations show that someone earning £250,000 and with dividends of £40,000 a year now pays nearly £30,000 more in income and dividend tax compared to ten years ago. Moreover, while ten years ago they could have significantly lowered their tax bill by making a large pension contribution of up to £225,000, today they can only add £10,000. Buy-to-let, which until the rule changes was often seen as a relatively simple and fairly tax-efficient way of investing for the future, is now far less attractive.

Against this backdrop of increasing tax and restrictions, along with ISAs, where the annual limit now stands at £20,000 a year, VCTs stand out as one of the last bastions of tax efficiency. These are the main benefits:

1. You get up to 30% income tax relief when you invest.

2. All dividends are tax-free. So, if a VCT pays a dividend of 5%, this is what you actually get in your hand. By way of comparison, to get the same income from a unit trust, a top-rate taxpayer would have to receive a gross dividend of more than 8%.

3. You don't need to declare VCTs – or any dividends you receive – on your tax return.

4. The allowance is generous and, importantly, simple: £200,000 a year for anyone.

Looking beyond the tax relief, interest in VCTs would not be so great if they were not also potentially appealing investments in their own right. The reason the government gives investors in VCTs such generous tax treatment is that the capital VCTs raise provides risk capital for small and growing businesses, on which the future growth of the economy depends.

The idea of supporting young and entrepreneurial companies strikes a chord with many investors. Ten years ago tech hubs, where young businesses looking to get off the ground can share office space and swap ideas, were rare. Today the major cities are brimming with them. The companies VCTs invest in represent our future. They are nimble and agile. They also create a lot of jobs. Small and medium-sized businesses (SMEs) are responsible for 60% of all private sector employment in the UK.

VCT funds raised 2017/18 tax year

VCT OFFER	SECTOR	DATE OPENED	CAPACITY* (£M)	RAISED IN 2017/18 (£M)	DAYS	£M TOTAL / DAY	AS AT
Foresight 4 VCT	Generalist	05/19/17	50	25.5	321	0.079	05 Apr 2018
Octopus AIM VCTs	AIM	06/16/17	40	40	151	0.265	Closed 14 Nov 2017
Unicorn AIM VCT	AIM	07/25/17	35.5	35.5	115	0.309	Closed 17 Nov 2017
Octopus Titan VCT	Generalist	09/05/17	200	200	199	1.005	Closed 23 Mar 2018
Albion VCTs	Generalist	09/06/17	32	32	180	0.178	Closed 4 Mar 2018
Mobeus VCTs	Generalist	09/06/17	80	80	169	0.473	Closed 22 Feb 2018
Downing ONE VCT	Generalist	09/07/17	30	30	194	0.155	Closed 20 Mar 2018
Puma VCT 13	Limited life	09/13/17	30	8.9	204	0.044	05 Apr 2018
Northern VCTs	Generalist	09/22/17	60	60	54	1.111	Closed 15 Nov 2017
Maven 3 & 4 VCTs	Generalist	09/22/17	40	39	195	0.2	05 Apr 2018
Hargreave Hale AIM VCT 2	AIM	10/02/17	4.2	4.2	46	0.091	Closed 17 Nov 2017
Baronsmead VCTs	Generalist	10/04/17	44.2	44.2	77	0.574	Closed 20 Dec 2017
ProVen VCTs	Generalist	10/20/17	7.2	7.2	61	0.118	Closed 20 Dec 2017
Calculus VCT	Generalist	10/23/17	5	2	164	0.012	05 Apr 2018

VCT OFFER	SECTOR	DATE OPENED	CAPACITY* (£M)	RAISED IN 2017/18 (£M)	DAYS	£M TOTAL / DAY	AS AT
Amati VCTs	AIM	10/30/17	20	19.8	157	0.126	05 Apr 2018
Pembroke VCT	Generalist	12/01/17	20	6.1	125	0.049	05 Apr 2018
Elderstreet Draper Esprit VCT	Generalist	12/07/17	10	3.6	119	0.03	05 Apr 2018
British Smaller Companies	Generalist	01/11/18	4.4	4.4	15	0.293	Closed 26 Jan 2018
Edge Performance VCT	Specialist	01/16/18	1.3	0.7	79	0.008	Closed 5 Apr 2018
Hargreave Hale AIM VCT 1	AIM	02/13/18	20	18.2	51	0.357	05 Apr 2018
Hazel Renewable Energy 1&2	Specialist	03/14/18	4.4	4.4	6	0.733	Closed 19 Mar 2018

Important note: These figures have been collated by Wealth Club. Wealth Club monitors the main VCT offers open to execution-only clients, not the whole market. The total raised (column E) does not match the official figure of £728m. This is because there are some smaller VCTs (e.g. advice only) we haven't included. Also, our figures reflect purely new funds raised, whilst the official figure also includes any dividends reinvested.

HAVE ANY OF THESE ENTREPRENEURIAL BUSINESSES TURNED INTO SUCCESS STORIES?

The most high-profile VCT success story in recent years has been Zoopla, the UK's most comprehensive property website. It was founded in 2007 and first received a VCT investment in 2009. Five years later, Zoopla Group floated on the London Stock Exchange with a value of £919m and soon became the first VCT-backed £1bn company.

Another example is SwiftKey, a London-based start-up founded by two Cambridge graduates that employed artificial intelligence to create a ground-breaking predictive smartphone keyboard app. It received its first VCT investment in 2010. Six years later, Microsoft acquired SwiftKey in a deal reportedly worth $250m.

More recently, Watchfinder, the leading retailer of pre-owned premium watches, was sold to Richemont, the Swiss luxury goods holding company, which owns brands such as Cartier, Montblanc, Vacheron Constantin, and Van Cleef & Arpels. Watchfinder first received a VCT investment in 2014 and subsequently grew rapidly. Turnover trebled between 2015 and 2018. The trade sale to Richemont was completed in July 2018. The size of the deal was undisclosed, but the VCT achieved its exit at 8.7 times the value of its investment.

Clearly, you don't come across a Zoopla, Swiftkey or Watchfinder every day. Some of the companies in which VCTs invest will fail, others will languish. Risk capital is called risk capital for a reason. That said, if you look at the past five and ten years, the average VCT has marginally outperformed the FTSE 100. When you factor in the tax relief, the returns are clearly even more attractive. However, as any investor knows, past performance is not a guide to the future.

HOW TO CHOOSE A VCT

The top-performing generalist VCTs over the last ten years are managed by companies such as Maven, Northern, Mobeus, British Smaller Companies and Baronsmead. If you had invested ten years ago and reinvested all your dividends, you could have at least doubled your money. However, much of the good performance in these cases has come from certain types of investment, principally management buyouts, which originally qualified for VCT tax relief, but are no longer allowed for new VCT investment under the latest rules.

Similarly, renewable energy provided very steady returns for many VCT investors until it was disallowed as a new investment in 2015. Because the original contracts to provide energy from wind and solar were underpinned by government-backed feed-in tariffs, the risk profile for such VCTs was considerably lower than it would otherwise have been. The government and HMRC sensibly retain the right to tighten the rules if a particular type of investment turns out to be sufficiently secure not to warrant tax relief.

WHAT DOES THIS MEAN FOR INVESTORS?

When you invest in a VCT you get shares in the trust, rather than a direct shareholding in the companies in which it invests. That means you get access to the whole portfolio, which for many VCTs still includes some of their 'older-style' lower-risk investments. However, any new money the VCT has raised since 2015 will have had to be deployed in younger and riskier companies.

Inevitably, as a VCT raises more money and starts to exit some of the older-style investments, the balance between older-style and new-style investments will progressively shift in favour of the latter. In practice, this means that over time VCTs can become riskier and the dividend payments may become lumpier and more irregular. On the upside, however, the more risk you take, the greater the overall returns potentially can be. Experience shows that VCTs only need a handful of big successes to more than compensate for the many others that never make the grade.

So what are the options for VCT investors this year? Broadly speaking, there are two types of VCT: **AIM** and **generalist**.

AIM VCTs, as the name suggests, invest in young, potentially fast-growing companies which are already listed on AIM. The stock market listing leads to greater transparency in valuations, but also to greater fluctuations in value compared to VCTs investing in unquoted companies. The leaders in this field include HARGREAVE HALE and UNICORN.

Generalist VCTs on the other hand invest predominantly in unquoted businesses. As mentioned earlier, some generalist VCTs, such as MAVEN, BRITISH SMALLER COMPANIES, MOBEUS and NORTHERN, have historically focused on relatively mature companies with a particular bias towards management buyouts, which typically still represent a significant, but decreasing, proportion of the portfolio.

This should mitigate risk and help fund dividend payments, but it also means the manager has had to change, in some cases dramatically, its investment strategy. Amongst this type of VCT, a trust such as Maven is one that offers a decent mix of old and new investments which could temper the risks for investors while still giving them the potential for exciting future growth.

At the other end of the spectrum you have the likes of OCTOPUS TITAN and PEMBROKE. These VCTs have always focused on much earlier-stage growth businesses. Octopus Titan in particular has been very successful. It was an early investor in the likes of Zoopla, Secret Escapes and Graze.

Whilst it is one of the riskier VCTs, in our opinion if any VCT is going to end up investing in the next Facebook, it will probably be Titan. No other VCT has had the same level of success in spotting rising stars and supporting their growth to realise a successful sale to the likes of Amazon, Microsoft and Twitter. But, of course, past performance is not a guide to the future.

WHO INVESTS IN VCTS?

The average age of our clients who invest in VCTs is 58. The youngest is 20, the eldest 100. 82% are male, only 18% female. They invest £36,585 on average across a number of VCTs per tax year. The average amount invested in each VCT is £13,912. We don't record occupation, but those we speak to who invest are typically professionals such as doctors, lawyers, higher earners in the City, business owners, but also head teachers and civil servants. What do they all have in common? Nearly all are affected by the pension restrictions in some way.

For someone who doesn't have sufficient assets or earnings, and doesn't clearly understand the risks, VCTs are unlikely to be a suitable investment. Young, small companies are more likely to fail than older and larger ones. If something goes badly wrong for a small company, it is much harder for it to recover than it is for a large and well-established company. They are also a lot more illiquid, as are the VCTs themselves.

However, if you have sufficient assets elsewhere, you have already used your pension and ISA allowances, and you have a certain level of financial sophistication, then VCTs may well be a worthwhile option for you to consider. As a rule of thumb, VCTs should be no more than 10% to 15% of your total portfolio. Typically, your money will be spread over 30 to 60 companies, which provides an important degree of underlying diversification.

Secondly, just as professional venture capital investors find it difficult to know in advance which start-up businesses are going to become their biggest successes, so investors in VCTs should consider spreading their capital across more than one trust. We always suggest you consider spreading your annual investment over a number of VCTs, preferably with different investment strategies, to further diversify your risk. Don't forget you also have a 30% cushion in the form of tax relief should things go wrong.

ONE FINAL THOUGHT

If you are looking to invest in a VCT this year and see one you like, don't hang around.

Deploying money in qualifying companies is always a painstaking task for VCT managers. It is time-consuming and requires lots of research and due diligence. Recent rule changes mean VCT managers have to deploy the capital they raise more quickly than in the past. At the same time, there is growing demand from investors for all the reasons outlined above. Capacity will be limited, which means that this year, as in the previous two years, popular deals are likely to fill up fast, well before the end of the tax year. Therefore, if you see a deal you like, you should invest whilst you can.

ALEX DAVIES *is the founder and CEO of Wealth Club, the UK's largest investment platform for experienced investors. It specialises in researching and analysing tax-efficient investments, including VCTs and Enterprise Investment Scheme offers. Investors can apply for VCTs online (Wealth Club was the first service to offer this) and benefit from full initial discounts and annual rebates of up to 0.25% for three years.*

HUNTING FOR EXTREME RETURNS

JAMES ANDERSON, *joint manager of Scottish Mortgage Investment Trust, talks about the implications of Professor Hendrik Bessembinder's game-changing research into long-term share price returns.*

G ENERALLY I PREFER our research to appear irrelevant. The further it is from being a direct debate about the merits of a company as an investment the happier I tend to be. Obliquity is superior to confrontation. Walking is preferable to staring at a computer screen. Much of the most valuable research is deeply indirect in its investment implications and surprising in its eventual impact. Most commentators, brokers, intermediaries and consultants are deeply offended by such musings. That's their problem.

But occasionally direct assault has its virtues. This particularly applies to academic input. It can have the ability to stand outside the moment. It certainly has the ability to free itself from the preconceptions, self-interest and necessary operating dogma of practitioners and industry insiders. The very absence of skin in the game can be a virtue. Radical reappraisal is possible. Sometimes external authority gives the necessary evidence and context to build on uncomfortable and unexpected rumblings of our own.

Such has been our experience of working with Hendrik Bessembinder of Arizona State University. In early 2017 Professor Bessembinder released his initial drafts of a paper entitled 'Do Stocks Outperform Treasury Bills?'* The

---

* Bessembinder, Hendrik (Hank), 'Do Stocks Outperform Treasury Bills?' (28 May 2018). *Journal of Financial Economics (JFE)*, Forthcoming. Available at SSRN: ssrn.com/abstract=2900447 or dx.doi.org/10.2139/ssrn.2900447

"AS OUR FINANCIAL INDUSTRY MARCHES FIRMLY AND UNANIMOUSLY UP ONE HILL, WE'RE RUNNING DETERMINEDLY IN THE OPPOSITE DIRECTION. IF WE ARE RIGHT, THAT IS A COMPELLING COMPETITIVE ADVANTAGE."

title itself is heretical. It is a central assumption of modern portfolio theory, as taught to all students, that because equities are more risky they must have higher rewards. This is drummed into the heads of the record 227,031 candidates who registered for the Chartered Financial Analyst (CFA) exams in June. But Bessembinder showed that "slightly more than four out of every seven common stocks have lifetime buy-and-hold returns, inclusive of reinvested dividends, of less than those on one-month Treasuries.

> "When stated in terms of lifetime dollar wealth creation, the entire gain in the US stock market since 1926 is attributable to the best-performing 4 per cent of listed companies."

As he put it to me this is "just a collection of facts". It's not fake news. If this was the character of the US market in the past how much more might it be the path in the global and digital future?

But if this is right then our task is transformed. Our job is solely and simply to find and invest in the stocks that are capable of producing the extraordinary returns of the 4%. Everything else is best put aside. But what characteristics might the companies need to produce these returns? What attributes in turn do we need to hope to identify them? As Bessembinder writes, "The returns to active stock selection can be very large. If the investor is either fortunate or skilled enough…" So the natural course of affairs was for us to build a relationship with the professor so that we could learn how to become skilled (or lucky).

Fortunately my colleagues are now experts in providing sufficient freedom and support, both financial and intellectual, that we can progress towards regular contact in such instances. So in March I found myself sweltering in Tempe rather than freezing in Edinburgh in order to discuss these matters. Tom Slater, joint manager of SCOTTISH MORTGAGE INVESTMENT TRUST, had preceded me. Although we both found that Professor Bessembinder veered to academic caution rather than fund manager exuberance, there was still a great deal of importance to digest.

The two main areas of research that we have agreed to work with the professor on at this early stage are focussed on expanding data to the rest of the world (we are helping with the limited data sources) and trying to find common factors behind both the 4% of the companies that have created all the returns and the even more remarkable 90 companies (out of over 24,000) that have contributed half the wealth created in US equities since 1926.

The biggest lifetime US wealth creators (table from original paper)

COMPANY NAME (MOST RECENT)	LIFETIME WEALTH CREATION ($M)	% OF TOTAL	CUMULATIVE % OF TOTAL
Exxon Mobil Corp	1,002,144	2.88%	2.88%
Apple Inc	745,675	2.14%	5.02%
Microsoft Corp	629,804	1.81%	6.83%
General Electric Co	608,115	1.75%	8.57%
International Business Machs	520,240	1.49%	10.07%
Altria Group Inc	470,183	1.35%	11.42%
Johnson & Johnson	426,210	1.22%	12.64%
General Motors Corp	425,318	1.22%	13.86%
Chevron Corp New	390,427	1.12%	14.98%
Walmart Stores Inc	368,214	1.06%	16.04%
Alphabet Inc	365,285	1.05%	17.09%
Berkshire Hathaway Inc Del	355,864	1.02%	18.11%
Procter & Gamble Co	354,971	1.02%	19.13%
Amazon Com Inc	335,100	0.96%	20.09%
Coca-Cola Co	326,085	0.94%	21.03%
Du Pont E I de Nemours & Co	307,976	0.88%	21.91%
AT&T Corp	297,240	0.85%	22.77%
Merck & Co Inc New	286,671	0.82%	23.59%
Wells Fargo & Co New	261,343	0.75%	24.34%
Intel Corp	259,252	0.74%	25.09%

Prof Bessembinder's calculations show that just 20 companies have accounted for 25% of the total lifetime wealth created in the US stock market between 1926 and 2016.

It's this second question – in both versions – that has begun to unearth potentially crucial insight. It looks as if there could well be common factors behind the brilliance. Although many stocks with the most stellar returns now appear ex-growth (Exxon Mobil), or once mortally wounded but now surgically reassembled (GM), at the start of their lives they were all participants in markets that would become very large and that they entered if frequently not first then at early stages (this has been the case from Exxon Mobil to Google). As these names indicate, titanic founder-owners or at least missionary leaders are the enduring pattern.

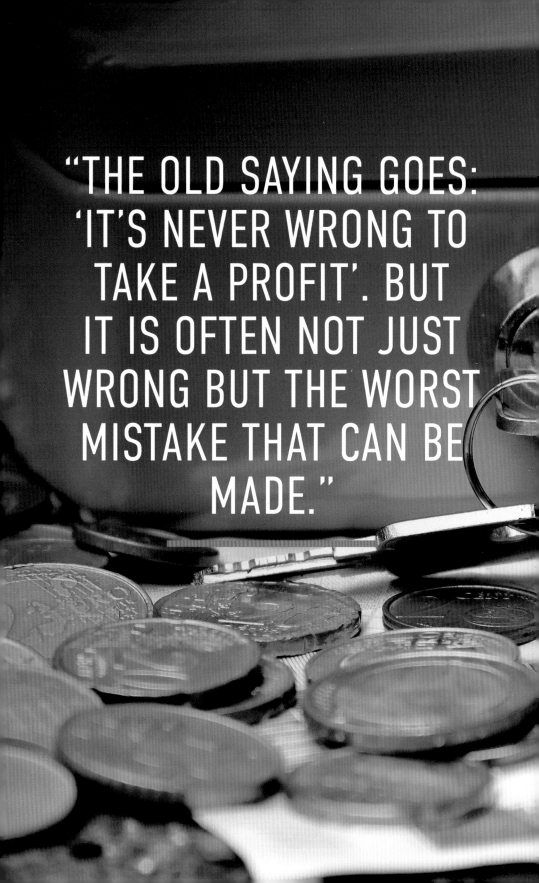

"THE OLD SAYING GOES: 'IT'S NEVER WRONG TO TAKE A PROFIT'. BUT IT IS OFTEN NOT JUST WRONG BUT THE WORST MISTAKE THAT CAN BE MADE."

This is no assemblage of FTSE-100-style companies boasting CEOs with three-year tenures. Moreover these companies have not been run with slide-rules; they acknowledge doubt and embrace emerging opportunities. As Bessembinder was talking about this my mind went automatically to Jeff Bezos, enthusing 20 years ago about the 'weirdness' of how the inputs to his business got better and cheaper every year – but that even he had no clue as to what that would mean.

In a sense much of this is predictable, even if it's more acute and structural than we surmised. What is more striking and even more exciting is the attributes that the professor believes that investors in their turn need to possess in order to identify the truly great potential companies. Just like the company founders themselves, he thinks the skills we need are centred on dreaming of a grand future, backing great people and coping with twists and turns and ups and downs.

His explication seems to us to run very counter to perceived market wisdom. It certainly casts doubt over the strong preferences of most investors for predictability and certainty. But still more, his perceptions indicate that our job is much more about imagination and vision and the qualitative assessment of leadership skills than it is about the hard analytic numbers and financial mastery that the 227,031 are being examined on by the CFA. The hope – or inspiration – that Professor Bessembinder provides us is that, as our financial industry marches firmly and unanimously up one hill, we're running determinedly in the opposite direction. If we are right, that is a compelling competitive advantage.

But there's one last essential to the professor's current thinking. Identifying the great investments isn't enough. As Hendrik Bessembinder makes plain, it is the long-term compounding of their share prices that matters. This seems to us to require an additional set of skills, such as the creativity to imagine greatness discussed above. The compelling urge among ordinary humans for sure, but far more damagingly amongst that odd sub-breed that are fund managers, is to take profits and lock in performance.

As the old saying goes: 'it's never wrong to take a profit'. But it is often not just wrong but the worst mistake that can be made. I first wrote a note asking if Amazon had gone up too much at $77 a share. Thankfully the conclusion was that there might be more to go for at that juncture. We're still resisting the temptation around $1,700 a share. Professor Bessembinder is reinforcing such convictions.

JAMES ANDERSON *is a partner at Baillie Gifford and co-manager of the UK's largest investment trust, Scottish Mortgage.*

———————————

THE NEXT GENERATION

ALEX DENNY *and* CLAIRE DWYER *give a millennial perspective on the attraction of investment trusts for a younger generation of investors.*

Why might investment trusts appeal to younger investors?

Alex Denny: I'm flattered to have been described as a millennial. I suppose I just about qualify having been born in the early 1980s! There is actually another term that has been created for people around my age which is 'Xennial'; lost somewhere between Generation X and those who don't remember a world before the internet. I like to think that this helps me to identify well with both older and younger groups.

Knowing what I know now, it is obvious to me that investment trusts should appeal to younger investors for the same reasons that they appeal to older ones. Put simply, they are an excellent vehicle for investing in assets (of almost any type) for the medium or long term. Younger investors obviously have longer investment horizons than their parents. They have longer until they retire (and, dare I say it, die). It follows that they have most to gain from the excess returns which investment trusts can make over many other types of investment funds across economic cycles.

The challenge with younger investors often isn't about persuading them about the merits of investing in investment trusts, but persuading them about the merits of investing at all. Many young professionals in their 20s or 30s find themselves heavily in debt. Student loans, mortgages and credit card debt mean that many live their lives with liabilities which far exceed their assets.

Being 'cash poor' is a difficult position from which to begin investing and, in truth, for those with expensive unsecured debt such as credit cards, it is very sensible to pay these debts down before beginning to invest in risk assets. An average APR of 23.1%[*] for a credit card is hard to beat consistently with any investment.

However, once those expensive debts have been paid down, there is clear evidence that younger people are not putting enough of their income aside for their future needs. One recent report suggests that a millennial would need to have accumulated the equivalent of at least £260,000 at retirement (rising to £445,000 for those who don't own a property) to enjoy even a basic income thereafter.[†]

Of course, whether in debt or not, with auto-enrolment in a pension scheme now mandatory, all young professionals are doing *some* compulsory saving. Their pension pot is bound to build up over time as their employers contribute to it. There is a wealth of academic evidence that on average and over the longer term investment trusts produce returns that outstrip bank interest rates, inflation, stock market indices and many other types of fund.[‡]

That has certainly been the case over the last ten years. An investment of £10,000 into FIDELITY SPECIAL VALUES PLC in 2008 would have been worth £36,000 ten years later. That is equivalent to a return of 13.5% per annum and compares to the £21,000 you would have had from investing in an FTSE All-Share index fund. £10,000 grown in line with RPI inflation meanwhile would be just £12,300 today.[§] With an ever-growing need for people to save for their own futures, investing in a vehicle with such a long track record of success would seem an obvious choice for the younger investor.

Claire Dwyer: While the investment trust has a long and distinguished pedigree as a vehicle, the portfolio themes that managers are capitalising on as we edge through the 21st century are distinctly modern. It's hard not to think that they should be capturing the imaginations of millennial investors more than they are. If the electric lightbulb was once the miracle, it's now surely the internet and its underlying algorithms. Around the world consumption is shifting towards digital,

---

[*]   Source: *Which,* June 2018: www.which.co.uk/news/2018/06/credit-card-interest-rates-on-the-rise-how-to-find-the-best-deals

[†]   Source: www.theguardian.com/money/2018/may/16/average-person-will-need-260000-for-retirement-says-report

[‡]   Source: AIC and CASS Business School.

[§]   Source: FE Trustnet – to 31/08/2018.

cashless and mobile transactions, especially in Asia where app-savvy millennials are shaping the future direction of the continent's economies.

Dale Nicholls, who runs FIDELITY CHINA SPECIAL SITUATIONS PLC, likes to point out that the country's transition to a consumption-led economy and a rising middle class is throwing up a host of new investment opportunities. Disposable income per capita in China has more than doubled in the past decade, while retail sales continue to rise at a double-digit pace.

In a recent catch-up Dale mentioned his interest in a couple of Chinese companies experimenting with innovative, lucrative and tech-enabled models like live-streaming, where consumers of online content can purchase virtual gifts for the online hosts they follow. Many younger investors will be experiencing these sorts of developments first hand. I've been sent a virtual pet monkey myself.

China's *Jiulinghou*, or 'post-90s' generation, born in the 1990s, now number more than 200m. They'll have grown up in one-child households in the digital era and are now in their late teens to early 30s. For this generation the rate of economic growth has been eye-watering and compared with previous generations this cohort has greater disposable income at a younger age and a marked propensity for online spending.

The point I am making is that the millennial generation has a chance not only to enjoy the wonders of the internet age in their daily lives, but also to profit from investing in the changes that they and their counterparts on the other side of the world are helping to make to the way that society operates and goes about its business. Doing well by doing good, if you want to philosophise about it.

Do you have advice to younger investors when picking an investment trust?

AD: My first piece of advice to younger investors is simply 'make sure you pick something'. Don't just leave cash in the bank and watch it lose its value in real terms. When saving for retirement, I would echo Steve Webb, the former pensions minister, who came up with a simple acronym. 'SUM': *Start* as quickly as you can. *Up* your contributions when you get a pay-rise. *Max* out on what your employer will give you by putting more in yourself.

Of course, pensions aren't the only place that young people can save or invest. The choices available in most defined-contribution pension plans are woefully thin. So my next piece of advice is to consider where, or what tax wrapper, you hold your money in. If it is a pension you're after and you have accumulated a decent size of assets already, then a self-invested personal pension (SIPP) may provide you with a better choice, including the ability to put your money into investment trusts.

If you think you may need the money before retirement (to buy a house, a car, or start a family etc.) then an individual savings account (or ISA) is probably the best tax-efficient choice. The fact that you won't have to pay any tax on the income or capital gains you make is an extraordinarily valuable gift from the government – one of the few that directly benefits young people. The more years you are able to put money into an ISA, the more valuable that benefit becomes.

While you may envy the fact that your parents have gained so much from being able to buy a house when they were young and watch its value soar, the ability to invest up to £20,000 a year without having to pay any tax on the income or capital gains is potentially just as golden an opportunity for you and your contemporaries – and certainly something your parents would have loved to have been able to do. It is a shame that this is not as widely appreciated as it should be.

If you have made this choice and are looking at investment trusts, I would start with a core portfolio option, a trust that diversifies broadly across the investment spectrum. Within the UK, a UK-focused investment trust makes sense, as would a global or European trust. This can then be added to over time with trusts that invest in other regions or asset classes to add diversification to your portfolio.

My personal view is that younger investors with long time horizons should focus on potentially riskier asset classes (such as equities) which have higher growth potential over market cycles. Often, the media focus too heavily on dividend yields and the income which can be earned from an investment. This may be great for older investors, but is often a distraction for investors with multi-decade time horizons. Yes, you will have to learn that shares prices can rise and fall from year to year, but you have so many years of saving ahead of you that you can afford to sit through the down years and give your money the time to let the gains accumulate.

Research and then choose a manager with a process that you can understand and that feels intuitive. There are great tools and lots of information about the range of investment trusts from online platforms, such as Fidelity's own or Hargreaves Lansdown and others. Websites such as Morningstar and Trustnet also have tons of searchable and sortable data. Most also offer apps that allow you to keep track of the markets and your favourite funds on your smartphone.

As a millennial, thanks to the internet you have the huge advantage of not just having better information than most professional investors had access to 30 years ago, but also the priceless advantage of knowing how to find and manipulate online data sources without difficulty. You can certainly use your familiarity with the digital world to make the most of your finances.

Lastly, I would recommend that younger investors (and all investors generally) keep regular but not-too-frequent tabs on the progress of their investments. Markets can and will fall as well as rise, and the temptation to change an investment just because it has fallen in value can sometimes lead investors to make irrational choices. What you want to know is that your investment manager is sticking to his or her process, that it still makes sense, and that you have faith in them over the longer term. Everything else is just noise.

How are developments in platform technology likely to impact who is buying investment trusts and how they go about it?

AD: Basically it is getting cheaper and easier! Over the past few years, most investment platforms – which are essentially websites that allow you to research, buy and store all your investments in one place – have been improving the way they offer access to investments listed on the stock exchange. Real-time dealing allows investors to see and choose the price at which they invest, monitoring the level of demand for shares and whether they are trading at a premium or discount.

Importantly, pretty much all platforms these days allow low-cost regular investments (monthly or quarterly etc.) as well as dividend reinvestment plans. This means that investors can benefit from investing on a regular and steady basis, which averages out short-term swings in price and break downs their investment into manageable chunks that can be timed to coincide with their salary. This is all light years ahead of the cumbersome paper-based process which used to absorb hours of time and effort for earlier generations.

Increased automation has led to faster and more accurate dealing, while reducing the costs, which can often be simple one-off cash-sum fees or maybe a set percentage of the whole deal value. The Association of Investment Companies (AIC) has recently launched a useful fees-comparison tool which allows you to work out which platform would be the most cost-effective for the size and types of deals that you would like to place. It may make sense to start out with one of the cheaper options and then trade up as your portfolio increases in size and sophistication.

How important is socially responsible investing to younger investors?

CD: I certainly think it's fair to say that sustainable – or socially responsible – investing is of special interest to younger investors. A recent paper on the subject by Ernst & Young suggests that millennial investors are nearly twice as likely as those in other age groups to invest in companies that target specific social or environmental outcomes. This is a good argument for active investing – and in particular, the investment trust, where you have not just the fund manager, but the board monitoring the composition of the portfolio.

Financial data such as accounting statements often do not provide the level or type of information required to make sure environmental, social and governance (ESG) issues are being appropriately considered. The early iterations of ESG investment strategies generally took quite a blunt approach to sustainable investing – simply excluding 'sin' sectors like gambling and tobacco, or by attempting to deliver a particular benefit or impact.

More recent approaches are more nuanced and sophisticated, often making quantitative assessments of key ESG metrics. Our view at Fidelity is that high standards of corporate responsibility make good business sense and have the potential to protect and enhance investment returns and to this end we have a dedicated team of global ESG specialists to provide guidance. The more money that flows into socially responsible investment vehicles, the more influence they will be able to bring to bear on how business operates and the more power to change the world they will acquire.

And changes to corporate governance?

CD: Much ink has been spilt on the subject of board diversity, both at the company level and the investment trust itself. The UK's public companies will need to significantly up the number of women appointed to their boards in the next couple of years if they are to meet government-backed targets. While progress has been made, its pace has arguably been too slow, and this is an aspect of governance that portfolio managers and boards alike are monitoring closely for developments.

The global financial crisis exposed serious deficiencies in corporate governance and I think the fact that this occurred just as many millennials were entering the workplace is significant. Ten years on there's a greater demand for transparency and accountability. Another reason I think an investment trust should appeal to this group of investors is the ability for them to make their voice heard as shareholders. It's always encouraging to hear new ideas and have a healthy

"MILLENNIALS HAVE THE MOST TO GAIN FROM THE EXCESS RETURNS WHICH INVESTMENT TRUSTS CAN MAKE OVER MANY OTHER TYPES OF INVESTMENT FUNDS ACROSS ECONOMIC CYCLES."

degree of challenge at annual general meetings. With open-ended funds that potential doesn't exist in the same way.

What are the implications of the evolving pension market for millennial investors?

AD: At industry level, we are seeing a sea-change in how pension money is invested. It is unfortunately not necessarily to the benefit of millennials. Not only are millennials faced with a complex regulatory maze of annual and lifetime allowances (the former of which is pretty generous and the latter unjustifiably limiting), they are of course widely denied access to the guarantees of the defined-benefit schemes available to their forebears.

It's easy to see why the defined-benefit pension has had to change. One need only look at the recent collapse of Carillion, the giant outsourcing company, to see the risks that an underfunded pension scheme poses to the benefits of its members. It is not hard to argue that a defined-contribution scheme, which offers no guaranteed future benefits, but is fully independent from the fortunes of the sponsor employer, may provide a better outcome than a defined-benefit scheme which fails all of its members.

However, the shift from defined-benefit to defined-contribution schemes has had some unintended consequences. In the past investment managers of defined-benefit schemes were given the task of taking risk-based asset allocation decisions to help achieve their long-term investment targets. To that end they often turned to investment trusts to provide enhanced investment returns or diversification into illiquid asset classes.

Defined-contribution pension schemes, by contrast, tend to focus much more on cost than on value, and the trustees are limited in the range of options they can provide. To the best of my knowledge, there are no defined-contribution schemes in the UK which offer members access to investment trusts. If you want to have those wider investment options, investors are effectively forced to transfer to a SIPP. That is something for millennials to agitate about at your workplace!

ALEX DENNY *is head of investment trusts at Fidelity and* CLAIRE DWYER *is an associate director in the same team.*

————————————

PROFILES

"WE ARE TRYING TO PRESERVE A STANDARD OF LIVING OVER THE LONG TERM."

THE UK'S LONGEST SERVING MANAGER

According to the Association of Investment Companies, PETER SPILLER, *of the Capital Gearing Trust, is the longest-serving manager of an investment trust in the UK. He has been running this specialist vehicle for 36 years and has no plans to retire any time soon.* JONATHAN DAVIS *went to talk to him.*

THE FIRST THING to say about Peter Spiller is that while his investment trust is relatively small, with a £265m market capitalisation, and still not widely known, he is far from an obscure figure in industry circles. Having started as a broker at Capel Cure Myers, he soon moved on to the blue-blooded broking firm Cazenove, where he remained a partner until 2000. He took over the running of Capital Gearing in 1982 to take advantage of what he saw as a myriad of discount and arbitrage opportunities in the investment trust sector.

Since then, despite progressively making its investment strategy more conservative in order to align with changing market conditions, the trust has put together a remarkable record of strong performance. The shares have compounded at an annual rate of nearly 15%, comfortably thrashing any relevant index and all other long-lived trusts. Unlike many trusts managed by larger investment groups, for whom the pursuit of scale is increasingly important, for most of its life Capital Gearing has remained small by choice.

The annualised rate of return achieved by Capital Gearing Trust outranks most long-lived investment trusts

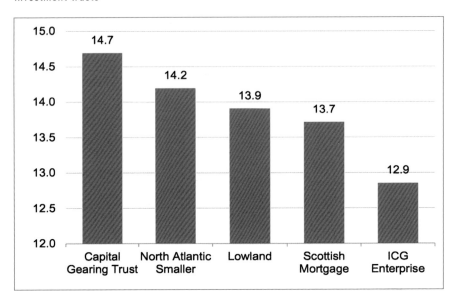

Source: Morningstar, Marten & Co. Annualised NAV return April 1982 to August 2018.

With a tight shareholder register, dominated by a relatively small but knowledgeable circle of City insiders, for many years the shares traded at a sizeable premium, reflecting the lack of liquidity – there were rarely any sellers – as well as the trust's strong performance record. In 2016, however, with one eye on the management succession, and another on wider changes in the trust sector, the board successfully introduced a policy of issuing new shares to meet demand and eliminate the premium. The trust has since increased its issued share capital by 2.2×.

The obvious place to start a conversation with a man who bought his first investment trust shares as a private investor in the early 1970s is to ask how the investment trust sector has changed in the near five decades that he has been following it. One striking feature, he says, is that the aggregate market value of investment trusts back then was twice as large as the unit trust (open-ended) sector. Today, it is only a quarter the size of the open-ended equivalent.

The difference in the growth rate he attributes in part to the "blatant bribery that open-ended funds used to use, getting intermediaries to put their clients into the funds, but it was also in large part because investment trust directors did not really do their job. They regarded their job as to make sure that the trust was honestly run and that it continued in existence, but that was it, more or less, full-stop. Discounts were just seen as a function of supply and demand at the time. Growing the trust was not part of their agenda."

The active discount controls that are now commonplace were not permitted until new rules came in in 2000, so it is true, Spiller says, "that boards were not, in a position to do the sorts of things they can do now". In fact he is inclined to be more critical of investment trust boards today for not doing as much with their new powers as they might. "We've seen significant progress with a number of trusts buying in stock when the discount's big, and the more progressive ones going on to a zero discount model, but not everyone is doing as much as they could".

Spiller is well known as a recent tireless advocate of the zero-discount model, and it is the noticeable trend towards that approach which makes him "much more optimistic now that trusts can grow". The ability to issue and buy back shares, when combined with "the undoubted fact that investment trusts have done better in performance terms than OEICs", provides a solid platform for future growth, "even if the advantage over OEICs is diminished because the cost difference has come down a lot". (This is a reference to the fact that since the Retail Distribution Review in 2013 open-ended funds can no longer include commission to brokers as a direct charge to investors in the funds.)

Spiller takes issue, however, with the argument that platforms such as Hargreaves Lansdown are unable to promote investment trusts heavily because of the illiquidity of many investment company shares. "For trusts with a zero discount model, the liquidity that is relevant is not the liquidity of the trust", he points out, "it is the liquidity of the underlying securities or assets that they own. That message has not really got across to platforms. It's a pity."

The way that Spiller has invested Capital Gearing's assets has changed dramatically since he started out. Along with some core larger holdings, part of the portfolio has always been committed to exploiting small but profitable anomalies in the way that the shares of listed investment trusts are priced in the market, drawing on his long experience and encyclopaedic knowledge of the sector. He was one of the first to appreciate, for example, that there was a turn to be made by anticipating the market's reaction to investment companies being promoted or relegated from market indices. (There were two trusts in the FTSE 100 index and more than 50 in the FTSE 250 index, as at 1 October 2018.)

Opportunism was a factor behind Capital Gearing's formation and there are still a number of 'special situations' that the trust seeks to exploit to boost its return. The portfolio includes a number of holdings in obscure trusts that most investors have never heard of, but which may for whatever reason, Spiller and his colleagues believe, be trading at the wrong price. Trust enthusiasts like nothing better than spotting obscure opportunities to profit from movements in discounts. Those opportunities are not, however, as common or as large as they once were.

> "When we started there was deep pessimism in the financial markets because equities had behaved so badly, and bonds had behaved so badly for such a long time that it created tremendous opportunities in investment trusts. Why? Because that pessimism was expressed in large discounts. There were scores of trusts trading on discounts of more than 20%. Not only that, but pessimism was also expressed through the market's reaction to gearing of any kind. Gearing was viewed as obviously enhancing risk, which it does. That meant, however, that one of the instruments which worked very well for us in the early days was capital shares. Capital shares have inherent gearing and largely for that reason, they stood at very, very big discounts – in other words at very attractive valuations.

> "I remember doing the calculations. They weren't very difficult calculations, but this was long before computers. We were able to buy capital shares where the return would still be adequate even if the real value of equities were to fall by 10 or 20%. The great advantage of gearing then was that at that stage the real value of the debt was going down by about 7% every year. The dynamics of how that worked was deeply misunderstood by the markets". [*Editor's note:* capital shares were one of the different share classes that investment trusts issued in order to cater for different investor requirements before the split capital trust scandal largely consigned such structures to oblivion.]

The proportion of the trust's assets committed to equity investments is very different today. When Spiller took over running the trust, back in the 1980s, almost the entire portfolio was in equities of one kind or another. Now the equivalent figure is no more than 25%. The percentage has been falling steadily for many years. Instead the portfolio is dominated today by cash and cash equivalents and, notably, sizeable holdings of US index-linked Treasuries (known as TIPS for short).

This radical change in exposure is primarily down to two factors – the state of the market and the risk tolerance of the trust's conservative shareholder base, of whom Spiller himself remains a significant member (his 4.7% shareholding is worth some £12.5 million). "Although the trust has evolved in the way it invests, it has always reflected my idea of the portfolio that an investor who has a long-term view, is risk-averse, and doesn't like drawdowns, should own. You can't not have drawdowns in the short term, but over time preservation of capital is what matters for this type of investor."

These days Capital Gearing is happy to be classified as an absolute return fund, aiming to make money in all kinds of market conditions. The current ultra-conservative asset allocation is also driven by Spiller's view that valuations of nearly all kinds of financial asset are very high and future returns likely to be poor as a result. "We work on the principle that when the outlook for returns is poor and the risk is high, you want very short duration in your portfolio. Back in 1982, prospective returns were very high, and the valuation model that we use now shows that you should have made something like a 16% per annum real return over the next seven years. Actually we did a bit better than that, but when valuations are that low, risk is also low and it is important to take advantage of that combination."

But what the model also indicates is that "if you want to have great long-term returns, you need to shift your assets around so that you're exposed to long-duration assets when they're very cheap and risk is low, and the reverse when they are not". Back in 1982, the values were "so fabulous that essentially the only thing you had to own was equities, because they've got the longest duration of all the main asset classes. Bonds were pretty good too back then, and they produced great returns, but equities were where the real value was".

Looking back, Spiller adds, "we were also helped in coming to that conclusion by the fact that the tax system in those days was extremely unhelpful to returns that came in the form of income". The tax system, fortuitously as it turned out, reinforced the decision to go for longer-duration equities. "It's difficult to recall how high taxes were then, even under Tory governments." In fact, he says, "it is just mind-blowing to think how poor we were!"

> "When I started, nobody cared what they were paid because the top rate of tax on income – the rate at which dividends were taxed – was 98%. What people cared about were their perks, such as their free car, their free petrol, their free gardener, whatever. Everyone had much better cars than their overall economic situation justified, as everything was hugely distorted. It's wonderful that all that has evaporated."

But what we have now instead is just as dispiriting as far as future returns are concerned, he believes. In contrast to the 1980s, when equities were dirt cheap, on the same valuation model the prospective longer-term real yield from equities today is "effectively zero". Not only are earnings multiples sky high, but the prices of all financial assets have been heavily distorted by quantitative easing and other central bank policies since the great financial crisis.

The real yield on TIPS has fallen from more than 4% at its peak in 2000 to less than 1% today; low real yields point to weak medium-to-long-term returns, Spiller warns

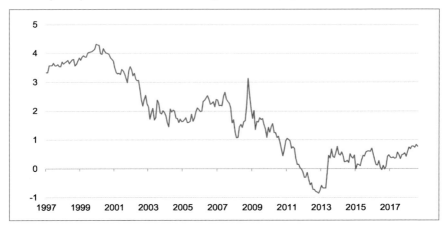

Source: Bloomberg, Marten & Co. US 10-year index-linked bond yields 1997 to date.

"QE has been very powerful in a number of respects. It has served to distort both the real economy and the price of all financial assets. The price of houses is distorted, the price of equity is distorted, the price of bonds is distorted – everything is distorted. I think that the central banks now have a tiger by the tail. So the Bank of England says it would like to raise short-term interest rates, which is fine, but it knows it can only do it by very small amounts by historic standards, because anything more will have such a devastating effect on the mortgage market that it just can't be allowed to happen."

He mentions Andrew Sentence, the economist and former Monetary Policy Committee member who has been on the hawkish tack on interest rates for a long time. "He has been saying that interest rates would need to go up gradually to something like 3 or 4%. In my view, they simply can't do that. They absolutely can't. And the worry has to be that if inflation does accelerate, it will be very difficult to stop it, because there is no strategy for controlling inflation which doesn't involve short-term interest rates going up."

That really has quite alarming implications, and "makes the prospect of a Corbyn government really frightening. If we also have to throw in fiscal incontinence from Mr McDonnell [Labour's shadow chancellor], the central bank is not at all well-placed to do anything about it. It's very far from certain that we're going to get a Labour government, but I think it might be very alarming if it happened. If confidence were undermined and we had capital flight, there would be concerning consequences for UK financial markets".

Mapping Capital Gearing's asset allocation demonstrates how its portfolio has continued to evolve in response to trends in valuations and market dynamics. "By the time we got to the turn of the century, equities were looking pretty rich and we thought that their prospective returns would be quite poor. But bonds still had very good prospective returns at that stage and so we had a much more bond-orientated portfolio. We had long bonds, 30-year bonds. The volatility was not hugely different from equities, but there was much better underlying value. That worked extremely well."

> "If we fast-forward to today, because of the distortions caused largely by QE, the prospective returns on all financial assets are extremely poor. You should not be worrying about the prospective return on equities: the outlook for bonds is much worse! With the exception of TIPS, which we think remain very interesting, we are looking at a prospective return on bonds which is so bad that it is off the page by historical standards."

It is unlikely however, he says, that the trust would ever go back to the kind of portfolio it had in 1982, even if valuations were as appealing as they were then. Why? "Because in many other respects the world has become an easier place to invest, at least as we speak at the moment. There are no exchange controls, and taxes are much more reasonable. All this might change, of course, but under current circumstances, even if we went back to 1982 values, we might still have more of a spread of assets than we did then. We were 100% in equities then. We'd probably go to a maximum of 80% today."

One reason for that is there are newer instruments investors can now use to achieve their objectives. Spiller mentions exchange-traded funds (ETFs), low-cost passive securities that can replicate almost any style or regional exposure you can imagine, as the prime example. "We have instruments available to us now, like ETFs, that we did not then. Did you see that Fidelity recently came out with a fee-free ETF? ETFs have made investment in some ways much easier, much cheaper and much more efficient than it was before."

But aren't there hidden risks in ETFs, primarily liquidity issues, that investors may not fully appreciate? Spiller does not dissent, but says perspective is needed. One of the reasons that ETFs have been able to flourish is that they are such an easy way to pursue a momentum strategy – that is, buying sectors or styles that have been performing well. "Momentum is a factor that has worked really well over the last 20 years – much to my chagrin, really, as I'm a sort of fundamentalist. More and more money is in that strategy, including from hedge funds, and a lot of it is expressed through ETFs."

What Spiller worries about is that when momentum does turn negative again, as one day it will, it will make the downward moves even bigger and faster. "After all an ETF just owns what it's supposed to own, and if some of those are very illiquid, it's going to be problematic if they get redemptions. So I do worry that ETFs in high-yield bonds, for example, will find that there is really no buyer of some of the things they want to sell, especially in circumstances where people start to get frightened about credit quality."

Liquidity is a bigger issue in general than it was, he concedes, in part because of regulatory changes, and that was highlighted when a lot of open-ended property funds had to stop dealings after the shock of the Brexit referendum vote. But the risk needs to be kept in perspective. "The residual risk is not extreme, on our analysis. To be honest, I'd be quite surprised if it turned out to be a significant problem. It depends on the instrument of course, but if it's something like a Spider [the nickname of the massive ETF that tracks the S&P 500 index] I think the liquidity issues are exaggerated. The big ETFs are collateralised. There are a lot of risks in life and the more you know, the more you appreciate how many other risks there are. You just have to rate and size them properly, make sure you're not over exposed to the wrong ones. I don't think the potential illiquidity of ETFs is a big one."

The bond market is a much bigger concern, in Spiller's view. Real (inflation-adjusted) yields have come down so far that in the UK index-linked gilts have been trading on negative yields for several years. "I think I'm right in saying that real yields in the UK were around 4.5% in the 1980s, or were thereabouts in the early days of index-linked. Today, they're -1.5%. The market has gone completely mad!" Spiller blames "these crazy yields" on actuaries, who have "persuaded (or rather mandated) pension funds to buy them in order to match their liabilities".

"Of course, if you don't care about the health of the sponsor [the company whose employees the pension fund exists to benefit], and the pension fund is fully funded, buying index-linked on a negative yield makes perfect sense. I emphasise not caring about the sponsor, because in every other respect it's plain mad to invest long term at these negative real rates. If you invest in the long index-linked gilt, even assuming no costs and no taxes, what do you need to pay now to get a guaranteed inflation-proofed £1 to spend in 50 years' time? When I did the sums recently, you needed to spend £2.10! It's just unbelievable."

When global stock markets are rising strongly, Capital Gearing Trust tends to underperform; its objective is to make positive absolute returns, not relative outperformance

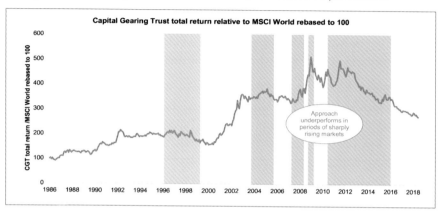

Source: Capital Gearing Trust out/underperformance compared to the MSCI World Index.

We move on from such absurdities to discuss the rise of alternative asset trusts, the biggest growth engine in the trust market. "It's something of an accident that they're called investment trusts," Spiller says. "The structure happens to suit, but they're very different kinds of assets. Many of them are completely illiquid. But I do think they give access to assets that are helpful for investors. We own a fair number. It's good that you can invest in green infrastructure, solar power or whatever, and they do offer streams of income that look pretty secure. They may not be in the case of the renewables. It depends on the power price, on which we have our own views, but that doesn't matter. It's still a valid instrument for investors."

"Yes, on the whole, I'm pretty positive about infrastructure of one kind or another. Of others that you might think of as alternatives, one that has been very kind to us, and is completely new, has been the ability to buy residential property in Germany. They're equities. So they're not going to be immune from moves in the equity markets, but they're probably a pretty low beta security. They have been terrific. It's wonderful that as investment trust investors we have these extra clubs in the bag."

They also have the attraction, he adds, of allowing you to benefit from the distortions in the price of money. "There is an interesting parallel with 1982, when gearing worked because the value of your debt in real terms was falling rapidly. Today, there isn't rapid inflation, but we have the wonderful example of a well-known public company whose commercial paper has traded at negative yields. Effectively someone is paying them to finance their buildings!

> "Just in the same way that investment trust analysts mark debt to market, I think when you're looking at the asset value of these companies, we can attribute some value to the fact that they can finance at extraordinarily low rates. That doesn't mean to say they should be highly geared. Obviously you have to have assets that you have confidence will hold that real value, or something close to it, but there's a value there that is underappreciated."

Is it not the case, I say, that the risks of some of the alternative asset trusts may be subtly increasing over time? Spiller agrees. "I think there's an issue for most of these alternatives in that there is a limited supply. What we observe, as in all history, when you've got something that works, but the managers want to get bigger, they go and buy (say) something overseas which they know less about, or they buy newer assets. If you take wind farm or solar, for example, each new generation of investments has less secure income than the past. For the substantial majority of the earlier ones the subsidy was fixed, but now it is not."

> "There's absolutely no doubt that the quality of earnings deteriorates from both those things. None of that makes them uninteresting investments, but it's a trend one needs to be aware of. The reality is that the opportunities change all the time. The opportunities were fabulous in investment trusts in 1982, they're much less interesting now as a general statement than they were then, but all sorts of other things have come up. I think on the whole I'm enthusiastic that the market has gone into these new asset classes. The fees are a bit high, but they will come down in time."

In the meantime Capital Gearing continues to hunker down in preparation for a less fertile time for investors. Spiller sums up his argument for caution. "Inflation is very low, but we think it will rise. Interest rates are very low; we probably think they will rise too. The P/E ratio is high and it's going to fall – that is not unrelated to the previous two points of course – and balance sheets are extremely ropy. It's also fair to say that as a general statement business in most of the Western world is extremely highly geared.

> "In those circumstances, the concern has to be not just that the valuations change for the worse, but that the structure is very fragile and correcting it will destroy a lot of value – although destroy it and then put it together again. That is how markets historically perform. They are cyclical, and prone to boom and bust".

So, I say, could this be a test of capitalism itself, as there was in the 1970s too?

"I do believe that capitalism itself has gone down a route which it needs to come back from. I am referring to the whole concept that the only thing that matters is shareholder value, clients are there to be exploited and the short term is far more important than the long term. All this has reduced the quality of earnings that companies make. It's very difficult to quantify, but if you're running a utility in the UK, to take an example, you've got earnings which have been achieved by deliberately obscuring prices.

"Essentially, there is an adversarial relationship with their clients, which has made them very unpopular. So, it is not surprising that when politicians talk about nationalisation, that resonates with their supporters. I do think these things have long-term consequences. That the quality of earnings is lower than it was is just one example, and that is quite apart from the accounting which itself has considerably exaggerated the declared earnings of companies. Most of the differences when you look at them in detail are absolutely indefensible."

Thank goodness, then, for the security of TIPS, which as I mentioned earlier make up a striking 25% of the Capital Gearing portfolio. It is not easy for UK investors to buy them directly, which is one reason why Spiller's team at CG Asset Management also run funds for institutional investors that exclusively invest in these instruments. Why does he think they are such a better safe haven than their crazily priced UK equivalent, index-linked gilts? "TIPS are a much better instrument because in America, almost the exact opposite pressure prevails, I think. Most pension funds in America, particularly the public ones, have an assumed rate of return of 7 to 8%. That looks and is ludicrous".

"But one thing it means is that if you're running a pension fund in America, the last thing you can buy is TIPS. Because unless inflation is 7% per annum, it is simply impossible to meet your target return by buying them. As a result, the pension funds, which are the natural buyers of index-linked government bonds, are effectively prevented from buying them! The good news is that as a result the TIPS market is throwing up much better value. The real yield is a positive 1.05%, compared to a negative 1.5% in the UK. We have 25% of the assets in TIPS. Obviously, in the short term, the currency is a source of volatility, but we like the protection that they provide from the particular risks that the UK faces. Definitely there's some risk there, but if what you're trying to do is preserve your standard of living over the long term, as we are, then we think this is the safest place to shelter."

The defensive positioning of Capital Gearing Trust has protected shareholders from significant loss in months when the MSCI World index has fallen (data since 2006, average drawdown in down months for the global index)

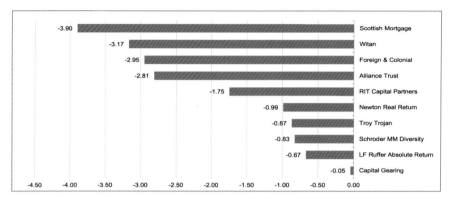

Source: Average percentage monthly drawdown in months where the MSCI AC World Index falls in value since February 2006.

Mind you, it is fair to say that Spiller has been in defensive mode for some time. Among other concerns, he remains deeply unconvinced about the viability of the euro and the whole European project. Given its defensive positioning, returns from Capital Gearing shares have inevitably lagged a long way behind those he achieved in the very different market conditions of its early life. But he has no plans to quit. "By far the most significant move that I've made recently has been to bring together a team that are 25 to 30 years younger than me. We work closely together and have done, in the case of most of the team, for eight years now. Hopefully I've got another five or six years to go, at least. When I retire, it means that the culture will not change, even though inevitably the investments will." For that to happen, all he needs is for markets to come off their unsustainable highs. Patience remains the watchword.

PETER SPILLER *founded CG Asset Management (cgasset.com) in 2000 and has been the lead manager of Capital Gearing Trust since 1982. He was previously a partner at Cazenove & Co Capital Management.*

THE YOUNG GUN

If Peter Spiller is the doyen of the investment trust sector, then KARTIK KUMAR *is the opposite – the youngest manager of an investment trust in the universe. The 28-year-old was appointed a co-manager of the Artemis Alpha Trust in April 2018.* JONATHAN DAVIS *talked to him to find out what he is about.*

A CAREER IN INVESTMENT management can start in many ways, but for Kartik Kumar it was a relatively conventional route by modern standards. While a student at Bristol University, studying for a degree in economics but uncertain about what career to pursue, he took a summer internship at Lazard Asset Management. While there he was given the task of analysing the fortunes of two companies in the same business. Those companies were the moneybroking firms ICAP and Tullett Prebon, both run at the time by powerful personalities, Michael Spencer and Terry Smith respectively.

Kumar spent six weeks looking at the two companies, an experience that included surviving a fact-finding session with the famously pugnacious Smith, now himself, as founder of Fundsmith, an extraordinarily successful fund manager. "That was quite an experience," Kumar recalls, "but I was so compelled by the work I had done – this was in the summer of 2011 – that I decided I wanted to buy some shares in ICAP. I didn't actually have much money, but I still tried to do it. Fortunately I got bogged down in bureaucracy – when I was back in university four months later, ICAP had fallen by around 35%, when I had thought it was a sure winner!"

"I was so intrigued by the fact that I could spend six weeks in what seemed like a very serious environment, working weekends, looking at two companies, and come up with a conclusion in which I had full conviction – and yet be entirely wrong. That's really what drew me into the investment business. I thought I wanted to try it again and get it right" – proof again of the wisdom of the useful old adage that what doesn't kill you will make you stronger.

Given such stubborn determination, it is perhaps not that difficult to see why John Dodd, now the chairman of Artemis, took a shine to this confident and intelligent young man and made him the firm's first graduate trainee in 2013. Born in India, brought up in Nigeria, where his father had moved to start a new business, and educated at boarding school and university in England, Kumar is the personification of two of the 20th century's most compelling themes, the onward march of globalisation and cross-border diversity. ("I am a bit of a mongrel" is his own low-key description.)

As it happens, though, it took a little time for Kumar to find a job in his newly chosen profession. There was no investment gene in the family, although his father, born in India, helpfully had a strong entrepreneurial streak, as evidenced by his move to Nigeria with his family. "My father did some terrifying things that I would never do. He moved the family to Nigeria and set up a tyre-retreading manufacturing business because he thought industry there would require retreaded tyres, which are more durable and cheaper than new tyres. I had first-hand experience of the difficulties of having a heavy manufacturing business in Nigeria, with not only oil price fluctuations but also – potentially more difficult – the risk of political interventions. So my father was a real entrepreneur. The way I look at it, the very definition of an entrepreneur is being willing to take on risk in pursuit of profit, and in my view that's what fund management is also about."

In the event, this unusual background stood Kumar in good stead when it came to applying for a job. His CV might not have looked that different to that of hundreds of other graduates looking to break into a lucrative fund management career, but his application did have one differentiating feature in the shape of a letter to the *Financial Times* that the editor of the 'pink paper' decided merited publication.

"I tried very hard to find a job in fund management, but I found it wasn't very forthcoming. I had a lucky break when I had the letter published in the *FT* when I was 20. I put it down on a CV and sent that to as many people as I could." Eventually it did the trick. Kumar was offered a job at a large firm about the same time that he was introduced to John Dodd, who quickly made him the offer to be the first graduate Artemis had employed.

And what was the letter about, I ask? "It was called 'Families that can't afford the luxury of a lightbulb.' I had read a piece in the *FT* that was talking about how ludicrous it is to have diesel subsidies in Nigeria when Nigeria is clearly an exporter of crude and is subsidising the import of diesel. I pointed out that if you removed these subsidies on diesel, without providing electricity, most poor families wouldn't have a way of having electricity in their house. You can't yank the rug out from under people like that. It was an Oxford professor who had written the article and I just said 'come on!' I was still in Nigeria at the time going, 'I'm not sure you know what you're advocating here'. It's great in theory, but I don't think it'd work that well in practice."

Challenging an academic theorist is not a bad qualification for a serious professional investor, one has to admit. What then did Kumar think he gained from his economics course at university? "I was always more interested in microeconomics than in macroeconomics. I had a particular interest in game theory. That is probably the most useful thing I learnt, because the premise of game theory is always to think strategically. If you look at the price that Sky has recently been sold for [via a knockout bid by the American cable company Comcast], that's a great example. An auction always extracts the maximum price from a buyer. So I think the application of thinking strategically in markets, companies or industries is hugely important. Directly or not, it's an incredibly powerful framework to remind yourself to use."

(At this point I could not resist asking what Kumar thinks game theory has to say about the likely outcome of the Brexit negotiations, which to the casual observer has always seemed to be a classic example of the so-called Prisoner's Dilemma, where two parties can still fail to arrive at the optimal cooperative solution in negotiations. His quick-as-a-flash answer: "I am not sure game theory has a framework for incorporating how an immense bureaucracy will behave.")

Having eventually found a foothold at Artemis, he was given a fluid training programme, as you would expect from an entrepreneurial firm that is still run by one of the four founders (who, I remember once being told, spent the first few weeks of setting up on their own playing table tennis in the absence of any money to run). "I got my first marching orders to go and work in the bond fund. I remember Adrian Frost [the long-serving manager of the Artemis Income fund and a City veteran of many years] turning to me when he heard that I was the first Artemis graduate and was starting on the bond team. 'Before you make any career decisions, look at what the yield is on the first-year Treasury!' It had fallen for the last 30 years. He said that didn't bode too well for future prospects…"

Armed with that useful advice, Kumar spent time working with the bond team, the global equity team and the smaller companies team before settling into a permanent role as assistant to William Littlewood, manager of the firm's global multi-asset fund, Artemis Strategic Assets. Littlewood, who made his name managing an income fund at Jupiter, is known for taking and holding on to high-conviction positions, often in defiance of conventional opinion.

"Will is very unusual in the way he thinks," Kumar says now. "I remember one of the first things he had me do was to try and work out what the value of Gazprom was, at which point John [Dodd] was standing in the corner of the room thinking, 'How on earth is he going to do that?' But Will and I got on extremely well. One thing is that Will read economics at Bristol, and he is also a big fan of game theory and that sort of thing, so we naturally got on very well. I liked the strategy and the way he thought."

Kumar thinks that he has learnt most from Littlewood in terms of understanding the role of psychology in timing an investment. "He has always said, 'Buy a good share on a bad day, buy a bad share on a good day.' He loves investing and he's always had a very strong understanding of when to make a purchase. Watching him in, say, August 2015, or February 2016, or the day after Brexit [all days when the market fell sharply] – seeing how he behaves on a day when the market is, in his view, throwing up bargains compared to a normal day is a sight to behold. Our dealers will often look at the deal sheet on the day after one of those days and think, 'Wow. For example, you didn't hold Diageo the day before, but bang – in August 2015 – you're in there at, was it, £16?'"

Having worked on the Strategic Assets fund for five years, how did Kumar come to be entrusted with a co-manager's role with ARTEMIS ALPHA? "When I was doing my rotation, I was given the odd project by John Dodd to look at, an opportunity he was looking at, and also particularly to help with monitoring some of our unlisted equity investments. My role just expanded organically. Artemis Alpha has always been run by John and Adrian Paterson – Adrian Paterson has worked with Will since the 1990s, they were at Jupiter together so they've got a strong relationship – and I'd occasionally find an idea. They would know what I was looking at for Will, and occasionally we'd say 'That looks like a really interesting opportunity for Alpha too. Why don't you buy it as well?' So we were sharing the knowledge and the work, and effectively my role expanded because the number of ideas that we thought were compelling for Alpha started to grow. I'd say I did this for about two years, maybe a little bit longer, before I was appointed co-manager of the trust itself."

Two factors combined to make the move a timely one. One is the impending retirement of Paterson, who has co-managed the Alpha Trust since it was taken on by Artemis 15 years ago. The second is that the trust, once one of the highest of high fliers in the trust universe, has in recent years suffered a striking loss of form, prompting the board, after consultation with shareholders and its managers, to announce a new strategy which it will be down to Dodd and Kumar to implement.

The discount at which the shares in Artemis Alpha trade tells the story of the need for a turnaround as graphically as anything. During its first decade, when the trust made a sparkling return of some 400% – well ahead of its peer group and double the return of the FTSE All-Share index – the shares consistently traded at or around net asset value. However, around 2014 results started to disappoint, the result of a combination of different factors. These included an above average number of holdings of energy stocks in a period when oil prices were on course to plummet from $100 to below $30 a barrel, the high proportion of difficult-to-value unlisted equities in the portfolio and a suspicion – so some observers clearly thought – that the managers, all busy with other responsibilities, might perhaps have taken their eye off the ball.

Artemis Alpha Trust – NAV and share price performance vs FTSE All-Share index

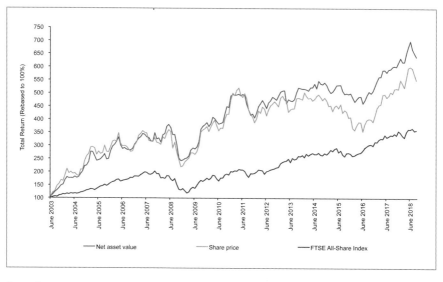

Source: Artemis.
Performance from 1 June 2003 to 30 September 2018.

The occasional premium then started to disappear, to be replaced by a discount that got as wide as 25% at its worst, prompting some influential shareholders to agitate for change. Had it not been for the fact that Dodd, Paterson and other managers at Artemis together own nearly 20% of the equity, it is doubtful whether the trust would have survived. In the event, the board decided to take remedial action and after consultation the new strategy – which includes a commitment to reduce the unlisted holdings from around 25% to less than 10% – was formally adopted in April 2018 and Kumar was given his chance to show whether his youthful promise would translate into a more senior and responsible role.

So what exactly, we ask, is his role now as co-manager, given that John Dodd continues to run both the firm and his other funds? "John and I work very closely. As you can imagine, we've got quite a strong relationship given that he brought me through the door on day one. What do I do? I meet a lot of companies, I think over 200 a year. For example, I'm going to Germany next week for two days to see companies that our largest investment, Rocket Internet, has invested in. I really like being on the ground, trying to pick up as much as I can about a company's culture, how it's being run and its competitive position."

"John clearly has tremendous experience, having been in the industry for over 30 years. So we work closely together in the sense that we bring the data back, have a look at it, analyse it and then make the decisions together with a view to constructing a portfolio with a number of interesting equities that we think are more valuable than the market is currently giving them credit for." The division of labour appears to be that Kumar is doing most of the stock research while his mentor, apart from the resource stocks which have always been his specialism at the firm, is there to ratify the decisions and oversee the overall composition of the portfolio.

Will it work? It is not as unusual as you might think for fund managers to start having a say in running money at such a relatively young age – Littlewood, for example, was 25 when he started running the Jupiter Income fund back in the 1990s. The saying, if you are good enough, you are old enough, is truer of fund management than many other professions, where experience is often an over-arching requirement for success. One benefit of the investment trust structure is that, when the discount has sunk as low as it had done with Artemis Alpha two years ago, there is not so much to lose from taking a new and bold initiative. An essential element of the new strategy is the board's commitment to offer shareholders an opportunity to exit at close to net asset value every three years.

Kumar speaks confidently about the chances of the new strategy paying off, as indeed you would expect him to do. As well as the commitment to reduce the holdings of unlisted equities, the managers intend to pivot the trust away from its historic focus on energy stocks and smaller companies. Instead the priority will be to unearth interesting opportunities across the market capitalisation scale, including up to 30% in non-UK stocks, using all the stockpicking resources of the Artemis team. A good example of this new approach was the decision to take a big holding in Tesco, following the accounting scandal which tarnished its name four years ago. It is unlikely that such a household name would have featured so prominently in the portfolio in the past.

As Kumar noted earlier, despite their very different objectives, there is already a significant overlap with the portfolio of Artemis Strategic Assets, Littlewood's fund, which has no investment trust equivalent. As the table shows, nearly half of the Artemis Alpha portfolio consists of names that also feature in the open-ended fund, though not always in the same proportion. The unquoted element of the portfolio has meanwhile already been cut to just under 12% (as at the end of September 2018), so that leg of the new strategy is already on the way to being fulfilled. The gearing has also been slashed and the number of holdings cut from more than 120 to 70, with more reductions to come.

Overlap in holdings between Artemis Alpha (ATS) and Artemis Strategic Assets (ASA)

	ATS	ASA
Rocket Internet	6.0%	6.9%
Tesco	4.9%	4.8%
Hurricane Energy	3.9%	6.2%
Dignity	3.3%	1.9%
Sports Direct	3.3%	2.5%
IWG	2.8%	1.3%
Inmarsat	2.6%	1.5%
Plus500	2.4%	4.6%
Dixons Carphone	2.4%	1.2%
Hornby	2.3%	0.3%
Fitbit	2.0%	2.2%
Delivery Hero	1.8%	1.8%
Nintendo	1.7%	0.6%
Vectura	1.6%	0.3%
GlaxoSmithKline	1.5%	4.6%
Criteo	1.4%	1.9%
Retail Money Market	1.3%	0.3%
JUST Group	1.0%	3.2%
Revolution Bars	1.0%	0.2%
Dick's Sporting Goods	0.7%	0.6%
Och-Ziff Capital Management	0.4%	0.8%
	48.2%	46.8%

Source: Artemis, data as at 31 August 2018.

The new management team is essentially looking for contrarian opportunities where a significant gap has emerged between the market's perception of a company and the reality of its circumstances as Artemis sees it after taking a closer look. "In our view," says Kumar "there are certain reasons why you might have this opportunity. It might be that a company is emerging from a rough patch and the market is behind the curve on the progress that's been made. It might be that the company is doing something more disruptive or creative than people are giving it credit for. (US technology companies are a good example of that.) It might be that the company is run by someone who we think has a strong focus on operational excellence and capital allocation. There's a really strong wealth of literature that demonstrates how that factor alone can lead to outsize returns over the long run. Our simple idea is that you look hard, you do the work and you wait patiently and act very opportunistically when you think you've got the right opportunity."

Okay, but are there not many other fund managers trying to do the same? "Yes. I realise that most fund manager strategies sound the same, and they should do because you're all trying to make money. But what I would suggest is that we are putting emphasis on factors that I don't believe other people are to the same degree. To give you one example, I believe we will be putting a larger emphasis on how management is allocating capital than many other people do, or that an index fund could ever do, given that it can't make a subjective opinion on the capabilities of the manager."

Bear in mind, he says, that capital allocation decisions can only really be judged in hindsight. "The substantial part is a judgement on what the likely outcome is going to be. For example, a return on capital metric wouldn't help you judge whether an acquisition is going to be good or not. The Comcast/Sky deal is a good example. Comcast lost 7% of its value the day after it announced its winning bid. Brian Roberts's track record as manager of Comcast is excellent. He tried to buy Disney a long time ago, and did buy NBC at the right time. The markets are suggesting that he's overbid; he might well have. But it's very difficult to tell at this stage. It's certainly unlikely that he has got a bargain." It is a good example of that game theory point that auctions tend to ensure that people have to pay up for what they want.

Another telling example he cites is what has happened to KAZ Minerals, whose shares can be measured against the price of copper and the much bigger commodity business run by Glencore. "KAZ Minerals has some great copper reserves and yet it halved in value quite recently because management thought it was a good idea to spend $900 million buying an asset from Roman Abramovich that he paid less than $100m for – and that is before they have to sink more money into developing the company's greenfield opportunity in Russia. There is no bit of analysis that you could've done on KAZ Minerals to suggest that its share price should halve, but if you had said that you were uncomfortable with the way management allocated capital, you might well have avoided it."

Asked for examples of a share other than the 5% holding in Tesco that the trust owns and which illustrate the new strategy at work, Kumar cites the aforementioned Rocket Internet, a German company which invests in other promising digital businesses, and in the UK, Dignity, the country's largest undertaking business. Artemis was one of the largest investors when Dignity was first listed on the stock market in 2014 and made some decent money from it. It later sold out, a wise precaution as the shares crashed from a peak of £28 in 2016 to a low of around £7.50 this year, at which point the trust bought back into the company (see box). Two other themes that run through the portfolio are holdings in several fund management companies (Liontrust, Polar Capital and Miton) and some large retailers (Sports Direct, Dixons Carphone Warehouse), on the view that the sell off in UK retail businesses with market-leading positions has been overdone.

It is too early to be certain that the new strategy is working. The best indicator of the progress that has been made with the new strategy is that the discount has been starting to narrow, reflecting an increasing confidence that the fortunes of the trust may be turning. It was down to 17% in September 2018 – and eliminating the discount, while not a formal objective, remains a key ambition. "This investment trust used to trade on a premium," says Kumar "and that's what we're determined to return it to. We think the new strategy has got the ingredients to achieve that." The board is helping the process, having obtained approval from shareholders to buy back shares in the trust and also undertaking to give shareholders the opportunity to tender their shares back to the company at a price close to net asset value every three years, starting in 2021.

Is Kumar daunted by taking on the responsibility of seeing this through at such a young age, we ask finally – and get, as you may have guessed from what has already been said, a straightforward and confident answer. "No. I'm absolutely up for the challenge. I'm very ambitious. I'm relishing the opportunity and enjoying the experience thoroughly. Our emphasis is on running this trust in a way to generate better and more consistent returns. My personal objective is to generate better performance, have that reflected in the rating and then take it on from there." If that turns out to be true, remember that you read it here first…

CASE STUDY: THE CASE FOR INVESTING IN DIGNITY

Dignity ticks a number of boxes for us. One is that the funeral industry has a very desirable characteristic of being completely unrelated to the economic cycle and also very predictable. You can chart out what demand for that industry is going to do for the next 20 years, because those factors were set in stone over 60 years ago [in other words, a function of mortality rates]. Dignity itself has some very attractive businesses. The crematorium business is effectively an infrastructure-type asset and it also has a very strong position in funeral care.

There's a third business, too, which is very interesting. That is the pre-paid funeral business which, because it's not on the balance sheet, I would argue that the market is putting a very low value to. It is effectively what Warren Buffett would call a 'float' business because people have pre-paid for a funeral, the company has the benefit of the economic surplus that that will generate and also has the certainty of the future business that that will provide.

When the company went towards £7 a share earlier this year, we believed there was a false perception that the company had effectively increased prices to a level at which it was so egregious that it would almost be bust if it tried to keep them at that level. When we looked at it in considerable detail we found a couple of things. One, it's quite hard to compare two funeral products. It's like trying to compare an expensive hairdresser with a cheap hairdresser. It's a service industry – not a homogenous product. Even though our observation would be that the company *had* increased prices too much, it has subsequently cut them. Our second observation was that the market seemed to be overlooking the value of the crematorium business. And our third observation was that management were clearly doing something about it.

When you put these factors together, our view was that this was an incredible opportunity to buy a very attractive business with fundamentally good long-term characteristics and we moved quickly to establish a position. This is really what this trust – and, more broadly, profit hunting – involves. It's saying we'll move opportunistically to buy if we think it is the right time, they're attractive long-term holdings and we have an in-the-moment reason for getting a bargain.

TOTAL RETURNS TO 30 APRIL 2018	3 YEARS	5 YEARS	10 YEARS	SINCE 1 JUNE 2003*
NAV per ordinary share	26.2%	41.7%	74.9%	552.3%
Ordinary share price	24.6%	19.5%	60.9%	459.1%
FTSE All-Share index	22.5%	45.6%	90.9%	253.0%

* The date when Artemis was appointed as investment manager.
Source: Artemis/Datastream

"OUR SIMPLE IDEA IS THAT YOU LOOK HARD, YOU DO THE WORK, YOU WAIT PATIENTLY – AND YOU ACT OPPORTUNISTICALLY."

Dignity share price performance

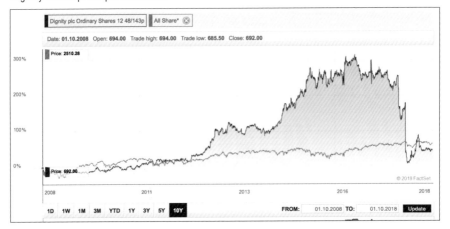

Tesco share price performance

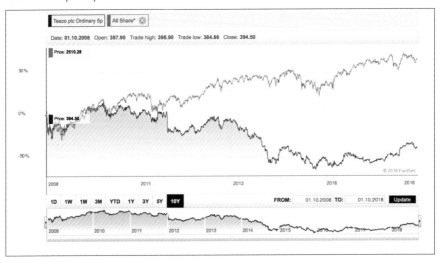

KARTIK KUMAR *co-manages the Artemis Strategic Assets fund with William Littlewood and Artemis Alpha Trust plc with John Dodd. He joined Artemis in 2012 after graduating from Bristol with a BSc in economics.*

RICH PICKINGS ON OFFER IN JAPAN

Portfolio manager NICHOLAS PRICE *has spent three years at the helm of Fidelity Japan Trust PLC, the value of whose shares doubled in that time. Here he explains how the investment environment in Japan has changed over the past two decades and why disciplined stockpickers are well placed to prosper in these conditions.*

BACKGROUND

I STARTED MY CAREER 25 years ago as a research analyst with Fidelity in Tokyo and I have been running Japanese equity portfolios for both domestic and overseas clients since 2000. What first brought me to Japan in the early 1990s was a deep interest in understanding how differently companies are run there compared with the West. Above all, I am interested in finding out what makes a business model and company successful, which in turn is what stands to make it a good investment.

I have always said that if you turn over enough stones in Japan, you will find some pearls, particularly among small and mid-cap companies. We have also seen the sell side of the investment business shrink since the introduction of Mifid 2 regulations, so the ability of analysts to cover these stocks appears to be declining, and that creates more opportunity for professional investors like us to find overlooked shares.

My investment philosophy is based on the belief that fundamental research can help to uncover and take advantage of market inefficiencies and add value to clients' portfolios. The prospects of individual companies and their comparative valuations can be predicted with a greater degree of accuracy than macroeconomic themes and factors, and that is why stock selection provides the best opportunity to capture added value.

My 'growth at reasonable price' approach utilises Fidelity's local research capability as well as its broader global research network. We have a team of 13 equity analysts on the ground in Japan, and with them, I typically make around 400 company visits every year, doing traditional 'bottom-up' research.

In addition to our internal research, I also conduct my own research, looking for under-covered names from multiple information sources, including venture capital companies, regulators, professors, and non-listed companies. I closely examine a company's business model, particularly its sustainability and the barriers to entry, followed by valuations, liquidity and the potential upside against the downside.

A key pillar of my investment approach is detecting signs of change in these kinds of area:

- fundamentals: for example, market share growth driven by the introduction of highly-competitive new products

- the environment: such as change in consumer mindset and greater willingness to buy online, which fuels strong growth in internet sales

- sentiment: to exploit gaps in investor perception, driven by excessive pessimism or euphoria

- valuations: for example, when changing from price-to-book (liquidation value) to price-to-earnings (going-concern value).

Understanding the businesses in which I invest involves talking to management, customers, vendors and competitors. It is important to ensure that I am buying their stocks at the right price. This means always being cognisant of valuations and where they stand relative to historical cycles, industry peers and the overall market.

It is important to recognise that one cannot be continually right with every investment decision. That means locking in performance gains when things are going your way and maintaining a strong sell discipline, trimming outperformers and recycling the proceeds into new ideas, retesting a mid-term growth thesis for signs of change, whether positive or negative, and moving on if there are more attractive opportunities elsewhere.

"BEING ON THE GROUND IN JAPAN HAS HUGE ADVANTAGES WHEN PICKING STOCKS. ALMOST HALF OF THE COMPANIES IN THE MID AND SMALL-CAP SPACE ARE NOT COVERED BY ANALYSTS."

THE IDEAL COMPANY

I try to be ahead of the market and get into a stock at the early stage of its growth story. I avoid stocks in which buy-side institutions already have large positions, as it means the discovery is already in the price. Essentially I am looking for companies with continuous growth over a three- to five-year period. I am after companies that can deliver returns on equity in excess of 10%, trade on attractive valuation multiples relative to both peers and their own history, and whose management is committed to enhancing shareholder returns.

In practice I tend to invest more in mid/small-cap growth companies, as that is where one can find better business models and higher returns on equity. Management in these companies also tends to be more incentivised towards delivering shareholder returns. Smaller companies, being relatively young and dynamic, are often able to create their own niche market and may therefore be capable of expanding their business regardless of a challenging external economic environment. Internet services, Asian consumption/finance and environmental themes are examples that have yielded rewarding investment ideas.

I particularly like companies which are dominant in mature domestic markets but are looking to utilise their expertise to expand overseas. As they transform from stable, domestic cash-generators to Asian or global growth stories, there is a good chance that such companies will be assigned a higher rating.

CHANGES IN JAPAN

Much has changed since I began covering Japanese companies in the early 1990s. Back then, domestic firms had relatively low margins and traded on high multiples. Since then the situation has been reversed. Valuations have come down while returns on equity have risen – the ideal combination. As a result, from a price/earnings perspective, Japan is now among the world's most attractively valued developed equity markets.

While the rate of change varies on a company-by-company basis, this commitment to broad-based reforms is clearly good news for investors. Notably, we continue to see encouraging signs of change in corporate mindsets, with Japanese companies increasingly focusing on greater capital efficiency. Historically, Japanese companies have been good at managing their businesses and profit-and-loss accounts, but less effective at managing their balance sheets.

There is now clear evidence of a concerted commitment to corporate reform and an integrated set of policies that are designed to encourage greater capital efficiency and return on equity. Japanese companies are delivering record levels of cash to shareholders. A common focus on returns on equity, the Stewardship Code, Corporate Governance Code and ROE-aware benchmarks have left traditionally conservative managements with no place to hide.

Ten years ago, only a dozen Japanese firms released integrated reports explaining their plans to increase long-term corporate value. That figure jumped to 341 last year, according to data from KPMG Japan. Only 45% of companies listed on the first section of the Tokyo Stock Exchange appointed outside directors in 2008. That has since grown to 99.7%.

Corporate Japan aggressively pursuing new business development

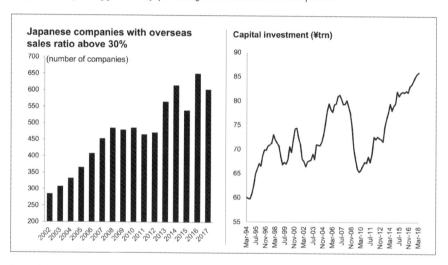

Source (left): eol (universe includes all listed companies in Japan and unlisted companies registered with eol; total of 3,632 companies). Data as of 31 December 2017. Note: eol, Inc. is Japan's No. 1 provider of corporate financial information. Source (right): Cabinet Office, GDP statistics (private non-residential investment, seasonally adjusted). As at 31 March 2018.

At the same time, companies are refocusing on their core competencies and many corporates, instead of sitting on piles of cash, are starting to deploy more of their surplus funds for investment. As long as returns from Japanese corporates continue to rise, we can also expect equities to rise, particularly as valuations remain attractive.

A SOLID ECONOMIC BACKDROP

This improving picture at the company level is supported by a generally positive macroeconomic backdrop. Employment conditions are strong, and the recent pickup in wage growth is supportive of Japan's move towards reflation. We are also seeing signs of the government gradually relaxing restrictions on foreign workers in Japan, which can create stockpicking opportunities in recruitment/staffing companies, for example, as well as providers of services for foreign residents.

Inbound tourism has been growing about 15–20% over the last few years, mainly due to Chinese tourists taking advantage of more relaxed visa regulations, and this has helped to sustain consumer spending. The influx looks set to continue, with Japan hosting the Rugby World Cup in 2019 and the 2020 Olympics.

Barring an external shock, Japan's economy appears therefore to be underpinned by positive fundamentals. Japan's central bank has made it clear that it will be lagging its global peers in terms of normalising monetary policy. The economic backdrop should provide a solid environment in which companies continue to grow and prosper, particularly in areas like services.

THE GATEWAY TO ASIA

Japan is also a gateway to the rest of Asia. Companies which develop strong brands nationally now look to expand across the rest of the region. The rise in tourism means that Asian people visiting Japan are increasingly aware of the best local brands, so when these companies go looking for new business in Asia they enjoy immediate recognition from consumers.

For example, Yamaha, the maker of musical instruments, is expanding into China, where it has got good traction as the middle class expands. It has a strong brand image and its management is raising margins by 1% a year. It is a good mid-term holding in the fund. The Chinese market for musical instruments is still quite a lot smaller than that of the United States, so Yamaha's large market share gives it a strong platform for growing along with the market. It is well-positioned to benefit as demand for luxury goods increases.

Musical instruments and audio equipment: Yamaha

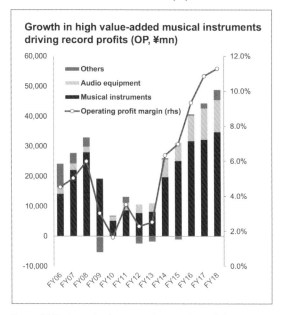

Source: Fidelity International, company data as of August 2018.

When I was a retail analyst at Fidelity in the 1990s, I covered Ryohin Keikaku, operator of the 'no brand quality goods' label Muji, as it expanded in Japan and then overseas. It did not do so well when it first went to the UK, but has since moved into Hong Kong, Singapore and China, accelerating its growth with the help of good merchandising. It's been a great long-term compounder for me.

Examples of strong profit growth: Ryohin Keikaku

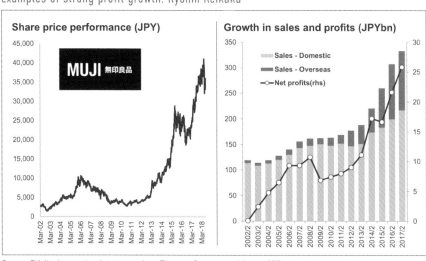

Source: Fidelity International, company data, Thomson Reuters as of August 2018.

I also own Makita, which is one of the largest power tool manufacturers in the world. As lithium ion battery technology improves, the company has continuous opportunities to keep on adding value and achieving steady increases in its pricing. It is currently expanding into the gardening market and working on offering more environmentally-friendly tools with greater battery capacity, a move that could increase Makita's market penetration by 50–60% over the medium term.

I'm always looking for companies which we perceive differently from the market. If our thesis is correct, we know we will benefit from a higher return. For example, I own Recruit Holdings, which is the number one online job site in Japan and also owns Indeed, one of the biggest search engines for jobs in the UK, which is showing strong growth.

Outside these larger and relatively well-known names, I see a lot of potential among smaller and medium-sized companies. Being on the ground in Japan has huge advantages when picking stocks. As almost half of the companies in the mid and small-cap space are not covered by analysts – there's a huge opportunity to discover hidden investment pearls.

NICHOLAS PRICE *graduated from Cambridge University with an MA in history and international relations and studied Japanese language at Keio University. He has worked at Fidelity International as a portfolio manager since 1999, where he manages three Japanese funds.*

SCOTLAND'S TRUST PIONEER

Historian and former analyst JOHN NEWLANDS *describes how Scotland's first investment trust came to be formed – and why it happened in Dundee, still today a major centre for the trust sector.*

D UNDEE TODAY IS a modern if small Scottish city, with a population just short of 150,000. Its civic motto – "One city, many discoveries" – is both a play on the name of the locally-built Royal Research Ship *Discovery*, which took Captain Scott to the Antarctic, and a reference to the city's remarkable record of scientific, medical and industrial innovation. The ship itself is in the process of becoming the centrepiece of a £1bn waterfront regeneration scheme for Dundee, involving the Victoria & Albert Museum. Dundee's history, on the other hand, might best be described as violent, chequered and bloody. Virtually every episode seems to have involved marauding forces from south of the English border.

A natural and relatively sheltered port, by the 12th century the city had become a centre for the import of wine, grain and timber. The main exports were hides and wool, the latter initially in the raw form but later being woven and dyed locally, marking the first steps towards a textile industry which became so dominant that the city gained the 19th century nickname of 'Juteopolis'. By the mid-19th century, two developments had turbo-charged Dundee's fortunes, turning the area into a trading and industrial powerhouse to rival any city in the British Empire at that time. The first step was the improvement and expansion of the city's docks; the second, the Industrial Revolution, bringing with it inventions from the steam engine to John Kay's flying shuttle to Edmund Cartwright's power loom, transforming manufacture, travel and trade.

Dundee had always been superbly situated, in terms of maritime trading, with easy access to shipping routes to Scandinavia and the Baltic, Germany and the Low Countries, and northbound through the Pentland Firth and out into the Atlantic. There was one major snag. The harbour was too small for larger ships, on top of which it was prone to disruption as silt, carried down the River Tay, caused sandbanks to build up. In 1770, the harbour was remodelled by John Smeaton, who introduced water tunnels to channel the silt away from the riverside and out to sea. The development of the port gathered speed after 1815. Several new wharves and docks were built from the 1820s onwards.

By the mid 19th century Dundee was benefiting from all Scotland's most successful industries, including shipbuilding, heavy engineering, fishing, whaling and most importantly its world famous textile business. By 1878, the Camperdown Works in Lochee, owned by Cox Brothers, had become the world's largest jute works, with a 22-acre site, its own railway branch line and employing 4,500 workers. The finished material was ideal for lower-cost products such as sacks and bagging and, by way of an aside, is undergoing a renaissance in the 21st century, as an ideal substitute for environmentally harmful plastic shopping bags.

Although Dundee was prospering, few would have considered it as a possible 'launch pad' for an innovative financial fund. What was to become the SCOTTISH AMERICAN INVESTMENT TRUST was a pooled investment scheme, the first investment trust to be launched in Scotland, that offered shares in a broad spread of investments, such that ordinary investors could reap the benefits of diversification with just a modest outlay. It was designed to focus on the leading emerging market of the day, the United States. This was at a time, it is worth noting, before the invention of electric light, the telephone or the motor car.

One young man by the name of Robert Fleming – still not yet 30 – had the vision to see the potential of this new instrument, and the character and determination to persuade enough local business people to invest to get his venture off the ground. Despite coming from a deprived background and having left school at the age of 13 to work as an office boy on a starting salary of £5 per year, he had quickly attained a position of influence in Dundee's textile industry. He was born in 1845 and began his life in Lochee in living conditions that can only be described as cramped, unhealthy and harsh. Conditions were so poor that five of Robert's brothers and sisters died in childhood, from diphtheria – three in 1843, before he was born, and two in 1859.

"ONE YOUNG MAN BY THE NAME OF ROBERT FLEMING – STILL NOT YET 30 – HAD THE VISION TO SEE THE POTENTIAL OF THIS NEW INSTRUMENT, AND THE CHARACTER AND DETERMINATION TO PERSUADE ENOUGH LOCAL BUSINESS PEOPLE TO INVEST TO GET HIS VENTURE OFF THE GROUND."

The family moved into Dundee itself in 1846, initially in Ramsay Street, and then in 1853 to a tenement close to Brown Street School, where Robert and his brother John were pupils and were given a basic education. During the summer holidays, the boys spent much of their time in the far fresher environment of Glen Shee, where both their two grandfathers lived. The two boys loved their time at Glen Shee so much, according to the Fleming family archives, that even after they had started working, in an era of the six-day week the pair thought nothing of catching the train to Blairgowrie on late Saturday afternoon and then walking the last 11 miles to Dalrulzion (or 13 if they were going to Glenkilrie). On the Monday, they would make the same walk in reverse, in time to catch the dawn train back to Dundee.

Although Robert's formal education ended at the age of 13, he had acquired a solid grounding in mathematics and bookkeeping, which served him well as his career developed. On leaving school he began work as an office boy with James Ramsay Jnr, a Dundee merchant based in the Cowgate, which that time was the commercial heart of the city. For his first year's work Robert was paid the princely sum of five pounds. His early duties included walking around the town with a packet of banknotes to pay accounts. Two years later, he joined Cox Brothers & Co., working in the mercantile office, where he first came to the notice of Thomas Hunter Cox, the partner response for financial matters, with whom he would later work closely in the management of the Scottish American Investment Trust and its successor issues. As local historian Bill Smith pointed out, "Fleming could not fail to appreciate the sheer wealth, power and influence of the partners … a revealing insight into a very different world".

Here the clerks maintained the firm's journals and ledgers, recording not just every aspect of the business but of the investment portfolios, kept in lockable files, which the partners administered for the firm and for themselves. It was during his time at Cox Brothers that Fleming began to take an interest in stock market matters and, as his surviving notebooks reveal, to maintain a list of the new issues market, covering both British companies and the large number of issues in London from foreign corporations.

After the passing of the Companies Act of 1862, which greatly simplified the procedures for forming limited liability companies, there was a surge of new issuance, into what, to begin with, were buoyant market conditions. Robert, meanwhile, was earning £100 per year before he was 20 and, as he recalled in a letter years later, "seeing before me illimitable wealth", he began to subscribe for new issues against the encouraging backdrop of rising markets.

All appears to have gone well initially but everything changed with the collapse of a leading London bank, Overend, Gurney & Co., on 'Black Friday' (11 May 1866). The shockwaves that followed took down many smaller firms, one of which was the Oriental Commercial Bank, in which Robert had invested the equivalent of several months' salary. The bank began to return its drafts unpaid and, within a few more weeks, had been placed in the hands of the liquidators.

Having bought the bank's shares part-paid, not only did Fleming have to sell all his other investments to meet the bank's calls, but it took him five more years to pay the remaining balance. It was the toughest of early lessons and, he admitted many years later, "one of these experiences that one never forgets."

Before the end of 1866, Fleming left Cox Brothers and joined the Dundee merchants, Edward Baxter & Son, as a clerk. By the time Robert entered his service Edward Baxter was 75, and still running the firm which, in addition to its extensive lending and investment activities in the US, involved the direct exporting of textile products to Dundee's overseas markets, bypassing agents in Liverpool and London. Gaining the confidence of Baxter, who was a wealthy and influential local figure, as well as the American Vice-Consul in Dundee, was Fleming's 'big break'. Edward Baxter died in July 1871 at the age of 80, leaving net assets of just over half a million pounds, equivalent to more than £50m today. He had retired from business four months earlier, at which stage he had appointed his solicitor, David Small, as Factor and Commissioner, "to act for me in the management of my estates and generally to manage my affairs and conduct my business". In the same document, Baxter recommended that Small should continue to employ "Robert Fleming my present Clerk and Book-keeper at such salary as he should consider reasonable". Robert Fleming's notebooks from this period suggest a continuous quest for self-improvement. He not only maintained his close study of the financial markets but read widely, attended as many talks and lectures as he could and resolved in his notebook "to study the art of conversation", a skill in which he felt he fell short. During the winter, he frequently went to the theatre, and recorded attending two balls.

By 1872, Fleming, his early misadventures in the new issues market well behind him, was once more active in the financial markets, dealing both on his personal account and behalf of a number of clients, including two of his fellow clerks at Edward Baxter & Co. The scale of his transactions grew larger, to the extent that his stockbrokers' commissions alone totalled £130 for the first ten months of 1872. Meanwhile, his desire to improve and learn was undimmed. His continuing studies of financial markets and any news reports thereof soon led him to the formation and success of the Foreign & Colonial Government Trust, which was regularly reported upon in the Scottish financial press.

A third issue is announced of "The Foreign and Colonial Government Trust" to the extent of £1,000,000, in 6 per cent. Certificates of £100. The issue price is £92, thus giving £6 10s 5d interest. This Trust has met a want, by enabling investors, whether small or large, to apply the principle of average to investments in Foreign Securities. It is obviously more prudent, in placing money in Stocks which pay a high rate of interest, to divide the investments so as to make one insure the other. The object of the Foreign and Colonial Trust is to enable any one to do this with a minimum of trouble and expense, as for each £100 invested the subscriber virtually becomes a holder of *pro ratâ* investments, none exceeding £10, in some 15 or 20 of the Foreign Stocks most currently negotiated on the London market ; and beyond this he receives a bonus when his Certificate is drawn for payment, and a share in the ultimate reversion, whatever it may be, when the Trust is wound up. The scheme has been so favourably received that two previous issues have been already absorbed.

Extract from the Money and Share Markets column of the *Dundee Advertiser* of 2 May 1871.

The clipping above, or one very similar, is likely to have triggered the 'light bulb moment' which led Fleming to propose a similar investment trust launch in Dundee. Not for him, though, the government stocks that made up F&C's founding portfolio. Through his association with Edward Baxter, he had gained a close knowledge of US investments and built up a range of contacts on the other side of the Atlantic. Fleming's brainchild, the Scottish American Investment Trust, was the result. He recalled:

"Dundee had not, up to that time been a financial centre, and we went to the printer in grave doubt of success with a proposed issue of £150,000. But such was the confidence in the Board, which consisted of four of the best men in the town – John Guild, John Sharp, Thomas Cox and Thomas Smith – that on the first day the British Linen Bank was flooded with applications, to such an extent that … it was decided to withdraw the prospectus and print a new one, with a capital issue of £300,000. This was also largely oversubscribed. … At the start, it took the form of a trust with a trust deed, the terms of which were printed on the back of bearer certificates of £100 each".

Fleming knew that there was a great deal of money in Dundee looking for attractive investment returns. He also knew that the United States was not just the land of opportunity but desperately short of the capital to develop railroads, coal and iron companies and civic utilities. At the same time, his costly lessons following the collapse of Overend, Gurney seven years earlier had made him wary of incautious investment. He believed that only investments secured on a railroad's land and equipment, i.e. mortgage bonds, should be acquired, and then only if that railroad was paying a dividend on its ordinary stock, or if the bonds were guaranteed by another railroad.

It says something about his personality and strength of character that he was able to persuade John Guild, a local merchant with interests in insurance and shipping, to become the trust's first chairman and his former employer, Thomas Hunter Cox, one of the most prominent local figures of all, to become a trustee, along with two other leading businessmen, John Sharp and Thomas Smith. The first formal meeting of the trustees took place in Thomas Cox's offices on 1 February 1873, when Fleming, let us recall, was still only 28. The minutes state that:

> "It was proposed to consider the establishment of a Trust similar in principle to the Foreign & Colonial established in London by Lord Westbury … Mr Fleming had previously brought the subject under consideration of the gentlemen present individually, giving them a sketch prospectus of the nature of the business, and the working of the proposed trust".

The trustees engaged Shiel & Small as their solicitors, where a further meeting took place on 5 February in Bank Street. Mr Shiel indicated that "The trust deed as it now stood was a very perfect one, resembling very closely the Foreign & Colonial trust deed which no doubt Lord Westbury had considered very carefully" The British Linen Company's Bank was appointed as banker to the trust, while Robert Fleming himself became its secretary.

The prospectus described the intended issue of £150,000, in certificates of £100 each and paying interest of 6% per annum; any surplus income would be used either to redeem certificates or to purchase additional investments. The trust initially had a life of ten years. The new trust was to invest in: "The bonds of states, cities, railroads and other corporations in the US, but chiefly in the mortgage bonds of railroads." Among other requirements, the annual general meeting was to be advertised in at least two daily newspapers published in Dundee and one in Edinburgh. Entry to the AGM was also to be strictly controlled: "no person shall be permitted to be present who does not produce his certificate ... and shall vote in proportion to the value of the certificates produce by them".

The launch of the trust was an immediate success, being oversubscribed by 60%. Rather than scaling down allotments, it was decided to increase the size of the issue – and, those involved with investment company documentation in the 21st century might note with astonishment, a revised prospectus was issued the same day. When applications closed five days later this, too, was oversubscribed, causing the *Dundee Courier & Argus* of 11 February 1873 to declare that "this splendid success is a remarkable indication of the estimation in which the Trustees are held ... as well as the soundness of the project itself".

The Cunard liner SS *Abyssinia*, in which Robert Fleming made his first transatlantic crossing. His original booking had been made in the RMS *Atlantic*, which struck rocks and sank off the coast of Nova Scotia with a loss of 560 lives. Abyssinia herself was destroyed after a fire in a cargo of cotton mid-Atlantic in 1891.

A TRANSATLANTIC CLOSE CALL

With the successful launch in the bag, and on the admirable principle that the only reliable source of information is personal original research, plans were put straight into force for Robert Fleming to visit the US and gain first-hand knowledge of the investment opportunities on offer. On 12 March 1873, Fleming left Dundee for London, where he spent a few days gathering information before heading back north to Liverpool, ready to make his first transatlantic crossing. He was armed with letters of introduction to key bankers in Boston, Philadelphia and New York. Thomas Cox had also written ahead to his New York advisers, the cumbersomely-titled Brown Brothers and Kidder, Peabody. As it turned out, Fleming had not only been provided with excellent references but endowed with a goodly measure of luck. He had originally intended to sail in another vessel, RMS (Royal Mail Ship) *Atlantic*, which sank with huge loss of life on 1 April 1873, having struck rocks off the coast of Nova Scotia.

Fleming reached New York on 26 March after a voyage of ten days. Three days later, the first of his numerous cables and letters was sent back to Dundee. These frequent communications either confirmed purchases made, to what must have been a pre-arranged plan, or asked for approval to invest, using a series of codewords. For example, in one of his letters Fleming recommended five separate railroad mortgage bonds, to which the Trustees replied by cable, "Letter 7th April [1873] received: BADAJOZ, TALAVERO, INKERMAN, BALACLAVA." Each of these four words (all names of European battles) was a code for approval to purchase, typically $60,000 of stock, in a certain railroad security. Interestingly on this occasion Fleming's fifth code word, WATERLOO, was missing from the reply from Dundee. This meant that his proposal to invest in the Missouri, Toledo, Wabash & Western Railroad had, for whatever reason, been turned down by the Trustees.

FIRST INVESTMENTS

The first recorded investment made by the trust was $83,000 of First Mortgage Gold Bonds of the Cincinnati, Richmond & Fort Wayne Railroad, purchased through Maitland, Phelps & Co of New York. The price was 91 cents, with a 7% coupon, giving a yield of 7.7%.

The trust's ten largest investments in July 1873

NO.	TEN LARGEST PORTFOLIO HOLDINGS AS AT 2 JULY 1873	PRICE	VALUATION (US$)	% OF TOTAL INVESTMENTS
120,000	Michigan Central Railroad 7%	99¼	119,100	7.6
110,000	St Louis & Iron Mountain Railroad 7%	95	104,500	6.6
100,000	New York & Harlem Railroad 7%	100	100,000	6.3

NO.	TEN LARGEST PORTFOLIO HOLDINGS AS AT 2 JULY 1873	PRICE	VALUATION (US$)	% OF TOTAL INVESTMENTS
105,000	Philadelphia & Reading Coal & Iron Co. 7%	90	94,500	6.0
100,000	Pacific of Missouri Railroad 6%	86¼	86,250	5.5
80,000	Detroit & Bay City Railroad Co. 8%	99½	79,600	5.0
83,000	Cincinatti, Richmond & Fort Wayne Railroad 7%	94	78,020	4.9
75,000	Dunkirk, Warren & Pittsburg Railroad 7%	103½	77,625	4.9
70,000	St Louis City Bonds 6%	97	67,900	4.3
70,000	Cleveland & Pittsburg Railroad 7%	93	65,100	4.1
TOTAL % INVESTED IN 'TOP TEN':				55.2

In the table above, which lists the ten largest investments which had been made as at 2 July 1873, the founding investment of Cincinnati, Richmond & Fort Wayne Railroad 7% Mortgage Bonds, which had been bought at 91, had advanced in price to 94. Eight of the ten holdings were railroad securities, one was a coal and iron company issue and one a civic bond. The total of $872,595 for the ten holdings represents some 55% of the total portfolio value of $1,577,495, the latter figure equating at the prevailing exchange rate to approximately £280,000.

The timing of the launch proved testing, to say the least. Just as the investment of the £300,000 raised was almost complete, the so-called 'panic of 1873' developed in the US, heralding the start of a depression that lasted for six years. Railroad stocks were badly hit, to the extent that several thousand miles of US railroad went into receivership in the next four years. Fortunately the Trust's founding investments had been chosen with care. Fleming and the trustees had prudently chosen to ignore the bonds of new construction railroad branch lines, which were yielding between 9% and 11%. Instead, they had gone for the older, dividend-paying railroads running on established trunk lines. These safer bonds typically paid 7% – still a handsome premium on the returns available from domestic investment.

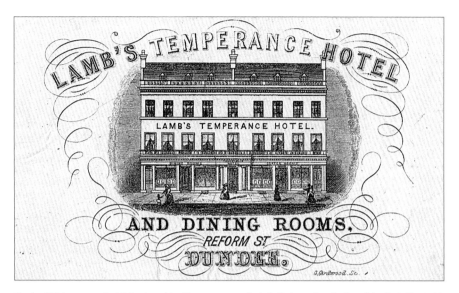

Early AGMs were held in Lamb's Temperance Hotel (later simply Lamb's Hotel) at 64, Reform Street, Dundee. The building was later used for many years as the head office of Alliance Trust. Since 1916 it has housed an upmarket coffee shop.

Looking back at the events of the previous year at the trust's 1874 annual general meeting, held in Lamb's Hotel, Reform Street, the trustees noted that:

> "In its origin the panic of 1873 was largely due to an excessive construction of new railroads … with the collapse of the Houses engaged in financing these operations, Railroad securities of all classes were subjected to a test unprecedentedly severe. Under such circumstances, the trustees have gratification in being able to report that in no case has there been the slightest irregularity or delay in payment … the market value of the securities forming the trust fund has been more than maintained".

FOLLOW-ON ISSUES

The first issue, as it retrospectively became known, not only survived its difficult early years but led to a second issue in September 1873 and a third in October 1875. Each of the follow-on issues was for £400,000. Robert Fleming remained as secretary to all three trusts for 15 years, before turning his attention to London, where he formed the Investment Trust Corporation Ltd in 1888. Despite US market turbulence for much of 1870s, the 'First Scottish' paid 6% annually on the certificates of all three issues with monotonous regularity until 1879. Each issue accumulated reserve funds of £26,000, £37,000 and £16,000 respectively, while the investments of the first issue had become worth £350,000 over and above their £1,000,000 book value, despite the general economic depression of the time. This was a creditable achievement – although, Robert Fleming later admitted, some of the railroad bonds purchased in the early years had given him sleepless nights. The historian J. C. Gilbert was to describe the First Scottish's overall performance in its early years as "a brilliant achievement … an example of the advantages to be derived from investment by experts".

In 1879, the first major change in the trust's history took place, not through voluntary action but because of a ruling in the English courts. In the case of Sykes v. Beacon (1878), Sir George Jessel, Master of the Rolls, ruled that investment trusts formed under trust deeds were "associations of more than 20 persons for the acquisition of gain". They were therefore not legal, unless registered under the Joint Stock Companies Acts of 1862 and 1867. Although the ruling applied solely to trusts registered in England, the advice of eminent counsel in Edinburgh was that it was only a matter of time before the issue was tested in the Scottish courts. Urgent action was required. Fleming and the trustees put in motion the process of converting the trust issues to the limited company form. A complication was that, as the certificates were bearer instruments, the names and addresses of many of their owners was not known. The only way to proceed was to advertise widely in the local area, inviting the holders of all three issues to attend a meeting in Dundee – as ever, at Lamb's Hotel – and hope for a majority vote.

The results of the proposed conversion were reported to shareholders on Wednesday 18 June 1879, when they were informed that:

> "In consequence of litigation in the English Courts, the result of which seemed to point to the illegality of the present constitution of the Trust, the Trustees summoned an aggregated meeting of the holders of Certificates of all the Trusts, to consider the steps necessary to be taken toward the protection of their interests. A numerously attended meeting had been held on 11th March, when it was unanimously resolved to convert the Trust into a Joint Stock Company … the conversion has proceeded so far as to leave its completion no longer doubtful. Out of 2,967 Certificates outstanding, 2,907 have already been surrendered in exchange for shares in the First Scottish American Trust Company Limited and the outstanding 60 Certificates are expected to be converted at an early day."

MOVING FORWARD AS LIMITED COMPANIES

The three trust issues were duly and separately registered as the First, Second and Third Scottish American Trust Companies Limited. The new articles of association gave the directors powers to authorise borrowing by the company, for the purposes of investment, not exceeding 10% of the capital of the company. However, no preference stocks or debentures were issued for over 30 years (unlike, for example, the Dundee land trust companies which eventually formed the Alliance group). Robert Fleming remained as secretary to all three companies, the offices of which stayed at 1, Royal Exchange Place, while the four founding trustees, all still going strong, became directors. The investment remit was still confined to the bonds or other obligations of the railroads, other corporations, states or municipalities, and of the US government itself.

Each of the directors was required to own not fewer than 30 shares in each of the three issues, meaning that each director had to allocate at least £9,000 to meet the requirements of his triple roles. This was a substantial commitment at a time when the *Dundee Advertiser* was offering "two self-contained dwelling houses of six apartments each" in Broughty Ferry, near Dundee and standing in substantial grounds, priced at £1,000 for the entire site. The day-to-day process of managing the investment portfolio, by now some 50 holdings, quickly resumed. As before, any adjustments were invariably either confirmed by, or made on the advice of, Fleming himself, who continued to visit the US at least once per year and sometimes more often. At the 1882 AGM, held at Lamb's Hotel and reported in detail in the *Dundee Advertiser* of 26 May 1882, the chairman reported that things were going well:

> "We are able to continue the rate of 8% to which the dividend was raised last year ... we are also able to add £2,000 to the Reserve Fund. (Applause); that we have again lengthened the average date to which the bond run, to 23 years; (Applause) and that Mr Fleming sailed for New York six weeks ago ... to investigate the merits of a number of profitable exchanges in our investments, with the view of improving the position of the Company ... these exchanges have now been carried out. (Applause)."

INVESTMENT BACKDROP IN THE US

In the 1880s, the US was very much a mixture of the modern and the 'wild frontier'. The major cities were booming and yet, further out, it was literally still the era of the Wild West. Take 1881. On the one hand, the Standard Oil

Company was being set up to host the fortunes of John D. Rockefeller. On the other, Wyatt Earp and Doc Holliday were shooting it out at the OK Corral. Just a few weeks before said gunfight, Sioux Chief Sitting Bull had finally surrendered to US troops at Fort Buford, North Dakota, after months of fighting, some taking place close, rather worryingly, it might be surmised, to the construction site of the Great Northern Railway that eventually ran from St Paul, Minnesota, to Seattle. This sort of tale gives credence to the story that an early representative of the other pioneering Dundee-based financial enterprise, Alliance Trust, came under bow-and-arrow attack while riding out on the Omaha Trail.

It was against this unsettled backdrop that the company's portfolio had been created and against which it clearly needed the most careful and regular monitoring. An examination of the meticulously-maintained contemporary accounts, still accessible today in bound ledgers in the archives of Dundee City Council, strongly suggests that in Robert Fleming the directors had found the right man for the job. The impeccably presented annual reports, for instance, always included that rarity among 19th-century accounts, a narrative, written not by the chairman but by Robert Fleming himself. The chairman's commentaries were published too, via the placing in the *Dundee Advertiser* of a verbatim transcript of every annual general meeting, including all the questions raised and a summary of their answers, these articles also being copied and retained in the relevant ledgers.

By 1886, the Company held 55 different investments, the identity of which, as was normal at the time, was not revealed in the annual accounts. On this occasion, unusually, an indication of the true asset value thereof was revealed. At that year's AGM, it was reported that "a careful calculation of the present market price (after providing for the dividend now recommended) is equal to £169 5s 10d per fully paid share of one hundred pounds". One director, Thomas Smith, had died earlier that year, being replaced in 1887 by William Ogilvy Dalgleish, who was the chairman of Baxter Brothers, marking the first boardroom change since the company's formation.

IMPROVING MARKET CONDITIONS

Market conditions in the US had begun to improve and some of the higher quality railroad bonds were beginning to look, to use a current phrase, fully priced. As John Guild noted in his 1886 chairman's remarks, this had been picked up in a recent *Economist* article, which suggested that the owners of railroad mortgage bonds were in danger of forgetting that in the fullness of

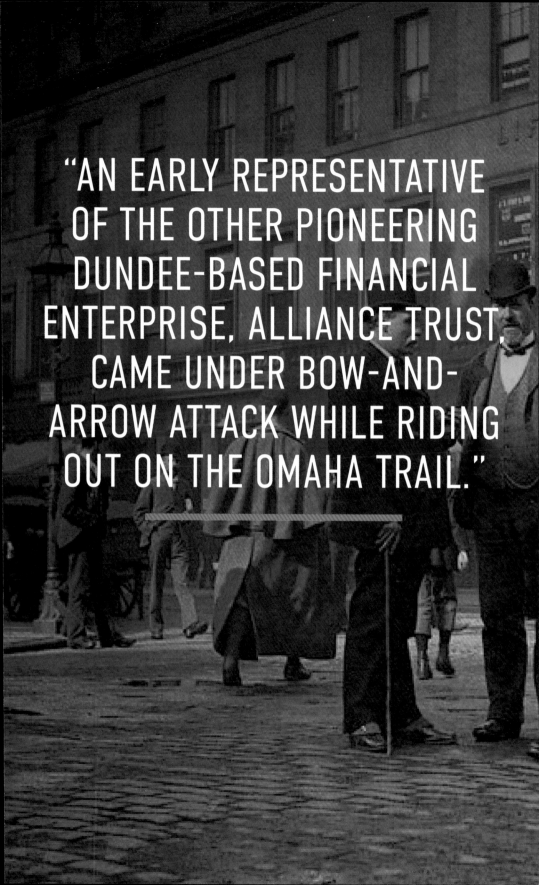

"AN EARLY REPRESENTATIVE OF THE OTHER PIONEERING DUNDEE-BASED FINANCIAL ENTERPRISE, ALLIANCE TRUST, CAME UNDER BOW-AND-ARROW ATTACK WHILE RIDING OUT ON THE OMAHA TRAIL."

time, repayment would be made at face value only. "In strictness", Guild noted, "they ought to lay a certain proportion of interest aside each year to meet the shrinkage of the principal – this is just what we have all along recognised and acted upon … every penny of the £49,000 of reserve fund has been made up of surplus revenue." As well as keeping back a proportion of interest received for a rainy day, the chairman also reported, the average date at which investments became repayable had been extended to 27 years, effectively locking in returns, on the assumption of no defaults, until June 1913.

This prudent policy – plus, of course, the focus upon US bond investment – goes some way to explaining the way that the effects of the 1890 Barings Crisis, often described as the most serious financial event for UK investors in the 19th century, seem to have caused barely a ripple of concern when described to shareholders at that year's gathering in Lamb's Hotel. Whereas other investment trusts, particularly those formed in London during the late 1880s' 'trust mania', suffered significant losses and in some cases went to the wall, investors at the 1891 AGM were politely being told that:

> "The market value of the investments does not show as well as it did – it is down about 2¾% since last year … [however] the income is sufficient to pay the usual dividend of 8¼% … and beyond that provides £1,000 to add to the Reserve fund. … Amidst the general disturbance of prices and insecurity in values, I think the shareholders of this Company need not distress themselves about the state of the share market, but quietly hold to a good investment which yields thcm a steady income with ample security".

Robert Fleming was listed as company secretary for the last time in the 1890 accounts, after which he was described as advising secretary – and then, from 1897, simply as 'London Correspondent'. Fleming's trusted but hitherto unmentioned clerk, Adam Hunter, became company secretary in his place. Hunter, though a low-profile figure in the company's history, assisted Fleming from the very start, succeeded him as company secretary in 1890 and later became a director, serving until 1936 – a mind-boggling 63 years after joining the company, presumably as a very young man.

The company might have been insulated from the main effects of the Barings Crisis but the depression that affected the US economy in the 1890s was a different matter. The first sign of major trouble came with the collapse of the Philadelphia and Reading Railroad in February 1893, leading to a run on the banks. This in turn caused a loss of confidence among European investors in US stocks, causing prices to fall. In the fallout, 500 American banks and 15,000 businesses closed, in addition to which the Northern Pacific Railway, the Union Pacific Railroad and the Atchison, Topeka and Santa Fe Railroad all failed.

The Company's conservative borrowing policy meant that it did not suffer to the same extent as other, more highly geared, trusts in this period. The investment portfolio had been diversifed further to 80 holdings. The 1893 accounts merely make mention of "three defaults this year, of small amounts, but which we feel will ultimately be paid … we have been able to continue the 8¼% dividend and propose, with your consent, to add £1,000 to the Reserve fund." The following year, under the sub-header 'A SINGULARLY FORTUNATE COMPANY', it was revealed that total income received over the past year had fallen by "£1,171, or 7s 10d on each share of £100".

By 1895, although some of the effects of the depression had worked through, causing the dividend to have to be reduced to 7¾%, the worst was over and US stock prices were on the turn. In an era when the disclosure of true net asset values was an infrequent event, the chairman Edward Cox declared that "compared with the high water mark of 1892, there was a depreciation [by mid-1895] of 10% of the capital", a more than decent outcome following one of the worst economic crises in US history.

The mood of optimism, albeit always phrased in cautious terms, was maintained as the new century approached. The recovery was slower to come than had been hoped, judging by the 1897 accounts, which talked in terms of "as yet, few signs of visible improvement" in the US. The dividend, on the other hand, had been restored to 8¼% and now £1,000 was to be committed to reserves, after a gap in such payments of two years. On this occasion a special visitor, Mr George Coppell, senior partner of Maitland, Coppell & Co., the Company's New York bankers, was invited to Dundee to address the 1897 AGM, saying:

> "My firm, as your bankers and agents in New York, has been connected with the Scottish American Investment Trust Companies from the very origin of their business … I wish the condition of [these companies] were at all symbolic of the actual conditions in the United States; but there must be something peculiar to the management of this Company which makes it able to present so favourable a statement and declare so handsome a dividend, both which are almost exceptional in these days".

UNEXPECTED QUESTION

The three investment companies, in short, had withstood the US recession years remarkably well – so well, in fact, that the following year a shareholder, Mr A. M. Guild, found cause to take exception to the annual "indulging of blowing trumpets over the success of the Company" which, he said, had an unwieldy shape and suffered from difficulty in marketing which, he felt, was depressing the price. It might have been wise 25 years ago to denominate the shares at £100, he suggested, but these now stood at £176 and the units had outgrown themselves. Perhaps, he argued, it was time either to divide each £100 share into ten shares of £10 or, alternatively, to convert each share into £100 of stock, which would be tradeable in smaller amounts. To judge by the minutes, the directors were in no hurry to implement such a radical change. It was not until 1905 that the original 3,000 shares of £100 each were converted into £300,000 of stock.

Taking stock of the 27-year-old company's position in early 1900, the investment portfolio of 99 fixed-interest securities by now had a remarkable average duration of 33 years. Total assets, as recorded on the balance sheet, were some £389,386, of which £387,938 was accounted for by the "Investments in Railroad and other bonds, &c." The covering text on the other hand referred to the par value of the securities being £561,055, "which is equal to £196 4s 6d per fully paid share of one hundred pounds". This tends to bear out a comment made in the Dundee press at much the same time, alluding to the directors' known tendency to apply "ultra conservative valuations".

The company's ten largest investments in May 1900

NO.	TEN LARGEST PORTFOLIO HOLDINGS AS AT 1 MAY 1900	VALUATION (US$)	% OF TOTAL INVESTMENTS
1	Duluth South Shore & Atlantic 5%, 1937	91,840	3.1
2	St Paul Minn & Alban (Montana) 4%, 1937	83,430	2.8
3	Toledo & Ohio Central Western Division 5%, 1935	78,750	2.6
4	Flint & Peremarquette (Port Huron Division) 5%, 1939	73,500	2.5
5	East Tennessee Virginia & Georgia 5%, 1930	69,600	2.4
6	Burlington Cedar Rapids & Co. 5%, 1936	69,000	2.3
7	Internation & Great Northern 6%, 1919	58,310	2.0
8	Chicago & Erie 5%, 1932	50,160	1.7

NO.	TEN LARGEST PORTFOLIO HOLDINGS AS AT 1 MAY 1900	VALUATION (US$)	% OF TOTAL INVESTMENTS
9	St Paul & Northern Pacific 6%, 1923	45,500	1.5
10	Union Elevated of Chicago 5%, 1945	43,200	1.4
TOTAL PERCENTAGE INVESTED IN 'TOP TEN':			22.3

A total dividend of 8¼% was paid for the year, and another £1,000 placed into revenue reserves, which now totalled £67,000. The company was in robust shape, therefore, as the new century moved ahead – starting off, not for the first or last time in history, with a series of booms, busts, leading into war, plus, on this occasion, one of Donald Rumsfeld's 'unknown unknowns', in the form of the San Francisco earthquake of 1906, which ruptured 296 miles of the San Andreas fault, destroyed 80% of the city, took more than 3,000 lives and led to the "Panic of 1907". The earthquake turned into a market-wide sell-off in US investments, not to mention a currency crisis so serious it led to the creation of the Federal Reserve.

The earthquake was followed by five days of raging fires, and a wave of insurance claims totalling an estimated $235 million, equivalent to approximately $6.5 billion today, rippled back to the insurance underwriters' floor in London. In time, this money re-crossed the Atlantic in the form of international gold flows, destabilising the exchange rate. This in turn caused the Bank of England to take defensive measures. When a stock manipulation scheme involving the United Copper Company failed, market fear set in and within three weeks the New York Stock Exchange had fallen 50% from its peak the previous year.

Back in the infinitely calmer surroundings of Lamb's Hotel, Dundee, Edward Cox was able to tell shareholders in 1906 that "none of their Company's investments were interested in any San Francisco undertaking, and in spite of the heavy falls in prices which followed that terrible disaster … the valuations of their securities showed a nominal fall of less than £4,000 from the record valuations last year". The following year, a depreciation of 3¾% was reported … "investors must be content with a dividend of 8 and three-eights per cent and the placing of £2,000 in the Reserve fund".

In 1908, Robert Fleming returned from a trip to the US, presumably to make a first-hand analysis of how bad things really were. He told the Investment Trust Corporation, Edward Cox told the Dundee AGM, that America was "still as safe as a field for investment as any". Mr Cox continued, "of course it is disappointing that the value of the Company's securities has depreciated to the extent of 6.8% … but it is fully expected this depreciation will disappear before long." Another major US financial crisis had come and gone, with no immediate impact beyond the temporary cessation of dividend increases. Investment valuations had fallen, certainly, but by far less than wider US equity markets and with every prospect of longer-term recovery. Moreover not a single portfolio default had occurred. The legend of Dundonian financial conservatism had been well and truly laid.

JOHN NEWLANDS *is the author of* Put Not Your Trust in Money, *a history of the investment trust industry from 1868 to the present. The trust that Robert Fleming founded, now known as Dunedin Income Growth Investment Trust, will celebrate its 150th anniversary in 2023.*

————————————

ANALYSING INVESTMENT TRUSTS

by JONATHAN DAVIS

UNDERSTANDING TRUSTS

KEY TERMS EXPLAINED

INVESTMENT TRUSTS (AKA investment companies) pool the money of individual and professional investors and invest it for them in order to generate capital gains, or dividend income, or both. These are the most important factors that determine how good an investment they are:

SHARE PRICE

The price (typically in pence) you will be asked to pay to buy or sell shares in any investment company. You want it to go up, not down.

SPREAD

The difference between the price per share you will need to pay if you want to buy and that you will be offered if you wish to sell – can be anything from 0% (good) to 5% (bad).

MARKET CAPITALISATION

The aggregate current value of all the shares a trust has issued – in essence, therefore, what the market in its wisdom thinks the investment company is worth today.*

NET ASSET VALUE (NAV)

The value of the company's investments less running costs at the most recent valuation point – typically (and ideally) that will be yesterday's quoted market price, but for some types of investment trust it might be one or more months ago.

---

* The market is not always wise and would be a duller and less interesting place if it were.

NET ASSET VALUE PER SHARE

This is calculated, not surprisingly, by dividing the NAV (see above) by the number of shares in issue. You can compare it directly with the share price to find the discount.

DISCOUNT/PREMIUM

When the share price is below the investment company's net asset value per share it is said to be trading 'at a discount'; if it trades above the NAV per share, then the trust is selling 'at a premium'.

DIVIDEND YIELD

How much a trust pays out as income each year to its shareholders, expressed as a percentage of its share price.

THE FUND MANAGER

The person (or team) responsible for choosing and managing the investment trust's capital. Will typically be professionally qualified and highly paid. How much value he or she really adds is hotly debated.

THE BOARD

Investment companies are listed companies, so they must comply with stock exchange rules and appoint a board of independent directors who are legally responsible for overseeing the company and protecting the interests of its shareholders, which ultimately means replacing the manager or closing down the trust if results are no good.

GEARING

A fancy word for borrowing money in order to try and boost the performance of a company's shares – a case of more risk for potentially more reward.

FEES AND CHARGES

What it costs to own shares in an investment trust – a figure that (confusingly) can be calculated in several different ways. More important than it sounds on first hearing.

SECTORS

Investment trusts come in many shapes and sizes, so for convenience are categorised into one of a number of different sectors, based on the kind of things that they invest in.

PERFORMANCE

A popular and over-used term which tells you how much money an investment trust has made for its shareholders over any given period of time – by definition, a backward-looking measurement.

TOTAL RETURN

A way of combining the income a trust pays with the capital gains it also generates (you hope) over time, so as to allow fair comparisons with other trusts and funds.

RISK AND RETURN

Riskier investments tend to produce higher returns over time, typically at the cost of doing less well when market conditions are unfavourable and better when they are more helpful. Risk comes in many (dis)guises, however – some more visible than others.

IS THERE ANY DIFFERENCE BETWEEN AN INVESTMENT COMPANY AND INVESTMENT TRUST?

Basically no. Strictly speaking, investment trusts are investment companies but not all investment companies are investment trusts. Feel free to use either term interchangeably, without fear of embarrassment.

CLOSED-END FUNDS

Investment trusts are an example of what is called a 'closed-end fund', meaning that its capital base is intended to be fixed and permanent (unlike unit trusts and OEICs, which take in and return money to investors on a daily basis and are therefore called open-ended). The distinction is no longer quite as important as it was, as it has become somewhat easier for investment companies to raise new money through share issues.

INVESTMENT TRUST SECTORS

There are no fixed rules for what an investment trust can invest in. The trust's strategy does, however, have to be outlined in a prospectus and approved by shareholders if, as does happen, the board wishes to change that objective at a later date.

For convenience, and to help comparative analysis, trusts are grouped into a number of different sectors, based on their investment focus. New trusts are launched on a regular, if cyclical, basis. Certain periods are characterised by a spurt of new issues in a particular segment of the market.

Property trusts and hedge funds, for example, were popular in the run up to the financial crisis in 2008. Income-generating trusts from alternative assets, such as infrastructure, have been particularly popular since then.

There have also been some notable new conventional equity trusts launched in recent years by big-name fund managers with strong personal followings. Examples include Anthony Bolton in 2010 (FIDELITY CHINA SPECIAL SITUATIONS), Terry Smith in 2014 (FUNDSMITH EMERGING EQUITIES) and Neil Woodford in 2015 (WOODFORD PATIENT CAPITAL). Each one of these raised several hundred million pounds at launch. In 2018 Terry Smith launched a second investment trust, one that invests in global equities, under the name SMITHSON.

At the same time there are regular departures from the investment trust universe, as funds either close down or return capital to shareholders, typically (though not invariably) as a result of indifferent performance or where the trust has a predetermined wind-up date. The way the universe of listed trusts looks can therefore change significantly from decade to decade.

One important difference in the last two decades is that it has become easier for trusts to grow through a process known as 'secondary issuance'. Essentially trusts that are popular with investors can now, provided they have the necessary shareholder approvals, more readily issue additional shares without the need to produce an expensive legal prospectus.

It is nothing like as simple as the daily process by which open-ended funds can issue or cancel units in their funds, but it does enable trusts to tap into additional demand on a regular basis. SCOTTISH MORTGAGE is the most striking example: it has raised an additional £600m of capital in this way since January 2017. Many of the infrastructure funds have also grown rapidly through this route.

The majority of the £1.88bn of assets in investment companies, however, remains in traditional equity and multi-asset funds ('conventional trusts'), as the following table, using the categories adopted by the Association of Investment Companies (AIC), shows.*

The tables after this analyse each of the main component groups.

---

* Excludes the small number of split capital trusts, which are too few these days to merit a separate listing.

Table 1: Breakdown of investment trusts by type

TYPE	TOTAL ASSETS (£M)	MARKET CAP (£M)	NO OF COMPANIES	AVG TOTAL ASSETS (£M)	AVG MARKET CAP (£M)	SHARE OF TOTAL ASSETS	SHARE OF COMPANIES
Conventional	123,446	107,068	214	577	500	65.6%	53.0%
Specialist	40,504	38,144	84	482	454	21.5%	20.8%
Property	19,759	15,376	40	494	384	10.5%	9.9%
VCTs	4,328	3,953	66	66	60	2.3%	16.3%
TOTAL	**188,036**	**164,541**	**404**	**465**	**407**	**100.0%**	**100.0%**

Source: AIC Statistics, 31 August 2018.

The sectors are ranked by the number of trusts in each one and also on two measures of size – total assets and market capitalisation (both in £m).* The two figures differ for two reasons:

1. the first includes assets funded by debt, whereas the second measures only the value of the shareholders' interest, as determined by the market

2. the impact of discounts – a discount reduces the market capitalisation relative to the asset value.

A breakdown of the 15 largest sectors in the conventional equity space – 190 trusts, accounting for 96% of total assets – are shown in the following table.

Table 2: 15 largest conventional trust sectors

SECTOR	TOTAL ASSETS (£M)	MARKET CAP (£M)	NO OF COMPANIES	AVERAGE TOTAL ASSETS (£M)	AVG MARKET CAP (£M)
Global	29,539	26,925	20	1,477	1,346
Private Equity	16,586	16,178	21	790	770
UK Equity Income	12,133	10,477	23	528	456
Flexible Investment	9,094	7,396	17	535	435
Global Emerging Markets	6,861	5,711	11	624	519
Asia Pacific – Excluding Japan	6,487	5,598	15	432	373

---

* Note that some other research providers you may come across use somewhat different ways of breaking down the sectors.

SECTOR	TOTAL ASSETS (£M)	MARKET CAP (£M)	NO OF COMPANIES	AVERAGE TOTAL ASSETS (£M)	AVG MARKET CAP (£M)
UK Smaller Companies	6,005	4,982	20	300	249
UK All Companies	5,985	4,980	15	399	332
Country Specialists: Asia Pacific	5,590	4,363	9	621	485
Hedge Funds	5,550	3,733	9	617	415
Europe	4,081	3,554	7	583	508
Global Equity Income	3,334	2,982	6	556	497
North America	2,783	2,259	7	398	323
Japan	2,699	2,269	6	450	378
European Smaller Companies	2,045	1,742	4	511	435
TOP 15	**118,773**	**103,148**	**190**	**625**	**543**

The majority of the sector categories are self-explanatory. It is worth noting, however, that individual trusts within each broad sector category will often have somewhat different investment objectives and benchmarks. The 'flexible investment' sector is a recently added one that includes a number of trusts which invest across a broad range of asset classes. Most of these were formerly included in the global sector.

A notable feature of the table is that just under 20% of conventional equity trusts have the UK as their primary investment focus. Investment trusts from the very earliest days have always had a bias towards investment outside the UK and their external focus remains one of their key attractions.

The specialist sectors are also clearly identified by their name. Unlike the conventional trusts, which are mainly defined by their regional focus, the specialist sectors are grouped by industry. The specialist sector is worth looking at in more detail as it gives a flavour of the wide range of investment strategies which are available once you look beyond the conventional trusts. It is these trusts, along with those investing in property and private equity, that are now commonly referred to as making up the 'alternative asset' sector.

Table 3: Breakdown of investment trusts — specialist sectors

SPECIALIST SECTORS	TOTAL ASSETS (£M)	MARKET CAP (£M)	NO OF COMPANIES	AVG TOTAL ASSETS (£M)	AVG MARKET CAP (£M)	ASSETS/ MARKET CAP
Infrastructure	10,373	11,213	7	1,482	1,602	8.1%
Debt	8,601	7,890	29	297	272	-8.3%
Renewable Energy Infrastructure	5,623	4,993	8	703	624	-11.2%
Biotechnology & Healthcare	4,414	4,608	6	736	768	4.4%
Tech, Media & Telecom	2,711	2,687	4	678	672	-0.9%
Leasing	2,613	1,948	6	436	325	-25.5%
Commodities & Natural Resources	2,574	1,997	9	286	222	-22.4%
Small Media Comms & IT	1,089	932	1	1,089	932	-14.4%
Insurance & Reinsurance Strategies	736	510	2	368	255	-30.8%
Environmental	677	591	3	226	197	-12.6%
Financials	490	447	3	163	149	-8.7%
Forestry & Timber	354	146	2	177	73	-58.9%
Utilities	235	169	3	78	56	-28.1%
Liquidity Funds	13	13	1	13	13	-1.3%
TOTAL	**40,504**	**38,144**	**84**	**6,731**	**6,159**	**-8.5%**

Source: AIC statistics as at 31 August 2018.

The main distinction in the property sector table is between trusts that invest directly in property (that is, buy and sell the bricks and mortar themselves) and those that invest primarily in the shares of other listed property companies. The former by their nature are less liquid than the latter.

Table 4: Breakdown of investment trusts – property sectors

PROPERTY SECTOR	TOTAL ASSETS (£M)	MARKET CAP (£M)	NO OF COMPANIES	AVG TOTAL ASSETS (£M)	AVG MARKET CAP (£M)	SHARE OF TOTAL ASSETS
Specialist	8,756	6,841	16	547	428	44.3%
Direct – UK	7,587	5,884	14	542	420	38.4%
Property Securities	1,597	1,346	1	1,597	1,346	8.1%
Direct – Europe	1,352	1,104	6	225	184	6.8%
Direct – Asia Pacific	468	202	3	156	67	2.4%
TOTAL	**19,759**	**15,376**	**40**	**3,067**	**2,445**	**100.0%**

Venture capital trusts, as described earlier, are specialist investment companies that exist to support companies at an early stage of their development, in return for which shareholders in the VCTs are offered some potentially attractive tax breaks. Most of these trusts will be investing in unlisted securities, although an exception are the AIM VCTs, which mostly own shares listed on the Alternative Investment Market.

Table 5: Breakdown of investment trusts – VCT sectors

VCT SECTORS	TOTAL ASSETS (£M)	MARKET CAP (£M)	NO OF COMPANIES	AVG TOTAL ASSETS (£M)	AVG MARKET CAP (£M)
VCT AIM Quoted	764	704	8	95	88
VCT Generalist	3,165	2,921	40	79	73
VCT Generalist Pre Qualifying	152	117	3	51	39
VCT Specialist: Environmental	166	158	7	24	23

VCT SECTORS	TOTAL ASSETS (£M)	MARKET CAP (£M)	NO OF COMPANIES	AVG TOTAL ASSETS (£M)	AVG MARKET CAP (£M)
VCT Specialist: Healthcare & Biotechnology	5	4	1	5	4
VCT Specialist: Healthcare & Biotechnology Pre Qualifying	14	15	1	14	15
VCT Specialist: Media, Leisure & Events	45	23	3	15	8
VCT Specialist: Technology	15	11	4	4	3
TOTAL	**4,328**	**3,953**	**66**	**66**	**60**

Source: AIC Statistics, 31 August 2018.

It is instructive also to look at the way that the composition of the trust sector continues to evolve. Some of the biggest changes over the past five years are summarised in table 6 overleaf. The differences would become even more marked if you were to take the comparison back ten years (when the global financial crisis was at its height) or 20 years (when the industry looked even more different).

These are some of the most important changes between 2013 and 2018:

- The investment trust sector as a whole has nearly doubled in size over the last five years, with total assets rising from £100bn to £188bn.

- Measured by percentage change in total assets, the property sector has grown the fastest (up 180%), followed by conventional equity (90%) and then specialist trusts (52%).

- The biggest gains in absolute terms have still come from the conventional equity sector, the assets of which are £59bn higher than they were five years ago. Rising equity markets have been a big contributory factor.

- The size of the industry by market capitalisation has increased by slightly more than the total assets. The reason is that discounts have narrowed on average across all the main categories. The average discount has fallen from 16% to 13%.

Table 6: Changes in the makeup of the trust industry, 2013-2018

Source: AIC Statistics, data to 31 August each year.

TYPE OF TRUST	TOTAL ASSETS			MARKET CAP			NO OF COMPANIES			AVG TOTAL ASSETS			AVG MARKET CAP		
	2018 £M	2013 £M	%	2018 £M	2013 £M	%	2018 £M	2013 £M	%	2018 £M	2013 £M	%	2018 £M	2013 £M	%
Conventional	123,446	64,350	91.8%	107,068	53,353	100.7%	214	169	26.6%	577	381	51.5%	500	316	58.5%
Specialist	40,504	26,601	52.3%	38,144	24,294	57.0%	84	87	-3.4%	482	306	57.7%	454	279	62.6%
Property	19,759	6,976	183.2%	15,376	4,135	271.9%	40	21	90.5%	494	332	48.7%	384	197	95.2%
VCTs	4,328	2,837	52.6%	3,953	2,439	62.1%	66	104	-36.5%	66	27	140.4%	60	23	155.4%
TOTAL	188,036	100,765	86.6%	164,541	84,221	95.4%	404	381	6.0%	465	264	76.0%	407	221	84.2%

INDUSTRY STRUCTURE

While some investment trusts are managed directly by their board of directors, the great majority delegate the management of their portfolios to specialist fund managers, employed on annual or multi-year management contracts with a mandate to meet the trust's investment objectives.

These range from large investment management firms to small specialist boutiques. In the case of the big firms, they will typically launch and market their own trusts to investors as well as providing portfolio management and carrying out administrative functions, often centralising them. The smaller firms, especially those managing specialist trusts, by contrast may only have one or more funds that they look after.

Table 7: Largest management groups

MANAGEMENT GROUP	TOTAL ASSETS (£M)	MARKET CAP (£M)	NO OF COMPANIES	AVG TOTAL ASSETS (£M)	AVG MARKET CAP (£M)	% OF TOTAL ASSETS
Baillie Gifford	13,784	13,066	9	1,532	1,452	7.3%
JPMorgan Asset Management	11,583	9,793	21	552	466	6.2%
F&C Management	10,061	9,006	10	1,006	901	5.4%
3i Group	7,437	8,721	1	7,437	8,721	4.0%
Aberdeen Asset Managers	7,292	6,127	19	384	322	3.9%
Janus Henderson Investors	6,895	6,001	13	530	462	3.7%
FIL Investments International	4,378	3,426	5	876	685	2.3%
Invesco Asset Management	4,116	3,424	9	457	380	2.2%
Frostrow Capital	4,029	3,746	5	806	749	2.1%
InfraRed Capital Partners	3,760	4,022	2	1,880	2,011	2.0%

MANAGEMENT GROUP	TOTAL ASSETS (£M)	MARKET CAP (£M)	NO OF COMPANIES	AVG TOTAL ASSETS (£M)	AVG MARKET CAP (£M)	% OF TOTAL ASSETS
BlackRock Investment Management (UK)	3,597	2,872	10	360	287	1.9%
RIT Capital Partners	3,419	3,231	1	3,419	3,231	1.8%
Pershing Square Capital Management	3,183	1,896	1	3,183	1,896	1.7%
Willis Towers Watson	3,027	2,624	1	3,027	2,624	1.6%
Schroder Investment Management	2,778	2,367	6	463	395	1.5%
TOTAL TOP 15 TRUSTS	**89,339**	**80,323**	**113**	**791**	**711**	**47.5%**

Source: AIC Statistics as at 31 August 2018.

The management groups with the most trust mandates are listed here. The 15 largest groups manage just under half (47%) of total industry assets.[*] Only five firms out of more than 400 in total manage more than ten trusts, however. The average trust among the 15 largest management groups has £791m in assets, compared to the industry average of £465m. In 2018 Baillie Gifford, a private partnership based in Edinburgh, became the largest player in the investment trust sector for the first time, overtaking JPMorgan.

The trust with the highest total assets, Scottish Mortgage, accounted for around 4.4% of the industry total as at 30 September 2018. The 20 largest trusts on this measure accounted for about a third (32%) of total industry assets while the top 50 trusts accounted for 50%. In contrast, more than 100 trusts had less than £50m in assets, although this figure includes a large number of venture capital trusts, which are invariably (and by their nature) much smaller on average.

---

[*]   The data includes separate entries for Aberdeen Asset Management and Standard Life Investments, which completed a merger in 2018. Added together they are now the third largest single management group, with just over £10bn of assets.

Table 8: 20 of the largest individual trusts

	COMPANY	MANAGEMENT GROUP	SECTOR	TOTAL ASSETS (£M)	MARKET CAP (£M)	NET ASSETS (£M)	PREMIUM/ (DISCOUNT) (%)
1	Scottish Mortgage	Baillie Gifford	Global	8,294	7,868	7,609	3.2
2	3i Group	Self-Managed	Private Equity	8,243	9,210	7,368	24.3
3	F&C IT	F&C Investments	Global	4,285	3,942	3,931	-0.1
4	Pershing Square Holdings £	Pershing Square CM	Hedge Funds	3,716	2,814	3,716	-24.9
5	RIT Capital Partners	J Rothschild Capital Mgmt	Flexible Investment	3,412	3,177	2,976	6.5
6	Alliance Trust	Willis Towers Watson	Global	3,021	2,620	2,797	-6.6
7	Tritax Big Box REIT	Tritax Management	Property Specialist	3,020	2,174	2,097	3.6
8	HICL Infrastructure	InfraRed Capital Partners	Specialist: Infrastructure	2,773	2,766	2,702	1.6
9	Witan	Self-Managed	Global	2,418	1,975	2,015	-2.2
10	Templeton Emerging Markets	Franklin Templeton IM	Global Emerging Markets	2,334	1,832	2,122	-13.4
11	International Public Partnerships	Amber Infrastructure	Specialist: Infrastructure	2,086	2,131	2,049	3.7
12	Mercantile	JPMorgan AM	UK All Companies	2,066	1,690	1,879	-10.5
13	Caledonia	Self-Managed	Global	1,931	1,548	1,928	-20.4
14	Monks	Baillie Gifford	UK All Companies	1,922	1,825	1,813	0.7
15	Polar Capital Technology	Polar Capital	Specialist: Technology	1,875	1,801	1,839	-3.2
16	3i Infrastructure	3i Group	Specialist: Infrastructure	1,839	2,001	1,785	10.8

	COMPANY	MANAGEMENT GROUP	SECTOR	TOTAL ASSETS (£M)	MARKET CAP (£M)	NET ASSETS (£M)	PREMIUM/ (DISCOUNT) (%)
17	Fidelity China Special Situations	Fidelity Investments	Country Specialists: Asia Pacific	1,723	1,191	1,357	3.2
18	Riverstone Energy	Riverstone International	Specialist: Commodities	1,699	1,090	1,364	-20.9
19	Murray International	Aberdeen Standard	Global Equity Income	1,684	1,456	1,490	-2.5
20	City of London	Janus Henderson	UK Equity Income	1,654	1,517	1,489	1.6

Source: Numis Securities, data as at 30 September 2018.

The main takeaway for investors is that the investment trust sector is a genuinely diverse one, which offers a range of different kinds of opportunities. Half the trusts in the top 20, for example, were trading at a discount while the other half were trading at a premium at the point this data was compiled. Each of the 20 also has its own policy regarding borrowing to enhance returns, which largely explains the difference between the total and net assets figure.

The trust sector is also a competitive one, in which no management group has a dominant position. Most of the trusts in the top 20 have been operating for many years, but that is not universally the case. PERSHING SQUARE, HICL INFRASTRUCTURE, TRITAX BIG BOX and RIVERSTONE ENERGY have all been launched or listed on the London market relatively recently.

OLD WINE AND NEW BOTTLES

The first investment trust, FOREIGN & COLONIAL, was formed in 1868 and continues in existence today. It celebrated its 150th anniversary in 2018. A number of other investment companies have also been around for many years. Twelve can trace their histories back to the 19th century.

This is a list of some of the oldest vintage trusts which are also still in existence. There is no obvious correlation between age and size or quality of trust, although the mere fact of having survived for so long indicates that a trust has successfully established a niche in the market.

A number of these trusts were started by wealthy or successful families looking to invest their fortunes in a tax-efficient manner, but have since expanded to include outside investors as well. The first Scottish investment trust, DUNEDIN INCOME GROWTH, is profiled by historian John Newlands on page 207. It was founded to provide a home for the savings of wealthy textile merchants in Dundee.

"Longevity," notes market commentator Ian Cowie, "is no guarantee of success but investment trusts that have stood the test of time – such as surviving two world wars and the great depression – can offer some comfort to investors alarmed by the historic events we are living through today."[*]

Table 9: Vintage investment trusts

YEAR STARTED	TICKER	COMPANY	AVG PREMIUM/ (DISCOUNT) 2017/18 (%)	MARKET CAP (£M)	NET ASS. (£M)	YIELD (%)	BID/OFFER SPREAD (%)
1868	FRCL	F&C IT	1.5	3,931	4,285	1.5	0.2%
1868	INV	Investment Company	-5.3	17	17	6.3	2.3%
1873	SCAM	Scottish American	6.4	513	595	3.0	0.7%
1873	DIG	Dunedin Income Gwth	-8.0	423	495	5.1	0.7%
1881	JAM	JPMorgan American	-1.8	1,085	1,151	1.2	0.3%
1884	MRC	Mercantile	-5.1	1,879	2,066	2.7	0.4%
1887	SCIN	Scottish IT	-6.4	744	826	2.3	0.3%
1887	JPGI	JPMorgan Global Growth & Income	5.1	420	449	5.0	0.8%
1888	ATST	Alliance Trust	-4.0	2,797	3,021	1.7	0.2%
1889	EDIN	Edinburgh IT	-6.8	1,464	1,611	3.9	0.2%
1889	BTEM	British Empire	-7.2	935	1,029	1.6	0.2%
1889	FCS	F&C Global Smaller Cos	2.1	887	941	1.0	0.5%
1889	LWDB	Law Debenture	-5.2	814	928	2.9	1.0%
1889	MRCH	Merchants	1.4	573	681	5.0	0.9%

---

[*]   *Citywire Investment Trust Insider*, 17 September 2017.

YEAR STARTED	TICKER	COMPANY	AVG PREMIUM/ (DISCOUNT) 2017/18 (%)	MARKET CAP (£M)	NET ASS. (£M)	YIELD (%)	BID/OFFER SPREAD (%)
1891	CTY	City of London	2.9	1,489	1,654	4.2	0.2%
1898	ADIG	Aberdeen Diversified Inc & Gwth	3.3	400	460	4.2	1.0%
1905	BNKR	Bankers	1.3	1,142	1,210	2.2	0.2%
1907	MYI	Murray International	5.2	1,490	1,684	4.5	0.3%
1909	SMT	Scottish Mortgage	4.9	7,609	8,294	0.6	0.1%
1909	WTAN	Witan	-0.4	2,015	2,418	2.0	0.2%
1927	BUT	Brunner	-6.0	379	406	2.2	1.3%
1929	MNKS	Monks	5.4	1,813	1,922	0.2	0.2%
1929	JETG	JPMorgan European – Growth	-4.6	246	281	2.3	1.5%
1930	HFEL	Henderson Far East Income	4.7	445	481	5.8	0.9%
1905	TRY	TR Property	2.7	1,325	1,564	3.0	0.3%
1969	RIII	Rights & Issues IT	-6.5	200	200	1.3	1.0%
1972	EAT	European Assets	3.7	446	446	7.3	1.7%
1972	EUT	European IT	-7.0	414	414	2.5	0.7%
1923	MUT	Murray Income	-6.7	564	609	4.3	0.6%
1926	FGT	Finsbury Growth & Income	1.6	1,415	1,457	1.9	0.2%
1926	TMPL	Temple Bar	-3.1	910	1,029	3.4	0.3%
1927	DNDL	Dunedin Smaller Cos	-6.1	153	153	2.6	1.5%
1927	JFJ	JPMorgan Japanese	-4.9	845	980	1.1	0.5%
1929	SHRS	Shires Income	5.6	81	101	5.1	1.6%

YEAR STARTED	TICKER	COMPANY	AVG PREMIUM/ (DISCOUNT) 2017/18 (%)	MARKET CAP (£M)	NET ASS. (£M)	YIELD (%)	BID/OFFER SPREAD (%)
1945	III	3i Group	51.6	7,368	8,243	3.2	0.0%
1954	KIT	Keystone IT	-8.7	259	290	3.3	0.8%
1960	CLDN	Caledonia	-15.3	1,931	1,931	2.0	0.4%
1962	THRG	BlackRock Throgmorton Trust	-11.8	401	438	1.0	1.0%
1963	JCH	JPMorgan Claverhouse	-3.4	422	426	0.6	0.6%
1963	CGT	Capital Gearing	3.2	263	263	0.5	0.7%

Source: Numis Securities, data as at 30 September 2018.

Some individual trusts are also notable for having long-serving managers who have been running the trust's investments for many years. In some cases the managers also have significant personal shareholdings in the trust (see also Skin in the Game on page 282).

Here is a selection:

Table 10: Long-serving managers

MANAGER NAME	COMPANY	AIC SECTOR	FM START DATE	
Peter Spiller	Capital Gearing	Flexible Investment	01/01/1982	36 years 05 months
Simon Knott	Rights & Issues	UK Smaller Companies	01/01/1984	34 years 05 months
Angela Lascelles	Value and Income	UK Equity Income	11/07/1986	31 years 11 months
Matthew Oakeshott	Value and Income	UK Equity Income	11/07/1986	31 years 11 months
Hugh Young	Aberdeen New Dawn	Asia Pacific – Excl Japan	12/05/1989	29 years 01 months
James H. Henderson	Lowland	UK Equity Income	01/01/1990	28 years 05 months
Tim Levett	Northern Investors Company	Private Equity	27/04/1990	28 years 01 months

MANAGER NAME	COMPANY	AIC SECTOR	FM START DATE	
Alastair Conn	Northern Investors Company	Private Equity	27/04/1990	28 years 01 months
Richard M. J. Newbery	Aberforth Smaller Companies	UK Smaller Companies	10/12/1990	27 years 06 months
Alastair J. Whyte	Aberforth Smaller Companies	UK Smaller Companies	10/12/1990	27 years 06 months
Job Curtis	City of London	UK Equity Income	01/07/1991	26 years 11 months
Tim Stevenson	Henderson EuroTrust	Europe	01/01/1994	24 years 05 months
Martin Hudson	Mercantile	UK All Companies	01/01/1994	24 years 05 months
Katie Potts	Herald	Sector Specialist: Small Media, Comms & IT Cos	16/02/1994	24 years 04 months
Austin Forey	JPMorgan Emerging Markets	Global Emerging Markets	01/06/1994	24 years 0 months
Robin Boyle	Athelney Trust	UK Smaller Companies	19/06/1995	23 years 0 months
Adrian Lim	Aberdeen Asian Smaller Companies	Asia Pacific – Excl Japan	19/10/1995	22 years 08 months
Flavia Cheong	Aberdeen Asian Smaller Companies	Asia Pacific – Excl Japan	19/10/1995	22 years 08 months
Hugh Young	Aberdeen Asian Smaller Companies	Asia Pacific – Excl Japan	19/10/1995	22 years 08 months
Christopher Wong	Aberdeen Asian Smaller Companies	Asia Pacific – Excl Japan	19/10/1995	22 years 08 months

Source: AIC.

COMPARISONS WITH OPEN-ENDED FUNDS

It is not uncommon for the investment managers of trusts to manage other funds outside the investment trust sector at the same time. In fact, a number of managers start their careers managing different kinds of fund (typically unit trusts and OEICs, though also hedge funds) and if successful are encouraged to take over or start an investment trust with a broadly similar investment objective.

Adding an investment trust to their responsibilities gives successful fund managers the opportunity to take advantage of the benefits of the investment trust structure. These include being able to use gearing (borrowing) to enhance returns and take a longer-term view, thanks to the permanent (or semi-permanent) nature of investment trust capital. They can also use derivative securities such as futures and options for investment purposes.

These advantages show up regularly in comparisons between the long-term performance of investment trusts and that of open-ended funds with either the same manager or the same investment objective. Where trusts and similar funds can be directly compared, trusts typically show up with superior performance records.

The next table summarises the difference in the performance of directly comparable trust and open-ended equivalent sectors. The blue-shaded cells show the extent to which trusts have outperformed. It is fair to point out that such comparisons could be criticised by statisticians on the grounds that the two samples are very different in size and also may display what is called survivorship bias. However, academics at Cass Business School in London who completed a rigorous analysis of investment trust returns between 2000 and 2016 reported in 2018 that their research supported the superior performance of investment trusts. They found that, measured by NAV total return, directly comparable investment trusts outperformed their open-ended equivalents by an average of 1.4% per annum. A final version of their academic paper, extending their analysis back to 1994, is scheduled to be published in 2019.

Where a trust and an open-ended fund with the same mandate are managed by the same individual, it is rare for the trust not to do better over the longer term. The degree to which comparable trusts outperform does vary markedly however from sector to sector. In part that simply reflects the fact that some sectors only boast a small number of trusts. It is also important to look at how performance divergences in up and down markets.

Performance of closed-end funds vs open-ended funds (equity and property mandates)

	NAV total returns (annualised) Open-Ended funds			NAV total returns (annualised) Investment Cos			Price total returns (annualised) Investment Cos		
	1 yr	5 yr	10 yr	1y	5y	10y	1y	5y	10y
UK - Equity Income	5.9	8.0	8.4	1.3	1.0	2.0	0.1	(0.3)	2.5
UK - All Companies	8.7	8.5	8.4	(2.8)	2.1	3.0	0.7	3.6	4.2
UK - Smaller Company	16.6	14.6	13.1	(0.8)	0.1	1.6	2.3	0.9	3.0
UK - Equity & Bond Income	3.8	6.7	7.1	2.1	1.8	2.1	(1.5)	0.8	2.4
US - General	12.4	14.3	12.8	(0.3)	0.2	1.0	0.0	(0.9)	1.4
US - Smaller Company	17.3	14.1	14.9	5.0	(0.4)	1.6	1.1	(2.9)	2.1
Global - Equity	9.2	10.7	9.0	7.3	3.6	1.8	8.9	5.2	3.0
Global - Equity Income	4.1	8.9	9.3	(1.8)	(0.6)	0.9	(2.9)	(1.7)	1.5
Europe - General	4.1	10.2	7.8	5.2	2.4	1.9	1.1	2.1	2.2
Europe - Smaller Company	9.6	14.1	11.4	(4.1)	3.4	0.5	(7.7)	4.6	1.1
Asia Pacific - Ex Japan	5.3	9.7	9.7	0.9	1.0	1.5	2.0	1.3	1.8
Japan - General	8.2	9.6	8.9	11.0	4.3	2.9	11.3	5.6	3.7
Japan - Smaller Company	15.2	15.5	14.9	14.5	4.2	(1.2)	15.4	5.0	(0.8)
Emerging - Global	2.7	7.1	6.5	2.8	0.2	1.2	2.8	(0.4)	0.7
Technology	20.4	17.9	15.6	8.9	3.4	2.8	12.4	4.7	3.9
Property - UK	6.3	7.1	4.9	3.8	5.8	2.6	0.5	4.4	6.6

Note: Data to 6 July 2018. Blue shading indicates outperformance by ICs relative to open-ended funds. Source: Morningstar, Numis Securities Research.

PERFORMANCE ANALYSIS

A S WITH ALL investment funds, the performance of investment trusts turns on four main things:

- how much money the trust has made
- the way in which those returns are obtained
- how those returns are delivered – as income or capital
- the risk that is being taken to achieve the results.

The distinctive feature of analysing investment trusts stems from the fact that performance can be measured in two distinct ways:

- the rate at which the net assets of the trust grow
- the rate at which the share price of the trust grows.

As a broad generalisation, NAV growth is an indication of how well the manager is doing the job of managing the investments. The change in the share price reflects how well or how little the market likes what the manager is doing.

Because most trusts invest in shares and bonds that are listed on a stock exchange, both the NAV and the trust's share price can change from minute to minute as deals go through the stock market. Around half the universe of trusts consequently report their NAV on a daily or weekly basis.

Trusts that invest in less liquid types of asset, such as property or private equity, report less frequently – monthly, quarterly or six-monthly. The share price of the trust may still change on a daily basis, however, reflecting supply and demand for the shares.

Valuation reporting – NAV reporting frequency

Daily	186
Weekly	33
Fortnightly	1
Monthly	72
Quarterly	23
Six-monthly	76
Annually	1
TOTAL	**392**

Source: Numis Securities.
Some trusts report different holdings at different intervals – e.g. listed holdings weekly and unlisted monthly.

The only sensible way to measure how well a trust is performing is to look at the behaviour of its NAV and share price over longer periods of time. In the digital age, this kind of performance data – along with a host of other useful facts about each trust – is widely available for free on the internet.

It is relatively straightforward to sort this performance data into rankings as well. The AIC's statistics section provides a range of important information about nearly 400 trusts, including all the largest ones. The first page of the 'Analysing Investment Companies' link lists all 393 trusts in alphabetical order and provides additional data for all of them on eight different measures (shown as shaded tabs across the top of the table reproduced below).

A screenshot of the AIC website – 'Analysing Investment Companies' page

Overview	Discounts	Dividends	Share price total return	NAV total return	Charges/gearing	Trading	Volatility					
Name ↕			AIC sector ↕			Price (last close)	Price (bid) ↕	Price (offer) ↕	NAV ↕	Total assets (£m) ↕	Market cap (£m) ↕	
Baillie Gifford Japan Trust PLC			Japan			GBX	823.00	821.00	823.00	786.76	828.532	748.518
Baillie Gifford Shin Nippon			Japanese Smaller Companies			GBX	191.90	189.38	191.88	182.36	537.236	512.090
Baillie Gifford UK Growth			UK All Companies			GBX	169.00	169.00	171.00	187.02	281.505	254.380
Baillie Gifford US Growth Trust plc			North America			GBX	119.80	116.20	119.00	114.05	244.732	254.695
Bankers Investment Trust Plc			Global			GBX	845.00	848.00	850.00	869.13	1,134.142	1,036.027
Baring Emerging Europe Plc			European Emerging Markets			GBX	685.00	676.00	694.00	773.07	110.429	89.810
Baronsmead Second Venture Trust Plc			VCT Generalist			GBX	86.50	86.00	87.00	91.76	198.646	187.266
Baronsmead Venture Trust Plc			VCT Generalist			GBX	86.00	85.00	87.00	91.01	175.097	164.988
BB Healthcare Trust PLC			Sector Specialist: Biotechnology & Healthcare			GBX	137.00	135.50	137.00	131.94	434.012	425.629
BBGI SICAV S.A.			Sector Specialist: Infrastructure			GBX	147.50	147.00	147.50	130.10	750.944	851.354
Better Capital PCC Limited 2009			Private Equity			GBX	64.00	62.00	66.00	114.62	40.418	22.568
Better Capital PCC Limited 2012			Private Equity			GBX	11.00	10.00	12.00	25.93	82.465	34.986
BH Global Limited GBP			Hedge Funds			GBX	1,490.00	1,485.00	1,500.00	1,546.92	306.122	294.859
BH Global Limited USD			Hedge Funds			USD	14.90	14.70	15.10	15.55	32.579	31.217
BH Macro Limited GBP			Hedge Funds			GBX	2,305.00	2,300.00	2,310.00	2,398.11	338.569	325.424
BH Macro Limited USD			Hedge Funds			USD	23.20	23.00	23.40	24.42	49.740	47.255
BioPharma Credit C			Sector Specialist: Debt			USD	1.06	1.04	1.07	0.99	122.434	131.037
BioPharma Credit PLC			Sector Specialist: Debt			USD	1.07	1.06	1.07	1.01	697.533	738.050
BlackRock Commodities Income Investment Trust Plc			Sector Specialist: Commodities & Natural Resources			GBX	75.90	74.80	77.00	82.65	106.456	88.180
BlackRock Emerging Europe plc			European Emerging Markets			GBX	316.50	314.00	319.00	325.04	116.734	113.674

Total Results: 37

View: 20 per page ▢ 1–20 of 37 First | Previous | Next | Last

Company prices are updated every weekday after the close of trading. All figures are as at this last close, and on a cum income basis with debt valued at fair (unless otherwise stated). Performance returns are presented in GBP but price and NAVs are shown in the company's traded currency.

© Copyright 2018 Morningstar. All rights reserved.

MORNINGSTAR

Source: AIC – generic example – as at early October 2018.

By clicking on individual columns in each table it is possible to filter and rank the data on that page in various ways. For example, on the page shown above, you can sort all the trusts beginning with the letter B by NAV, total assets and market capitalisation. To do this you click on the little arrows in the header section.

By going to the other tabs you can also analyse and rank trusts on other important metrics, such as:

- the discount or premium at which the shares currently trade

- the level of gearing each trust employs (and the allowable range which the board has set)

- the costs of owning the trust (the 'ongoing charge'), expressed as a percentage of the share price

- the current dividend yield and the annualised rate at which dividends have grown over the previous five years.

There are two separate tables for historic performance. One measures the share price return over six different time periods. The second provides comparable data for NAV performance over the same time periods. For example, you may wish to see how trusts in the popular Global sector have performed in the last decade. By using the filters this would produce a table that looks like the following. It lists the ten trusts with the highest NAV return over ten years.

A screenshot showing filters in use on AIC's online statistics section

Company name ⬦	Management group ⬦	AIC sector ⬦	Traded currency	NAV	Discount / premium (%) ⬦	Gearing (%) ⬦	SPTR 3yr (%) ⬦	SPTR 10yr (%) ⬦	NAVTR 3yr (%) ⬦	NAVTR 10yr (%) ⬦	5yr div grth (%pa) ⬦	Div yld (%) ⬦
Global	Weighted average	Global	N/A	-	-1.16	6.05	92.44	360.95	84.66	262.02	2.63	1.29
Lindsell Train	Lindsell Train	Global	GBP	833.21	42.52	0.00	151.02	913.31	122.29	574.38	25.80	1.79
Scottish Mortgage	Baillie Gifford	Global	GBX	524.89	3.13	7.00	131.44	535.63	135.67	459.92	1.10	0.57
Independent Investment Trust	Independent Investment Trust	Global	GBX	679.77	-3.94	0.00	97.05	399.95	97.89	365.84	3.70	0.92
Edinburgh Worldwide	Baillie Gifford	Global	GBX	958.30	2.69	4.00	128.44	387.67	113.64	316.84	.	.
F&C Global Smaller Companies	F&C Management	Global	GBX	1,473.01	-1.56	3.00	59.46	342.37	64.77	310.33	12.50	0.99
Mid Wynd International	Artemis Investment Management	Global	GBX	524.50	1.98	0.00	73.44	291.78	75.09	245.24	7.90	1.04
Witan	Witan Investment Services	Global	GBX	1,127.07	-1.87	12.00	61.75	255.84	65.25	216.94	9.30	2.03
JPMorgan Elect Managed Growth	J.P. Morgan Asset Management	Global	GBX	868.83	-2.46	0.00	50.24	213.40	55.07	214.58	11.80	1.55
Foreign & Colonial Investment Trust	F&C Management	Global	GBX	723.45	0.08	8.00	84.09	244.05	72.89	209.90	3.70	1.49
Bankers	Janus Henderson Investors	Global	GBX	928.30	-3.16	3.00	64.87	229.94	69.25	208.97	35.00	7.04

Source: AIC – illustrative only.

A separate section on the AIC website enables you to find and compare specific individual trusts in greater detail, based on a range of specific criteria that you have set yourself. Equally important is that for each individual trust the AIC website provides links to the company's annual report and accounts, its half-yearly results and its latest factsheet. Nobody should invest in any trust without having looked at all these documents.

The annual report, in particular, is a must-read source of information. Company law requires the directors to provide a comprehensive report on the trust's performance and its financial results have to be audited by an independent firm of auditors and approved by shareholders at the annual general meeting. The report also discloses such things as directors' fees and shareholdings, management contract details and a full listing of the trust's investments.

INTERPRETING PERFORMANCE

There is a reason why the regulators insist that every piece of marketing literature issued by any kind of fund provider includes the phrase "past performance is no guarantee of future performance". The reason is that it is true.

While performance data gives you useful information about an investment trust's track record, and the way that it has been investing your money, that information in isolation is insufficient to tell you whether you should buy or continue to own that trust.

There are several reasons for that. They include:

- markets move in cycles and are unpredictable

- styles of investing come in and out of fashion

- superior performance in one period often does not repeat in the next

- managers of trusts can be and often are changed, making direct comparisons with earlier periods difficult

- unexpected events, such as political shocks and natural disasters, may throw a hitherto successful strategy off course.

What the regulators are keen to ensure is that less-sophisticated investors are not misled into thinking that a trust which has done particularly well in the past will continue to do so in the future. Their perspective is underpinned by many academic studies.

However, that is not the same as saying that past performance information has no value at all. Clearly it is essential for any investor to understand how a trust has performed in the past and to seek to establish why it has the track record it does.

At the very least it is important to understand the following:

- whether (and if so why) the trust's investment manager has changed over the track record period being looked at

- how far the performance of the trust has been affected by gearing (explained further below)

- how the trust performed during periods when markets were rising and when they were falling – it may be very different

- whether or not the trust has done better than a suitable benchmark, including the one chosen by the board

- how much risk the trust is taking relative to other comparable trusts and the markets in which it is investing.

DIFFERENCES BETWEEN SECTORS

Different sectors have very different characteristics, reflecting the different kinds of asset in which they invest. You can see this by looking at some of the key metrics for the broadest sector groupings.

Table 11: Key metrics of broadest sector groupings

SECTOR	YIELD (%)	MARKET CAP (£M)	AVG DISCOUNT (%)	NAV TOTAL RETURN OVER 10Y	OCR (INC PERF FEE) (%)
Japan	0.7	3,227	-2.2	291.4	0.92%
North America	1.6	2,435	-4.5	272.4	0.82%
Sector Specialist	2.3	15,479	2.1	248.3	1.57%
Asia Pacific	1.7	10,263	-10.3	213.9	1.59%
Europe	2.1	5,234	-6.0	208.4	0.95%
UK	2.7	21,988	-5.8	207.9	0.81%
Global	1.7	37,493	-3.4	194.5	0.81%
Infrastructure	5.0	12,882	4.7	165.4	2.12%
Emerging Markets	3.0	7,714	-13.7	102.2	1.32%
Hedge Funds	0.7	4,888	-17.5	94.0	4.08%
Property	4.1	26,362	2.4	66.6	3.01%
Private Equity	2.7	18,532	10.7	57.4	1.88%
Debt	6.8	13,777	2.9	37.1	2.68%

Source: Numis Securities, data as at 1 October 2018.

So, for example, the debt and infrastructure sectors on average have the highest yields but are among the most expensive to own. UK sector trusts have the lowest management charges, and hedge funds and private equity the highest. The level of discount also varies considerably.

These metrics can be usefully compared to the performance figures for the sectors, as follows, ranked by NAV performance over the past ten years.

Table 12: NAV growth

SECTOR	NAV GROWTH (%)				YIELD (%)
	1Y	3Y	5Y	10Y	
Japan	27.3	98.7	121.0	291.4	0.7
Private Equity	17.1	77.2	120.1	57.4	2.7
North America	21.3	91.3	114.7	272.4	1.6
Europe	8.4	64.1	86.9	208.4	2.1
Global	13.4	68.2	84.4	194.5	1.7
Asia Pacific	5.7	67.2	80.4	213.9	1.7
Sector Specialist	11.7	63.0	80.0	248.3	2.3
Property	11.6	37.6	74.9	66.6	4.1
Infrastructure	10.6	31.9	69.6	165.4	5.0
UK	5.8	35.2	56.8	207.9	2.7
Emerging Markets	3.9	62.0	38.8	102.2	3.0
Debt	10.2	23.6	34.7	37.1	6.8
Hedge Funds	13.2	6.4	24.2	94.0	0.7

Source: Numis Securities, data as at 1 October 2018.

This table highlights the fact that some sectors with the highest yields on average have among the the lowest returns (though this not true of infrastructure), and those with low yields tend to have performed better in NAV terms, though again the correlation is not precise.

Just as striking is the fact that the five-year returns from some sectors (notably property and private equity) are higher than their ten-year returns. This is because they were the sectors worst hit by the global financial crisis of 2007–09, which period is included in the ten-year figures, but not in the five-year figures.

This underlines the fact that certain types of asset do better in different market conditions. This can also be seen by looking at which sectors have performed the best in share price terms over different periods. (The disparity from year to year would be even greater if the rankings were done on a calendar year basis.)

Table 13: Share price performance

1Y	3Y	5Y	10Y
Japan	Japan	Private Equity	Sector Specialist
North America	North America	Japan	Japan
Sector Specialist	Private Equity	Sector Specialist	North America
Global	Sector Specialist	North America	Asia Pacific
Hedge Funds	Global	Global	UK
Private Equity	Asia Pacific	Europe	Europe
Infrastructure	Emerging Markets	Asia Pacific	Global
UK	Europe	Infrastructure	Infrastructure
Europe	UK	Property	Debt
Property	Infrastructure	UK	Property
Asia Pacific	Property	Emerging Markets	Private Equity
Debt	Debt	Debt	Emerging Markets
Emerging Markets	Hedge Funds	Hedge Funds	Hedge Funds

Source: Numis Securities, data as at 1 October 2018.

By tracking how different sectors – and the trusts within them – have performed over different periods, it is possible to build up a more detailed picture of the way they perform in different conditions.

ANALYSING INDIVIDUAL TRUSTS

As should be clear from the example of the global funds, there can be considerable differences between trusts in the same sector. Different sources of information may well give different levels of detail. Many trusts are happy to publish some of this data in a standardised format on their own websites, along with other company literature.

The returns that investment trusts make can be broken down into two key elements:

• income, which in practice means dividend payments

• capital gains and losses arising from share price movements.

Once a dividend has been paid, the money used to pay it is obviously no longer available to the trust to invest. The NAV of the trust therefore falls by the amount that it costs to pay the dividend to all the shareholders. If the investor decides to reinvest the dividend payment back into the trust, however, it will continue to rise or fall in value in line with the movement in the share price from the date of reinvestment onwards.

In practice, most investors keep the dividend payments (which are potentially liable to income tax) and wait to see how the share price of the trust performs over time.

Income returns are analysed in the next section. However, most data sources, including the AIC, use what are called total share price returns, which assume that the dividend is reinvested. This has the advantage of making it possible to directly compare the overall performance of different trusts – otherwise trusts that pay a higher rate of dividend would appear to have performed less well in share price terms than ones which paid little or nothing as income. However, for anyone who does need the dividends as income, it is important to remember that a total return figure includes the reinvested dividends.

Capital gains and losses from holding shares in investment trusts are relatively straightforward to track. The two most important numbers are the share price return and the NAV return. The difference between the two is primarily determined by the level of discount and the level of gearing.

When an investor sells shares for more than was paid for them, the gain is potentially liable to capital gains tax. There is an annual capital gains tax allowance which allows capital gains up to an annual limit (£11,700 per annum in the 2017–18 financial year) to be exempt from tax. Gains thereafter are paid at a rate of either 18 or 28% (2017–18 rates, which are liable to change in the Budget each year).

Gains made by investments held in an ISA or SIPP are, however, exempt from capital gains tax, although in the case of a SIPP they may become taxable if the money is taken out as income. It is the combination of income and capital gain (or loss) that determines the total return that an investor will make over time. Up to £20,000 can be invested into an ISA each year, a very valuable allowance.

It is just as important to look at past return figures of individual trusts in the same detailed way as was suggested when analysing sector performance. Key factors to analyse include:

- the contribution from gearing
- the movement in the discount

- the variation from calendar year to calendar year

- the volatility of the share price and NAV

- the fund manager's track record and experience

- performance against relevant benchmarks and peer group

- board policies on discounts and share buybacks

- the history and sustainability of dividends.

INCOME INVESTING

MANY INVESTORS TURN to investment companies to provide them with investment income. It is an area where the closed-end structure has distinct advantages over open-ended equivalents. However, it is also important to look very carefully at how a trust is generating its income, because not everything is always as it seems.

As with all companies, the way that income is distributed by investment trusts is in the form of dividends. These can be paid quarterly, twice a year or annually. In exceptional cases, trusts may also have an opportunity to pay 'special dividends' in addition to their normal regular distributions.

Dividends are set by the board of directors of a trust and typically announced at the time of its half-year and annual results. They will set the day the payments to shareholders will be made (the payment date) and also the date (the record date) on which shareholders will need to own the shares in order to qualify for that payment. Payments are typically paid a few months after the end of the accounting period to which they relate.

Example

In March 2018 FOREIGN & COLONIAL announced that it would pay a final dividend of 2.70p to all the shareholders on its register at the close of business on 28 March 2018. The dividend, it said, would be paid on 1 May 2018. Having earlier announced three quarterly interim dividends, that produced a total dividend payment in respect of the 12 months to 31 December 2017 of 10.4p.

The following table summarises the recent history of dividend payments made by Foreign & Colonial Investment Trust. Until 2013 F&C paid dividends twice a year. Now it pays four times a year. You can see the progression of the annual payment over time from 9.0p in 2013 to 10.4p in 2017.

Table 14: Recent dividend payments by Foreign & Colonial Investment Trust

YEAR ENDING:	31/12/18	31/12/17	31/12/16	31/12/15	31/12/14	31/12/13
Dividend payments						
Final:	-	2.70p	2.70p	2.70p	2.70p	2.70p
3rd interim:	-	2.70p	2.45p	2.30p	2.20p	2.10p
2nd interim:	2.70p	2.50p	2.35p	2.30p	2.20p	2.10p
1st interim:	2.70p	2.50p	2.35p	2.30p	2.20p	-
Interim:	-	-	-	-	-	2.10p
TOTAL for year:	-	**10.40p**	**9.85p**	**9.60p**	**9.30p**	**9.00p**

Source: Hargreaves Lansdown.

You may also notice that the first two interim payments declared for the current year (2018) amount to 5.4p, higher than the equivalent payments in 2017. This suggests that in the absence of surprises the overall dividend this year will add up to more than 2017's 10.4p when the third interim and final payments have been made. Maintaining and ideally growing the annual dividend over time is a priority for many boards. Because dividends are paid at regular intervals, shareholders in trusts with secure dividends can typically look ahead to see when the next payment is due.

TAXATION OF DIVIDENDS

Investment trust dividends are liable to income tax, unless held inside an ISA (individual savings account) or SIPP (self-invested personal pension), where no tax is payable and the income does not need to be declared on your tax return. Dividends from venture capital trusts are a special case and not liable to income tax at all if the holding is held for five years or more. The first £2,000 a year of dividend income was free of tax in 2018–19, but this allowance may be altered for future years by the chancellor in the Budget.

DIVIDEND YIELDS

The dividend-paying capacity of an investment company is typically described as a yield. So a trust that pays an annual dividend of 5p to each shareholder and whose shares are trading at 100p is said to have a yield of 5.0%. That is the income you will get if you buy the shares at that price.

When reading about the yields on different trusts, investors need to distinguish between different ways of presenting the figure. Yields are shown before any deduction of tax and in these examples assume a share price of 100p.

HISTORIC YIELD

Historic yield is based on the total amount of dividend that was paid in respect of the previous financial year. So if trust X has paid an interim dividend of 2.0p per share and a final dividend of 3.0p per share, it will have a total dividend of 5.0p per share. The yield is therefore 5.0%.

PROSPECTIVE YIELD

Prospective yield is based on the total amount of dividend that is expected to be paid in the current financial year, but has not yet been declared. This will typically be an estimate derived from either the company's public statements or from a broker's estimate. Say trust X is expected to pay a dividend this year of 6.0p; its prospective yield will be 6.0%.

TRAILING 12-MONTH YIELD

You may sometimes see a figure of this kind, which is based on combining the most recent dividends paid. If trust X paid a final dividend for 2017 of 3.0p and has paid an interim dividend of 2.5p for 2018 (but not yet declared its final dividend), it will have a trailing 12-month yield of 5.5%.

It is also possible to express the dividends a trust pays as a percentage of its NAV per share, not its share price. This will produce a different yield figure, depending on whether the share price is higher or lower than the NAV per share.

PORTFOLIO YIELD

Portfolio yield measures how much income (net of costs) is generated by the investment portfolio of the trust and can be compared to the amount of income that is being paid to shareholders.

A distinguishing feature of investment trusts is that they are required to pay out a minimum of 85% of the income from their investments as a dividend to their shareholders. They need to do this in order to preserve their investment trust status for tax purposes. This in turn allows them to buy and sell investments without having to pay capital gains tax on any profits.

Unlike open-ended funds, which have to pay out all their distributable income each year, they can, however, hold back up to 15% of their income each year as a 'revenue reserve'. In effect they can put aside some of the investment income they have received as a rainy-day fund to pay future dividends in years when their investment portfolio has lost money or done less well.

Many investment trusts have taken advantage of this privilege to sustain and grow their dividends consistently over time, drawing on revenue reserves in bad markets and replenishing them in good times. Shareholders benefit in this way from having a steady dividend stream they can rely on.

More recently, new rules have allowed trusts to pay dividends out of their capital reserves, not just their revenue reserves. This is a more contentious practice as it means that the dividends are being paid at the expense of capital gains that have been accumulated over time. They are not strictly income payments at all.

The key point to note is that the portfolio yield of a trust and its dividend yield can be – and often are – very different figures. This can be for a number of different reasons.

1. The portfolio yield is expressed as a percentage of the trust's net assets, not of its share price.

2. The trust may not pay out all its revenues in the form of dividends. It may hold some back as a revenue reserve.

3. The trust may, alternatively, choose to pay more out as dividends than it has earned, either by using accumulated revenue reserves or paying dividends from capital.

4. Trusts also differ in how much of their costs are paid out of income and how much out of capital.

DIVIDEND HEROES

A number of investment trusts, through careful management, are sometimes known as 'dividend heroes', having been able to raise their dividends every year for more than 20 years. This is the current list, according to the the Association of Investment Companies, as at October 2018.

Table 15: Dividend heroes

COMPANY	AIC SECTOR	NO OF CONSECUTIVE YEARS' DIVIDEND INCREASED
City of London Investment Trust	UK Equity Income	52
Bankers Investment Trust	Global	51
Alliance Trust	Global	51
Caledonia Investments	Global	51
F&C Global Smaller Companies	Global	48
Foreign & Colonial Investment Trust	Global	47
Brunner Investment Trust	Global	46
JPMorgan Claverhouse Investment	UK Equity Income	45
Murray Income	UK Equity Income	45
Witan Investment Trust	Global	43
Scottish American	Global Equity Income	38
Merchants Trust	UK Equity Income	36
Scottish Mortgage Investment Trust	Global	36
Scottish Investment Trust	Global	34
Temple Bar	UK Equity Income	34
Value & Income	UK Equity Income	31
F&C Capital & Income	UK Equity Income	24
British & American	UK Equity Income	23
Schroder Income Growth	UK Equity Income	23
Invesco Income Growth	UK Equity Income	21

Source: AIC/Morningstar. Correct as at 11 October 2018.

ASSESSING THE YIELD

It is probably clear by now that a whole number of factors need to be taken into account when looking at the yield of a trust you are interested in. A 5p dividend payment will always give you an income return of 5% if you buy a trust for 100p.

The yield figure (as a percentage) will, however, change as the share price goes up and down. If your trust's share price rises from 100p to 200p, but the dividend stays the same, the yield on that trust will halve from 5.0% to 2.5%. If it falls to 50p the yield will rise to 10%.

That is one reason why it is important to look at the total return of your investment – the combination of dividends received and capital gains (or losses) made.

Equally important is to form a view as to how well-supported and sustainable the dividend rate is.

- How much in the way of revenue reserves does a trust have – is the buffer good enough to keep the dividend going if the trust has a bad year?

- Is the dividend being paid partly or wholly out of capital? If so, what you receive as a dividend will be matched an equivalent decline in the NAV per share.

- Trusts that use gearing to increase their returns may also be overstating a trust's ability to pay their dividend on a consistent basis.

- Analysing how a trust allocates its costs will also help to reveal what the true dividend capacity of a trust is.

- Special dividends are by definition meant to be exceptional and probably won't be paid again in future years.

Here are two common metrics that are used to assess the value of particular trust's yield:

- **Dividend growth:** The rate at which a dividend is growing can be compared to the performance of the trust. If it is growing too fast, that is a warning sign.

- **Dividend cover:** A ratio that measures the extent to which a trust has generated enough income to pay its dividend in any given year. A figure of more than 1.0 means that trust has more than earned its dividend. A figure below 1.0 means that the dividend cost more to pay than the trust has earned.

Look at the example of Foreign & Colonial again:

Table 16: Foreign & Colonial dividends in more detail

YEAR ENDING:	31/12/18	31/12/17	31/12/16	31/12/15	31/12/14	31/12/13
Dividend metrics						
Dividend growth	n/a	5.58%	2.60%	3.23%	3.33%	5.88%
Dividend yield	n/a	1.60%	1.80%	2.10%	2.20%	2.40%
Dividend cover	n/a	1.12	1.07	0.88	0.72	0.85

Source: Hargreaves Lansdown.

Foreign & Colonial's dividend has been growing at a relatively modest rate of 2–3% per annum but that rose to 5.58% in 2017, similar to the rate of increase in 2013 and 2014. The dividend yield has fallen from 2.4% to 1.6% over five years. It has not been fully covered by earnings in three of the past five years, although the cover ratio is currently not so low as to cause alarm.

A report by analysts at Numis Securities[*] looking at the UK Equity Income and Global Equity Income sectors highlighted how many trusts have been using the flexibility they have over the allocation of costs and the use of revenue and capital reserves in order to enhance their dividend payments. It underlines again that careful analysis is therefore needed to be sure that the yields they offer are sustainable.

KEY THINGS TO REMEMBER ABOUT INCOME INVESTING

Investment companies have some unique advantages over other funds when it comes to delivering income:

- They can invest in a wider range of income-producing assets.
- They can smooth dividends over time, and even pay dividends out of their capital profits.
- They can use gearing to boost dividends as well.
- Investment companies can grow income over time to offset some of the impact of inflation.

They are intended as long-term investments and you should therefore be prepared to invest for at least five years, and preferably ten or longer. Your income, and capital, are at risk, and can fall as well as rise, and so they are not a substitute for deposit type investments and annuities. You should not invest in investment companies if you need a guaranteed income or if you cannot afford to lose your capital.

Source: AIC.

---

[*]   3 July 2017, 'A Blurring of Capital and Income'.

GEARING

▊▊▊▊▊▊▊▊▊▊▊▊▊▊▊▊▊▊▊▊▊▊▊▊▊▊▊▊▊▊▊▊▊▊▊▊▊

G EARING IS A fancy investment term for using borrowed money to enhance returns. This is something that investment trusts are allowed to do, but open-ended funds (unit trusts and OEICs) are not. It is therefore one of the ways in which investors in trusts can hope to obtain superior returns over time. In essence, the mathematics of gearing are very simple.

• If a trust can obtain a higher rate of return from its invested capital than the cost of the money it has borrowed, shareholders will benefit from additional gains.

• If the returns are less than the cost of borrowing, however, the shareholders will suffer a greater loss (or make a smaller gain) than would otherwise be the case.

Example

Trust A has £100m of shareholders money (equity capital) to invest.

The board decides to borrow an additional £20m at 5% per annum interest for a ten-year term. That means it has to pay the lender £1m each year in interest and repay the loan after ten years. At the outset, with the borrowed money, it now has £120m, instead of £100m, to invest.

The charts show how the NAV will look after ten years on two different, hypothetical outcomes.* In one case the investments return a constant 15% p.a.: in the other they lose a constant 10% p.a. (In reality, of course, the returns will be much lumpier than this.)

The results are shown in the following two charts. In the first case, the NAV of the geared trust grows from £120m to £537m, while that of the ungeared trust also grows – but only to £405m. The gearing has paid off. It has produced an additional 32% (£132m) of return.

---

* The example uses simplified assumptions about the timing of returns, investment and interest rate payments.

Impact of gearing over ten years (return 15% p.a.; interest rate 5% p.a.)

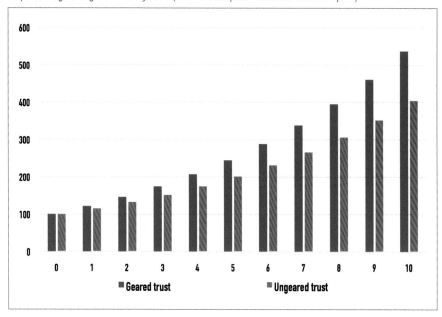

Impact of gearing over ten years (return of minus 10% p.a.: cost of debt 5% p.a.)

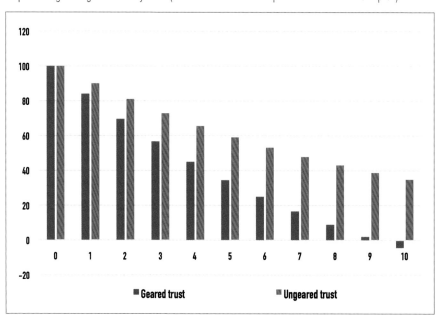

In the second case the ungeared trust falls to £35m after ten years, but the geared trust finds itself with assets worth less than its debt – it would become insolvent. (In practice, no doubt, the trust would have taken remedial action before reaching this point.) The gearing has wiped out 100% of the shareholders' equity. The ungeared trust would have made big losses, too, but would at least still be in business.

Another way of expressing the impact of gearing is to say that it amplifies the gains or losses that a trust stands to make. It follows that an investment trust with gearing is potentially more volatile and risky than an ungeared one, but with commensurate rewards if the investments produce a higher return than the cost of debt financing.

TYPES OF BORROWING

Trusts can borrow money in a number of different ways – as variable short-term borrowing (akin to an overdraft facility) or a fixed loan over a longer fixed term (more like a mortgage). The interest rate can also be a variable one or fixed in advance.

Interest rates have fallen sharply in the last 30 years and both short- and long-term borrowing has become cheaper and easier to obtain. The recent history of the WITAN INVESTMENT TRUST provides a good case in point.

- In 1986 it borrowed £44.6m in the form of a 30-year debenture. The interest rate it agreed back then was 8.5% per annum. The loan was repaid 30 years later in October 2016.

- In August 2017, Witan borrowed £30m at a rate of 2.74% fixed for 37 years. The 37-year term was believed to be a record for an investment trust in terms of time to maturity.[*]

- In 2016 it issued a £12m, 20-year loan at an interest rate of 3.29% and in 2015 it took out a £54m, 30-year loan at 3.47% per annum.

In effect, by the time the debenture was repaid Witan was paying more than 5% p.a. over and above current interest rates. Shareholders would have missed out on another 5% p.a. return had the trust been able to borrow at current rather than historic rates.

The total return Witan delivered over the 30-year term of its 1986 debenture was approximately 9% p.a. Given that the debenture cost 8.6% per annum, in this case the borrowing added little or nothing to shareholder returns.

On a more positive note, investment companies with long-term debt often publish an NAV with debt at par value and with debt at fair value. The debt at

---

[*] James Carthew, *Citywire Investment Trust Insider*, 17 August 2017.

par is based on the face value, whereas the fair value adjusts the value of the debt to reflect the moves in market interest rates since the debt was taken out.

For example, consider the historic debt of the EDINBURGH INVESTMENT TRUST, which has debentures paying an interest rate of 7.75% maturing in 2022. This would be highly attractive to a debt holder given current market interest rates. As a result, the fair value of the debt is higher than its par value.

Looking ahead, the low cost at which many investment trusts have been able to borrow recently might suggest that shareholders can look forward to much more impressive returns from gearing in future.

But interest rates are low for a reason. They have already helped to drive prices of most financial assets to much higher levels, and the implication is that future investment returns may also be much lower than in the past. If so, then gearing will have less effect and – if markets were to fall – add some downside risk, notwithstanding the low interest rates.

GEARING IN PRACTICE

In practice, gearing tends to be used sparingly across most of the investment trust sector. The main exceptions are trusts which invest in property, an asset class which lends itself more readily to the use of borrowing. The more secure and long-term a trust's investments are, the less the risk that comes from using borrowed money to enhance those returns.

Among mainstream equity trusts, some trusts use borrowed money as a near-permanent feature of their activities. Other trusts never use gearing at all, while a third group look to vary how much gearing they are employing in the light of market conditions and the terms on which borrowing is available.

An analysis of the gearing employed across the entire trust sector (approximately 500 trusts in total) shows that only around 60 were employing gearing of 20% or more at the end of Q3 2018. The standard way to express gearing is to measure the amount a trust has borrowed as a percentage of its net assets or capital employed.

A trust with £100m of equity and £20m of debt would therefore have potential gearing of 20%. The amount of cash (uninvested funds) that a trust holds is also important. The effect of cash is to reduce the level of gearing. So a trust with borrowing equivalent to 15% of its assets will have effective gearing of 5% (15% minus 10%) if it also holds 10% of its assets in cash.

The most highly geared trusts on this basis include specialist Guernsey-listed funds engaged in aircraft leasing, an activity once mainly carried out by banks, and a number of trusts that invest directly in property (with gearing of between 59% and 119%, against an average for the property sector of 24%).

Most of the trusts investing in listed equities had gearing of between zero and 20%. More than half the trusts in the analysis were not employing any gearing at all. Most boards of trusts, while often delegating tactical decisions on timing, set limits on the maximum amount of borrowing that can be employed by the manager of the trust.

Investors looking for income are often drawn to trusts that offer relatively high dividend yields. However, dividend payments may not always be as secure as they look. Trusts that use gearing or other ways to enhance their yields require particularly close scrutiny. A high level of gearing can be a red flag in these cases that the yield may not be sustainable.

WHAT IS NEGATIVE GEARING?

In August 2017 HgCapital, a private equity firm, had an £80m borrowing facility, but this had not been called upon. Its gearing was therefore zero. Only borrowings that have been used count. It also had 24% of its net assets in cash, so the effective gearing was negative (minus 24%). Because it earns little or no return, cash can act as a drag on future performance if it is not either invested or returned to shareholders. During market downturns, however, a high level of cash (negative gearing) can help to protect shareholders against losses.

DISCOUNT CONTROLS

MANY INVESTMENT COMPANIES have measures in place with which they attempt to control the discount and/or reduce discount volatility. Some trusts give a specific discount target, a level at which they promise to take remedial action. Others content themselves with a more modest statement of intent to keep the discount in mind.

Examples of discount control measures include:

BUYING BACK SHARES

If trusts buy back their own shares in the market at a discounted price, the effect will be to bolster the NAV per remaining share, leading to a lower discount. However, it means the fund's costs as a proportion of total assets will increase. Buybacks are not always a practical option for smaller trusts or those investing in illiquid assets (e.g. property).

RESTRUCTURING

If a trust's investment strategy has performed badly, a change of manager or the adoption of a new investment strategy may restore investor confidence in future performance.

MAKING A TENDER OFFER

A tender offer involves offering investors a chance to surrender their shares in return for cash, up to a certain aggregate number of shares in total (say, 15% of the issued share capital). The objective is to remove unhappy shareholders from the register in one go.

HOLDING A CONTINUATION VOTE

This involves giving shareholders a vote at a predetermined date in the future on whether the trust should continue. If a continuation vote is lost, the trust's assets will be liquidated and returned to shareholders. The idea is that if shareholders know they will get a chance to exit at NAV in a few years' time, it may prevent them selling out today.

Extreme volatility in markets can cause problems for mechanisms and 2008 is a good example of this.

For some investors, a stated discount control mechanism offers some reassurance that the board will be proactive when/if the discount widens significantly. But it doesn't guarantee that the gap will narrow. It may also help deter a challenge from aggressive activist investors.

DISCOUNT CONTROLS IN PRACTICE

It is now fairly routine for investment companies to adopt the power to buy back their own shares. This requires shareholder approval at a general meeting and more than two-thirds of the companies in the sector have obtained this approval. There is no doubt that many boards of investment companies are taking discount controls more seriously than in the past.

One reason is the emergence of so-called professional 'activist investors' who buy a block of shares and use that as leverage in trying to force the board of poorly performing trusts to take some action. There have been some notable examples of boards giving in to this kind of pressure in the last few years, including ALLIANCE TRUST and ELECTRA.

However, while some boards rigorously adhere to their discount control policy, many still allow themselves a degree of wriggle room to suspend the control mechanisms they have adopted in certain circumstances. It is important to check the wording of any policy closely to see if it's a hard-and-fast rule or simply a guideline, with scope for flexibility.

While adopting a policy of controls, many trusts have not yet felt the need to exercise this power, though in any given year a fair number do so. It is open to debate how far the greater adoption of discount-control mechanisms has been a factor in reducing the average level of discount across the sector.

Buybacks and tenders since 1996

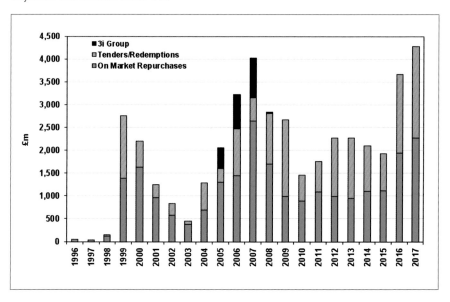

Source: Winterflood Securities, Morningstar.

According to Winterflood Securities, there are more than 50 trusts which have an explicit – as opposed to a non-specific – discount target, although these varied widely. However, of 51 trusts in one survey at the start of 2017, 19 were in breach of their specified targets at that date.

IPOS AND SHARE ISSUANCE

W HEREAS BUYBACKS AND tender offers reduce the amount of capital invested in the trust sector, in any year they will be offset by a combination of new and secondary issues by other trusts.

New issues, or IPOs (initial public offerings), are the mechanism by which new trusts are launched. The number and type of new issue varies enormously from one year to the next. The IPO process involves the issue of a prospectus and significant expense in the form of legal fees and corporate finance and other professional advice.

Investment company IPOs since 2000

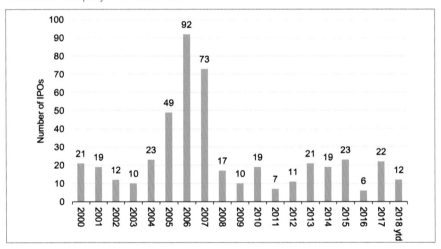

Includes Mobius IT, which started trading on 1 October 2018. Excludes introductions where no new capital is raised, e.g. Stenprop and Georgia Capital in Q2 2018.
Source: Numis Securities Research.

Secondary issues can take a number of different forms. The most common are placings of new shares and so-called 'C-share issues'. The first two mechanisms, which are less cumbersome and time-consuming than a new issue, both have the effect of allowing an existing trust to expand its capital base by growing the number of shares in issue.

Boards that have bought back their own shares also have the option of reissuing shares that they have not yet cancelled. A number of well-known trusts whose performance or style of investing have become popular in recent years have been able to issue a steady stream of new shares at a premium to NAV.

All issues of new shares have to be approved by existing shareholders, so as to avoid dilution of their interests. Many companies seek approval at their annual general meetings for the flexibility to issue new shares up to certain annual limits. The following chart shows that property and debt funds have raised the most over the last five years, although developed market equity funds are not far behind.

Fundraising by asset class in 2014–2018 (£m year to date)

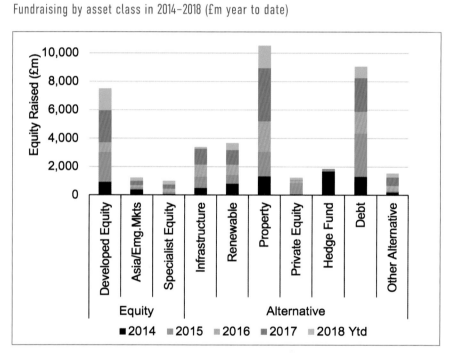

Source: Numis Securities.

THE 'MYSTERY' OF DISCOUNTS

W HY DO DISCOUNTS in investment trusts exist – and why do they persist? This is a question that has confounded academic researchers whose job is to study finance for many years.

According to a recent survey, more than 100 articles about this 'mystery' have appeared in learned journals over the past 30 years. Yet no convincing, all-embracing explanation has been forthcoming.

Indeed one distinguished American academic went so far not so long ago to say that "the mysterious case" of closed-end funds poses an "irrefutable challenge" to the whole of neoclassical economic theory.[*] Another described it as "a cause célèbre" in finance literature.

So what is the mystery? It is a puzzle to academics because it flies in the face of one of the core tenets of modern financial theory: the efficient market hypothesis. This says, in effect, that there are – or should be – no 'free lunches' in properly working financial markets.

If a closed-end fund like an investment trust consistently sells at a discount to its NAV, it means that it creates an opportunity for someone smart to make a quick and easy profit. All they need to do is buy all the shares and liquidate the portfolio, banking the difference.

Yet discounts, as we know, do persist and in many cases have done so historically for many years. Those quick and easy profits remain on the table for long periods of time. A related mystery is why, if this is the case, anybody buys a new closed-end fund when it is launched if they know that it is likely to go to a discount soon afterwards.

All sorts of theories have been put forward to explain this apparent paradox. They include:

- investor irrationality

---

[*]   Prof Stephen Ross, Princeton lectures (2002).

- management fees

- tax effects

- liquidity issues.

There is no space to review all these different explanations. A useful round up of the academic literature can be found in 'Closed-End Funds: A Survey' (2012), by Martin Cherkes of New York's Columbia University. His conclusion: the mystery has not been solved.

Fortunately, the mystery is of no great importance to investors. Recent years have shown that boards of trusts can and do take effective action to eliminate the discounts on their trust, either of their own volition or in the face of threatened activist pressure.

Some professional investment trust investors, such as Peter Spiller of CG Asset Management, argue that all investment trusts should actively pursue policies to eliminate their discounts.

Others, such as Nick Greenwood – who runs MITON GLOBAL OPPORTUNITIES, a fund that invests in other investment trusts – says that the opportunity to find great bargains (trusts that are selling at excessive discounts) is one of the best reasons for investing in the closed-end sector.

Simple observation shows that there is often a fairly direct link between trust performance and the discount. Look, for example, at these two charts of how the discount has moved in two of the larger sectors in the investment trust universe. In both cases the discount has narrowed significantly in recent years, having widened sharply during the big market sell-off around the time of the global financial crisis in 2007–09.

Performance (LHS) and discount (RHS) of UK Equity Income sector

Source: Thomson Reuters Datastream.

Performance (LHS) and discount (RHS) of Japanese sector

Source: Thomson Reuters Datastream.

Z-SCORES

How are z-scores calculated? The formula is:

$$\text{Z-score} = \frac{\text{(current discount - average discount)}}{\text{standard deviation of the discount}}$$

Example

Trust A is trading at a discount of 10% (minus 10%). Its average discount over the previous year has been 5% (minus 5%). The standard deviation of the discount over the same period is 2.5%.

Its z-score is therefore:

$$\frac{-10\% - (-5\%)}{2.5\%} = \frac{-10\% + 5\%}{2.5\%} = \frac{-5.0\%}{2.5\%} = -2.0$$

A negative z-score suggests that a trust is 'cheap' compared to its normal trading range. A positive z-score points to it being relatively 'expensive' to buy or sell at its current price.

A z-score of 2.0 or more (positive or negative) is particularly worthy of note and typically merits further investigation. It means that the discount (or premium) is more than two standard deviations away from its mean.

Z-scores can be calculated over any number of periods – anything from one day to one year or longer. The longer the time period, the more significant the reading may be. Short-term readings are more helpful for trading decisions.

The underlying assumption behind the calculation is that movements in discounts follow what statisticians call a normal distribution and revert to the mean over time. In practice this may well not be the case. In fact there is evidence that it is not true.[*]

INTERPRETING Z-SCORES

While they are certainly informative, therefore, z-scores always need to be treated with caution. Investors need to take into account a number of other factors which may be influencing the level at which shares are trading relative to their NAV.

Examples would be:

_____

[*]   See for example an article on *Seeking Alpha* by 'Left Banker' on 17 April 2017.

- the board announcing new discount controls or buyback commitments

- changes in the shareholder register (e.g. activist stakes or overhang from a major seller)

- portfolio developments not fully reflected in the NAV (e.g. the expected realisation of an unquoted asset).

It is also possible to study how current z-scores for different sectors compare to their historic averages.

Sample Z-scores – sector ranges, showing sector average and sector ranges of trusts above £150m (as at 31 October 2018)

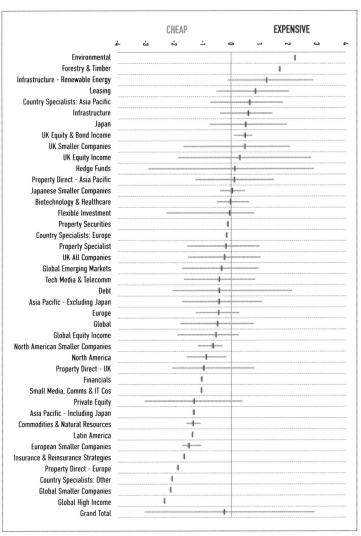

Source: Investec.

The width of the bars in this chart, produced by analysts at Investec, gives an indication of which sectors have been the most and which the least volatile in this respect. The orange bar shows the current z-score relative to the range as at the date of the sample (31 October 2018). Note that the majority of trusts had positive z-scores at this date.

It is not a surprise that the sectors with the widest range of z-scores are also those with the greatest volatility.

Sample Z-scores – cheap and expensive, showing z-score compared to their sectors range of trusts above £150m (as at 31 October 2018)

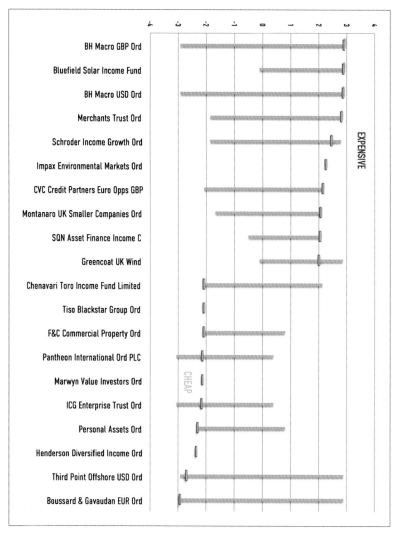

Source: Investec.

This chart summarises 20 of the largest trusts with the highest and lowest z-scores (and their range) at a date tested in October 2018. It is illustrative only – there is always movement from one month to the next. Remember that a positive z-score indicates a trust whose discount is well above its average trend while a negative z-score is the opposite. In other words, negative is often a positive from an investor's point of view!

DISCOUNT TRENDS

Discounts can vary considerably over time. A number of different factors, as already noted, can influence the level of the discount at any one time. Board policy, fund performance and market conditions can all have a bearing on the way that discounts move.

In recent years, as the impact of the global financial crisis has receded, both share and bond prices have been trending higher. While the discounts on many trusts widened sharply during the crisis, the general trend since then has been for them to have moved steadily higher on average.

For the last few years discounts on mainstream sectors have generally traded above their longer-term average of around 9% (shown by the black horizontal line in the chart). It seems probable that the trend towards greater use of discount controls has been one factor in this trend, along with the general buoyancy of equity markets.

Long-term sector average discount (excl. private equity)

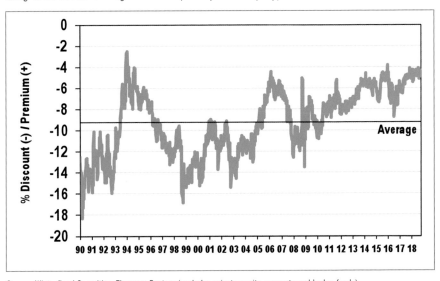

Source: Winterflood Securities, Thomson Reuters (excludes private equity, property and hedge funds).

The volatility of discounts – how far they move up and down in any given year – also varies from year to year.

Sector average discount ranges by calendar year since 2004

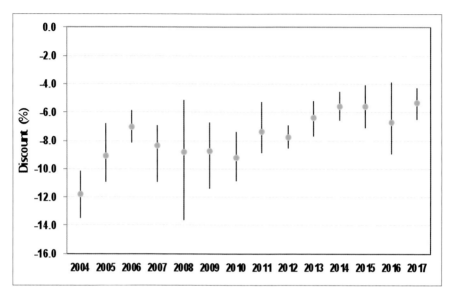

Source: Winterflood Securities.

Different sectors have different experiences, though. If you compare the average discount in the main global equity sectors you can see how they have moved in different ways over the last two decades. After the financial crisis in 2007–08, investors initially placed a higher value (= a smaller discount) on the equity income sector while trusts with defensive investment approaches have traded at a premium since 2015.

Global sectors average discount ranges since 2010

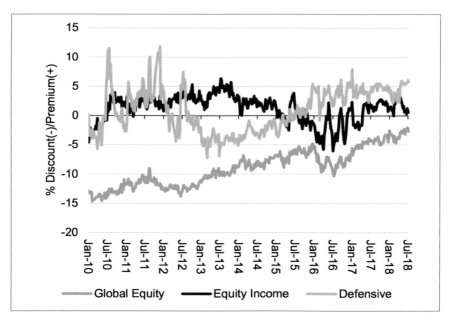

Source: Numis Securities Research, Morningstar.

The same effect has been visible with the recent appearance of a large number of alternative asset trusts, many of which as noted earlier offer relatively high yields but relatively little potential for capital growth. Many of these trusts were trading at premiums in autumn 2018, reflecting investors' greater appetite for income. The discount history of this kind of trust consequently looks rather different to that of conventional trusts.

SKIN IN THE GAME

A good question for investors to ask about any company (not just investment trusts) is the extent to which the interests of the managers of the company are aligned with the interests of the shareholders.

In an ideal world it would be comforting to know that those managing the company stand to gain or lose in the same way as those providing the capital for the business (which is what shareholders effectively do).

In the case of investment trusts, the two parties whose interests you most want to have aligned with yours as an investor are the board of directors and the individual fund managers who make the investment decisions.

In both cases it is usually a positive if they have substantial personal investments in their trusts. One exception may occur if an individual or institution holds such a large shareholding in a trust that they effectively control the company and can do what they want with it, whether sensible or not.

Directors of trusts are required to disclose at least once a year in the company's annual report and accounts the extent of their holdings in the trusts on whose boards they serve. It is also a stock exchange listing requirement they notify the market within 24 hours of any further dealings in their trust's shares. All significant shareholders must notify the market if they own more than 3% of the share capital in any trust.

While directors' interests are always available, it is less easy to discover how much the portfolio managers have invested in their trusts. They only have to disclose their shareholding if it exceeds 3% of the total issued share capital of the trust. Some choose to do so voluntarily.

Alan Brierley, investment analyst at Canaccord Genuity, does the industry a service by periodically compiling a summary of the shareholdings of directors and managers (where the latter can be ascertained). His last research on this topic, based on analysing 279 trusts, was published in April 2018. Earlier reports appeared in 2017, 2014 and 2012.

These are some of his headline findings from the latest survey:

- The total investment by boards and managers in the 2018 report was £2,043 million. While the evolution of the closed-end industry makes comparisons of limited value, and equity markets have been strong, this is materially higher than the total of £1bn in 2014 and £687m in 2012.

- 58 chairmen/directors have an individual investment in excess of £1m, while 67 managers or management teams have a personal investment in excess of £1m.

- 48 investment companies, or 17% of those analysed, have chairmen or directors who all have shareholdings valued at more than one year of their director's fee.

- 14% of directors have no investment at all in their trusts (vs 16% in 2014 and 19% in 2012). Excluding those appointed in the past year, this falls to 9% (vs 12% in 2014 and 14% in 2012).

The following table highlights trusts in which the managers (or management teams) have shareholdings in excess of £10m:

Table 17: Managers with a personal investment in excess of £10m at April 2018

COMPANY	MANAGER	VALUE (£,000)
RIT Capital	Lord Rothschild and family	336,781
Tetragon	Reade Griffith/Paddy Dear & management team	185,349
Apax Global Alpha	Management team	170,700
JZ Capital Partners	David Zalaznick/Jay Jordan	104,237
North Atlantic Smallers	Christopher Mills	97,149
Scottish Mortgage	Management team	82,900
Riverstone Energy	Management team	75,127
Pershing Square Holdings	Management team	74,212
Manchester & London	Mark Sheppard	56,177
New Star	John Duffield	45,784
Caledonia	Will Wyatt/Jamie Cayzer-Colvin	40,605
Aberforth Smaller Companies	Management team	38,429
Independent Investment Trust	Max Ward	30,066
Macau Property Opportunities	Tom Ashworth/Martin Tacon	24,952
HgCapital Trust	Management team	24,817
Jupiter European Opportunities	Alex Darwall	24,310
Value & Income	Angela Lascelles/Matthew Oakeshott	22,173
Hansa Trust	William Salomon	21,698
Syncona	Thomas Henderson	17,868
Aberforth Split Level Income	Management team	15,643
Capital Gearing	Peter Spiller	15,635
Artemis Alpha	John Dodd/Adrian Paterson	14,797
Primary Health Properties	Harry Hyman/Nexus Group	14,553

COMPANY	MANAGER	VALUE (£,000)
Montanaro UK Smaller Companies	Charles Montanaro & family	12,998
International Public Partnerships	Management team	12,969
Monks	Management team	11,500
Mid Wynd International	Simon Edelsten	10,345

Source: Canaccord Genuity, April 2018.

This year we also include a table showing which trusts have the most highly paid executive directors. By definition this is a relatively small group as most trusts outsource the management of the portfolio to external managers or advisers and most boards, as noted above, consist entirely of independent non-executive directors. Most of those on the list are self-managed trusts therefore.

Table 18: Highest paid executive directors

	COMPANY	APPOINTED TO BOARD	TOTAL REMUNERATION (£)	VALUE OF INVESTMENT (£)
Will Wyatt, Chief Executive	Caledonia Investments	2005	1,799,00	30,573,038
Christopher Mills, Chief Executive	North Atlantic Smaller Companies	1984	1,629,00	97,149,000
Lord Rothschild OM GBE	RIT Capital Partners	1988	1,365,288	336,780,947
Stephen King, Finance Director	Caledonia Investments	2009	1,257,000	865,613
Jonathan Murphy, Chief Executive	Assura	2017	1,232,000	1,385,749
Jamie Cayzer-Colvin, Executive Director	Caledonia Investments	2005	1,080,000	10,031,776
Tim Attlee, Acting Chief Executive	Empiric Student Property	2014	730,527	705,300
Andrew Bell, Chief Executive	Witan	2010	657,906	1,456,000
Michael Morris, Chief Executive	Picton Property Income	2015	617,893	47,164
Gavin Manson, Chief Financial Officer	Electra Private Equity	2017	300,000	126,143

	COMPANY	APPOINTED TO BOARD	TOTAL REMUNERATION (£)	VALUE OF INVESTMENT (£)
Lynne Fennah, Chief Financial Officer	Empiric Student Property	2017	205,038	46,813
Max Ward, Managing Director	Independent Investment Trust	2000	200,000	30,066,238
Neil Johnson, Executive Chairman	Electra Private Equity	2016	200,000	20,750

Source: Canaccord Genuity, April 2018.

BOARD COMPOSITION

The Canaccord Genuity report on board and manager shareholdings also provides some helpful data on board composition. Of the 283 trusts analysed, 93% of the directors could be classified as independent. Women accounted for 22.3% of investment company directorships, vs 15.2% in 2014 and just 10.2% in 2012. This compares with 24.5% of FTSE 350 company directors. Notably there are still 69 all-male boards vs just 12 in FT 350 index companies. Given that the government has announced a voluntary target of 33% female directors by 2020, trust boards are becoming less "pale, male and stale" as George Kershaw of Trust Associates puts it in his article (see page 77), but are still lagging the corporate sector generally.

MANAGEMENT FEES AND COSTS

F EW SUBJECTS HAVE aroused as much interest in the last few years in the fund industry as the issue of fees charged by management companies. Investment trusts, which for a long time have enjoyed a reputation for being cheap to buy and run, have found themselves under growing pressure to reduce their fees and running costs in order to stay competitive.

The competition has come from several directions.

- The growing popularity of low-cost index funds and exchange-traded funds, many of which charge much lower management fees than the average investment trust.

- The impact of the Retail Distribution Review (RDR), which since 2013 has banned unit trusts and OEICs, the main competitors to investment trusts, from paying sales commission to advisers who recommended them.

- More generally, greater transparency (and criticism) about the fees and costs that fund management companies have been able to charge historically.

These pressures have resulted in the investment trust industry moving towards a more standardised method of reporting cost information. The standard measure the industry had adopted now is the ongoing charge ratio (OCR), which attempts to calculate the operating costs shareholders in trusts are paying for the privilege of having their investments managed collectively.

This figure is expressed as a percentage of the trust's NAV and is published annually by each trust. The objective is to provide shareholders with an indication of the extent to which their annual returns have been reduced by the recurring operational expenses incurred by the trust. The figure excludes, however, the cost of buying and selling securities for the investment portfolio, which can vary significantly from trust to trust and from year to year.

Even though the OCR may appear to be a relatively small figure, research has demonstrated that even a 1% increase in the annual cost of running a fund of any kind can significantly eat into the returns it delivers over time. More importantly, funds whose recurring costs exceed 1% p.a. face powerful competition from passively managed funds, some of which charge 0.1% p.a or even less.

Given that the long-term historical return from investing in equities is around 7% p.a. in real (adjusted for inflation) terms, a trust's investment performance has to be exceptionally good to overcome a 2% p.a. cost disadvantage compared to a low-cost index-tracking fund.

Historically the annual charges of investment trusts have on average been lower than those of open-ended funds, not least because trusts were not allowed to pay standard 'trail commission' to advisers, as open-ended funds were until 2013. Trail commission before RDR of 0.5% p.a. was typically passed on directly to investors in open-ended funds as part of the fund manager's annual management charge.

Now that trail commission on new sales of funds has gone, the in-built cost advantage enjoyed by trusts has eroded. A well-functioning trust board will – or should – have cost control as one of its primary areas of focus, and many have taken steps in the last few years to reduce the annual management fees paid to their external managers.

A particular focus has been on eliminating performance fees, which allow managers of trusts to receive an extra fee in the event of the trust exceeding a specified return hurdle. More than 50 trusts have taken steps to reduce or eliminate performance fees and this trend is set to continue. Fidelity recently announced plans to use a different approach – so-called 'fulcrum' fees, by which the annual management fee rises or falls according to certain performance criteria – across its whole UK fund range. This idea may also spread to investment trusts.

As can be seen from the following table, sector average ongoing charges range between 0.8% and 1.94%, but individual trust figures are considerably more variable. Some large trusts, such as Scottish Mortgage (0.44% OCR), have used the benefits of scale to cut their fee to a historically low level. The OCR figure includes not just the investment management fee but a range of other costs, including legal fees, print costs and other administrative charges.

Table 19: Ongoing charge ratios by sector

SECTOR	EX PERF FEE	INC PERF FEE
UK	0.70%	0.81%
Global	0.78%	0.81%
North America	0.82%	0.82%
Europe	0.87%	0.95%
Japan	0.92%	0.92%
Asia Pacific	1.21%	1.59%
Sector Specialist	1.27%	1.57%
Infrastructure	1.30%	2.12%
Emerging Markets	1.31%	1.32%
Debt	1.60%	2.68%
Private Equity	1.69%	1.88%
Property	2.19%	3.01%

SECTOR	EX PERF FEE	INC PERF FEE
Hedge Funds	2.40%	4.08%

Source: Numis Securities at 28 September 2018.

The following table shows some of the trusts with the lowest OCRs – it is notable that none currently pays a performance fee. Woodford Patient Capital is the only trust which does not charge a management fee at all, but only a performance fee (which it has not yet earned). It is no surprise that most of these trusts are among the oldest and largest around. They benefit from economies of scale.

Table 20: Some trusts with low OCRs

TICKER	COMPANY	EX PERF FEE	INC PERF FEE
EAT	European Assets	0.14%	0.14%
WPCT	Woodford Patient Capital	0.18%	0.18%
HBMN	HBM Healthcare Investments	0.24%	0.24%
IIT	Independent IT	0.25%	0.25%
IVPM	Invesco Perpetual Select – Liquidity	0.35%	0.34%
FHIU	F&C UK High Income – Units	0.35%	0.35%
SMT	Scottish Mortgage	0.37%	0.37%
HSL	Henderson Smaller Companies	0.41%	0.98%
CTY	City of London	0.42%	0.42%
HGT	HgCapital Trust	0.42%	0.42%
BNKR	Bankers	0.44%	0.44%
RIII	Rights & Issues IT	0.45%	0.45%
SCIN	Scottish IT	0.47%	0.47%
MRC	Mercantile	0.47%	0.47%
TMPL	Temple Bar	0.49%	0.49%
BGLP	Blackstone GSO Loan Financing £	0.51%	0.51%
BGLF	Blackstone GSO Loan Financing	0.51%	0.51%
HANA	Hansa Trust A	0.51%	0.51%
FRCL	F&C IT	0.52%	0.52%

TICKER	COMPANY	EX PERF FEE	INC PERF FEE
MNKS	Monks	0.52%	0.52%
ARR	Aurora	0.54%	0.54%
JAM	JPMorgan American	0.55%	0.55%
JPE	JPMorgan Elect – Managed Growth	0.55%	0.55%
EDIN	Edinburgh IT	0.57%	0.57%
LWI	Lowland	0.57%	0.67%

Source: Numis Securities at 28 September 2018.

The next table shows some of the funds with the highest management fees. Specialist, property and private equity trusts tend to have the highest annual management fees and incur more expenses, in part because they are obliged to take a more hands-on role in managing the investments. High fees may then be rewarded by exceptional performance.

Table 21: Trusts with notably high OCRs

TICKER	COMPANY	EX PERF FEE	INC PERF FEE
JIL	Juridica Investments	n/a	12.51%
PSDL	Phoenix Spree Deutschland	3.17%	11.51%
MPO	Macau Property Opportunities	n/a	10.05%
NRI	Northern Investors	n/a	9.85%
ADAM	Adamas Finance Asia	n/a	9.31%
LXB	LXB Retail Properties	n/a	9.06%
BAF	British American	7.90%	7.90%
TPOU	Third Point Offshore – US$	2.98%	7.62%
3IN	3i Infrastructure	2.06%	7.18%
LTA	Altamir Amboise	7.05%	7.05%
SPPC	St Peter Port Capital	6.02%	6.02%
P2P	P2P Global Investment	4.90%	5.99%
ESP	Empiric Student Property	5.95%	5.95%
SERE	Schroder European Real Estate	5.91%	5.91%
DUPD	Dragon Ukrainian Properties	5.91%	5.91%

TICKER	COMPANY	EX PERF FEE	INC PERF FEE
YATRA	Yatra Capital	5.72%	5.72%
ECT	Eurocastle Investment	5.70%	5.70%
VOF	VinaCapital Vietnam Opportunity	2.34%	5.62%
GRIT	Global Resources	5.57%	5.57%
RMMC	River & Mercantile UK Micro Cap	1.28%	5.52%
ARTL	Alpha Real Trust	4.85%	4.85%
RC2	Reconstruction Capital II	4.08%	4.08%
JZCP	JZ Capital Partners	3.87%	3.87%
BHGG	BH Global – £	3.57%	3.79%
ASPL	Aseana Properties	n/a	17.64%
AA4	Amedeo Air Four Plus	n/a	19.21%

Source: Numis Securities at 28 September 2018.

A further complication in comparing the cost of ownership across the trust sector stems from the introduction of new EU regulations as part of an initiative known as Mifid2 which came into effect in January 2018. The PRIIPS rules* include, among other dictates, a requirement that investment trusts produce a 'key information document' (KID) for investors which includes a figure of their annual ownership costs (as well as future return projections under a range of scenarios).

The basis for calculating this figure is different in a number of respects from that employed in calculating the OCR or the 'total expense ratio' (TER), another method of calculating costs. Transaction costs are included, for example, but on a basis that analysts have shown produces some curious outcomes. Some trusts, for example, are recorded as having negative costs. Different companies also appear to calculate the figure differently.

To add insult to injury, these new KIDs are due to be extended to funds that are already compliant with the EU's UCITs rules, but not until January 2020. As those affected include many open-ended funds, the trust industry has protested strongly about the competitive disadvantage this appears to give to investment trusts. The UK's trade association of the open-ended fund industry has also

---

* PRIIPS stands for 'packaged retail and insurance-based investment products', the kind of clunking name that bureaucrats seem to love.

warned that the new KIDs may be seriously misleading and is calling for the extension of the new rules to be postponed until a better formulation can be found.

Analyst Charles Cade of Numis sums up the debate about which annual cost figure is best:

> "The TER covers management fees and expenses on a historic basis as a proportion of average net assets. Ongoing charges is similar but includes a broader range of expenses (including underlying fees – although not all funds include these). Neither includes performance fees, although they are often stated separately for the year.

> "The reduction in yield figure (RIY) required by the PRIIPS regulations includes management fees and performance fees (the latter averaged over three years). Also it includes portfolio transaction costs, as well as underlying costs of any fund investments, and interest charges.

> "The problem with the KID is that different funds do not calculate figures in the same way (transaction costs are negative for several funds). Many property funds show zero transaction costs whilst others are 8pc. Some do not include full underlying fund costs, and there is no benefit from gearing (but there is a cost)."

The message for private investors: costs are an important – though far from the only – factor in determining the results any investment fund can achieve. It probably makes sense for now to use the OCR as the starting point for comparisons, but treat anything you read in the KID with scepticism. Use the annual report to see what the actual running costs and transaction costs of your trusts are. You will also find there details of the annual management fee and performance fee (if any).

ALTERNATIVE ASSET TRUSTS IN DEPTH

We asked the top-rated analyst team at broker WINTERFLOOD SECURITIES *to summarise the key factors that investors should be looking at when analysing trusts in three of the most popular alternative asset sectors – property, infrastructure and renewables, and debt.*

LISTED PROPERTY INVESTMENT COMPANIES

By EMMA BIRD

INVESTING IN PROPERTY via collective vehicles allows investors to gain diversified exposure to an illiquid asset class without the need for a significant capital outlay. We believe that investment in illiquid asset classes, such as property, is ideally suited to the listed closed-ended fund structure. The permanent nature of these funds' capital means that managers can minimise 'cash drag' and avoid becoming forced sellers in difficult markets. While discounts may widen during periods of stress, shares can always be traded, albeit at a price that may differ significantly from NAV.

This stands in contrast to many open-ended property funds, which were forced to apply 'gates' in order to block redemptions during 2008/2009 and again in the aftermath of the Brexit vote in 2016. The listed funds also have the advantage of being able to smooth their dividend payments, as they have the ability to maintain revenue reserves and pay dividends out of capital profits.

Persistent UK inflation over recent years has coincided with a number of funds being launched with a focus on providing inflation-linked income. While interest rates have also risen, they remain low in a historical context. In this low-interest-rate environment, we believe that the dividend yields paid by property funds remain attractive.

There are numerous and varied funds within the investment trust property sector, ranging from diversified UK commercial property funds to those investing in individual specialist sub-sectors, such as supermarkets or care homes. Before analysing individual funds, investors should decide whether they are looking for broad and diversified exposure to the property sector or an opportunity to gain access to a niche area of the market.

If opting for a generalist fund, you should consider both geographic diversification and sector exposures within the portfolio. The UK commercial property market is traditionally split into four sectors: retail, offices, industrial and other.

In recent years, industrial properties have delivered the best capital growth, while the retail sector has lagged in the face of significant headwinds, particularly the growing dominance of e-commerce. This trend in relative sector performance is expected to continue.

Chart 1 shows the sector exposures of general UK commercial property investment trusts as at 30 June 2018. All the trusts have the ability to adjust their allocations in line with the managers' current outlook, though transaction costs can be a significant impediment to turnover.

Chart 1: UK direct property funds – sector exposure

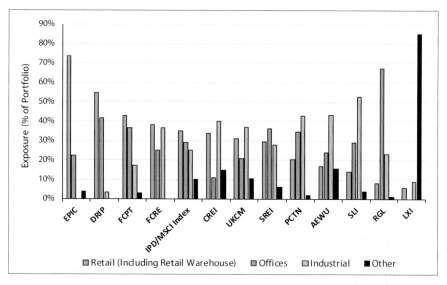

Source: Winterflood Securities, The Funds, data as at 30 June 2018 (except Index and LXI as at 31 March 2018; RGL as at 31 December 2017). Note: CREI's exposure is measured as a percentage of income. The full names of the individual funds are given at the end of this article.

Property funds often use gearing, or leverage, in an attempt to enhance both income and capital returns. While this boosts returns in periods of growth, it also increases risk as values will fall further in downturns, when compared to an equivalent ungeared fund. Investors should be cognisant of the amount of gearing used and we would suggest that more risk-averse investors focus on those with lower loan-to-value (LTV) ratios, defined as the amount of debt in the fund as a percentage of the value of the property portfolio. Chart 2 shows the net LTV ratios for the general UK commercial property investment trusts.

Chart 2: Listed UK direct property funds – net loan-to-value gearing

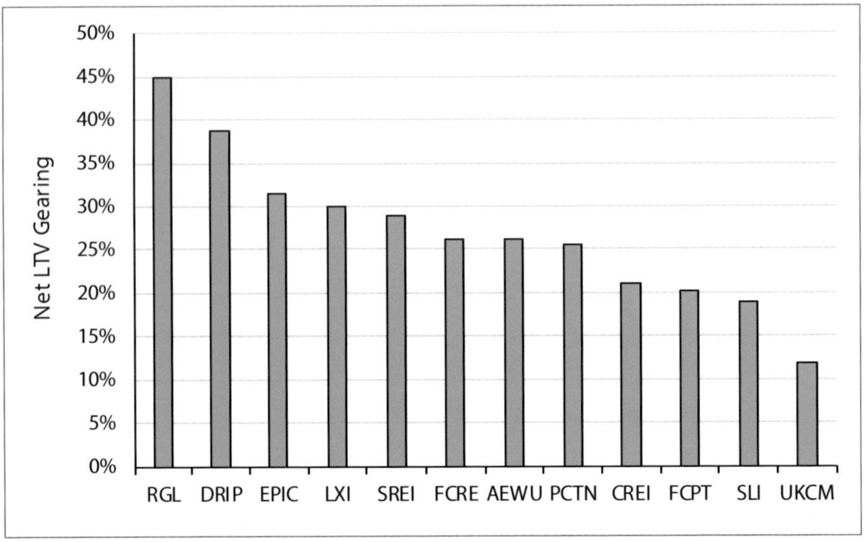

Source: Winterflood Securities, The Funds, data as at 30 June 2018 (RGL as at 31 December 2017; EPIC and LXI as at 31 March 2018; PCTN and SREI following post quarter-end activities). Note: the figure for AEWU is the gross LTV ratio.

In the current low-interest-rate environment, one of the key attractions of property investment trusts is their yield. We expect income to be the key driver of property fund total returns over the next couple of years. Another aspect to consider, therefore, is the prospective yield of a fund and the potential for dividend growth. Dividend cover, the extent to which annual dividend payments are covered by current year earnings, can give an idea of the likelihood that a fund's dividend can be maintained or even increased from year to year.

Charts 3 and 4 show the dividend yields and dividend cover of each of the general listed UK property funds, as at the end of August 2018. There are now also some options for investors looking for an income stream that is protected from inflation, with a number of funds, particularly those investing in specialist sub-sectors, targeting rents that are inflation-linked. This means that the funds' earnings should grow in-line with inflation each year, creating the potential for the dividend to grow at the same pace.

Chart 3: Listed UK direct property funds – dividend yields

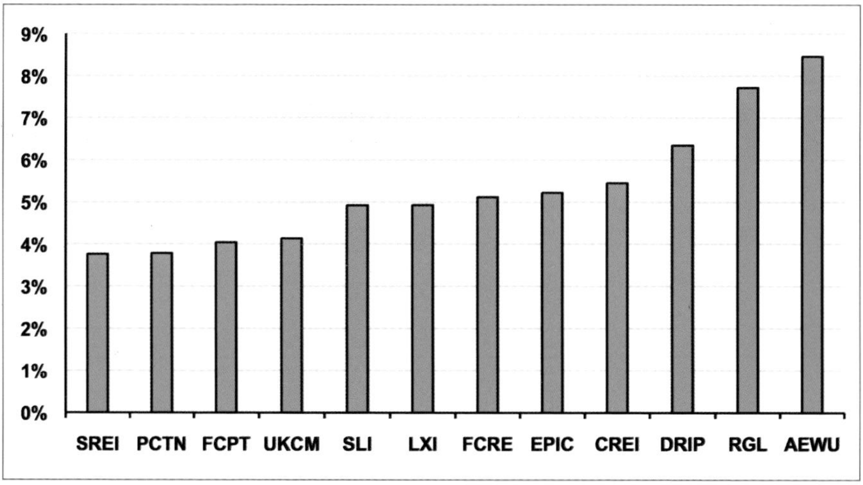

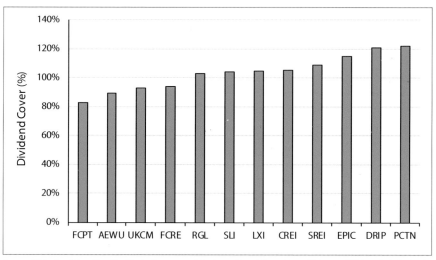

Source: Winterflood Securities, The Funds, Morningstar based on share prices as at 28 August 2018.

Chart 4: Listed UK direct property funds – dividend cover

Source: Winterflood Securities, The Funds. In respect of the latest financial year (as at 28 August 2018) for which the funds have published results.

Finally, while we would not expect the property market as a whole to deliver much in the way of capital growth in the near future, we think there are still opportunities for managers who are able to add value through active asset management. We therefore favour fund managers that have demonstrated this ability.

Table 1 gives some examples of specialist listed property funds with significant inflation linkage in their revenues.

Table 1: Listed property funds with indexed-linked income

TICKER	FUND NAME	% OF RENTS LINKED TO INFLATION
IHR	Impact Healthcare REIT plc*	100% (as at 30 June 2018)
CSH	Civitas Social Housing plc	100% (as at 31 March 2018)
SOHO	Triple Point Social Housing REIT plc	100% (as at 31 December 2017)
RESI	Residential Secure Income plc	100% (as at 31 March 2018)
SUPR	Supermarket Income REIT plc	100% (as at 30 June 2018)

Table 2: UK direct property funds

TICKER	FUND NAME
EPIC	Ediston Property Investment Company plc
DRIP	Drum Income Plus REIT plc
FCPT	F&C Commercial Property Trust Limited*
FCRE	F&C UK Real Estate Investments Limited
CREI	Custodian REIT plc
UKCM	UK Commercial Property REIT Limited
SREI	Schroder Real Estate Investment Trust Limited
PCTN	Picton Property Income Limited
AEWU	AEW UK REIT plc
SLI	Standard Life Investments Property Income Trust Limited*
RGL	Regional REIT Limited
LXI	LXI REIT plc

*Denotes a corporate broking client of Winterflood Securities.

EMMA BIRD *joined the investment trust research team at Winterflood Securities in 2015 shortly after graduating from the University of Nottingham with a first-class degree in economics.*

———————————

LISTED INFRASTRUCTURE INVESTMENT COMPANIES

By KIERAN DRAKE

S INCE THE LAUNCH of the first investment company dedicated to investment in infrastructure in 2006, the asset class has been one of the undoubted success stories of the investment companies sector. At the end of 2007 there were just three listed funds providing access to the asset class, with aggregate net assets of £1.6bn. At the end of August 2018, the sub-sector had grown to 15 funds with aggregate net assets of £15bn.

These funds can be broadly categorised as providing access to:

*   environmental infrastructure, primarily renewable energy production (BLUEFIELD SOLAR INCOME, FORESIGHT SOLAR, GORE STREET ENERGY STORAGE, GREENCOAT RENEWABLES, GREENCOAT UK WIND, JOHN LAING ENVIRONMENTAL ASSETS,* NEXTENERGY SOLAR, THE RENEWABLES INFRASTRUCTURE GROUP)

*   social infrastructure, such as hospitals, schools and roads (BBGI, HICL INFRASTRUCTURE, INTERNATIONAL PUBLIC PARTNERSHIPS, JOHN LAING INFRASTRUCTURE)

*   economic infrastructure, such as utility companies (3I INFRASTRUCTURE)

*   infrastructure debt (GCP INFRASTRUCTURE, SEQUOIA ECONOMIC INFRASTRUCTURE INCOME).

AN ATTRACTIVE SOURCE OF DIVIDENDS

Investors have been particularly attracted to the dividend streams derived from government-backed revenues via mechanisms such as the Private Finance Initiative (PFI) and Ofgem's renewable energy subsidies. The majority of assets held by funds in the sector have fixed lives and therefore, all else being equal, valuations that will gradually fall to zero. Examples include concessions to design, finance, construct and run public services such as hospitals or schools for a fixed term in exchange for regular payments until the asset is handed back to the relevant public body.

---

*   Corporate broking client of Winterflood Securities.

In the case of renewable energy assets, they tend to receive subsidies for a period of 20 years and the equipment that generates the electricity is expected to have a 25-year life. In both of these cases the individual assets have annuity-like properties, with capital invested at the beginning in exchange for a series of cash flows over a period, at the end of which the asset has nil value. It is therefore important to understand that the cash flows received from assets are not simply income yields, but also include the return of capital.

In practice funds have been able to avoid seeing their NAVs fall since launch as a result of a combination of factors. These include: reinvestment of part of their revenues not used to pay dividends into new assets, alongside new equity capital raised from investors; uplifts in capital value as demand for such assets has increased; and various asset management activities that have added value.

In a low-interest-rate environment, as well as delivering dividend growth the sector has consistently offered attractive dividend streams for investors. Many of the assets that the funds invest in have revenues that have some linkage to inflation. This has become increasingly important with elevated levels of inflation in 2017 and 2018. The majority of funds in the environmental infrastructure sub-sector target dividend growth in line with the rate of retail price index inflation. Part of their revenues are directly linked to RPI inflation, and there is an underlying assumption that the power price will be correlated to inflation over the long term.

As a result the premium ratings of these trusts increased in 2017/18 as inflation began to rise and the gap in ratings compared with social infrastructure narrowed. However, as inflation rose above 3%, the RENEWABLES INFRASTRUCTURE GROUP, one of the largest trusts in the group, dropped its commitment to an inflation-linked dividend and several other funds put their policies under review.

Dividend cover is therefore an important metric in the sector and ranges from approximately 1.1× to 1.7×. With the exception of the funds that focus on infrastructure debt, where dividend levels have been static, the other funds in the broader sector have also tended to generate dividend growth, although it varies by fund and few have consistently grown dividends ahead of inflation.

THE CHALLENGE OF ACCURATE VALUATION

The assets in which the funds invest are unlisted and relatively illiquid and so the closed-end structure of investment companies is particularly well-suited to the asset class. Being unlisted also means, however, that the assets are inherently difficult to value. The methodology adopted by the sector is a discounted cash flow (DCF) model. These models require a variety of assumptions to be made in forecasting the revenues and costs over the life of the assets, which is often measured in decades. Funds publish the sensitivity of their NAVs to changes in a variety of assumptions used in the valuation models.

The discount rate used to calculate the present value is one of the key inputs in the valuation and provides an indication of the expected return from the portfolio. The discount rate is often described as being a combination of a relevant 'risk-free rate', such as the yield on government debt, and a risk premium. However, in arriving at the risk premium consideration is also given to relevant market transactions.

Discount rates are not static but change in response to market conditions and investor preferences. The demand for income, or yield, in recent years has increased demand for the assets that the infrastructure funds have targeted. This rise in demand from buyers, combined with their often lower cost of capital, has helped to push up prices. Taking HICL INFRASTRUCTURE, the first listed infrastructure fund and the one with the longest track record as an example, the discount rates used in its DCF valuation models have generally fallen since 2010 (see chart 1). They have, however, remained in a relatively tight band when compared with the fall in the 'risk-free' rate (long-dated government bonds in this case), which has been a key driver of the demand for assets in the sector.

Chart 1: HICL Infrastructure – discount rate used in portfolio valuation

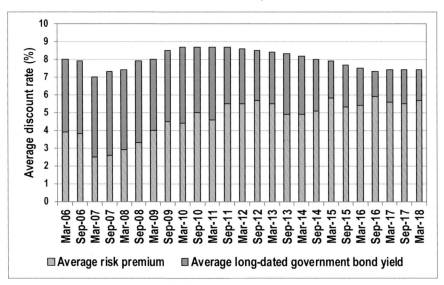

Source: Winterflood Securities, HICL Infrastructure.

The gradual reduction in the discount rate has enabled HICL to deliver stable NAV growth, with the added attraction of low correlation to equity markets. It is also an indication that valuations may be conservative, with the risk premium part of the discount rate now at elevated levels. Of course, the portfolio has changed with time as new assets have been acquired and so by comparing discount rates through time we are not necessarily comparing like with like. Nevertheless, the suspicion that valuations may be on the conservative side has also been supported by a small number of opportunistic disposals in the social infrastructure sub-sector at significant premiums to carrying value, as well as the takeover offer for JOHN LAING INFRASTRUCTURE in 2018.

With the Bank of England base rate rising in 2018 for only the second time in more than a decade, it is not unreasonable for investors to be concerned about the impact that rising interest rates could have on infrastructure funds. Given the expectation of modest and gradual increases in interest rates, the impact on NAVs is likely to be small in our view, and with demand for income likely to remain, the risk premiums within the discount rates should be able to absorb small increases in the 'risk-free' rate.

Chart 2: Infrastructure – NAV performance since 2015

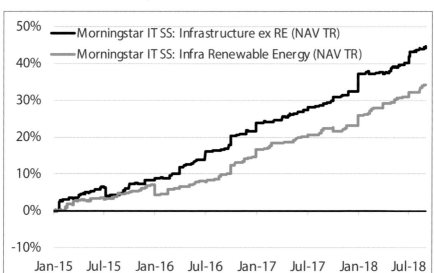

Source: Winterflood Securities, Morningstar. Data to 31 August 2018.

Chart 3: Infrastructure – ten-year premium/discount history

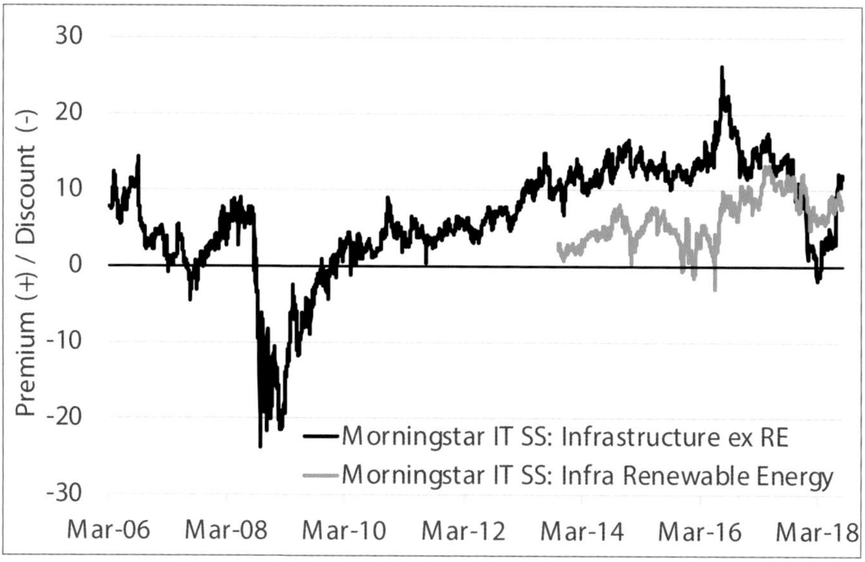

Source: Winterflood Securities, Morningstar. Data to 31 August 2018.

Both NAVs and share prices in the infrastructure sector have a low correlation with broader equity markets. However, share prices within the sector have at times been closely linked to movements in the bond markets. Driven by their dividend yields, many funds have consistently traded at significant premiums to NAVs that are generally only published semi-annually or quarterly. This is demonstrated in the chart below which compares the sector average rating with the yield on 20-year UK gilts (note that the yield is inverted: as the yield on gilts falls the demand for infrastructure funds increases).

Chart 4: Infrastructure ratings correlated to 20-year gilts

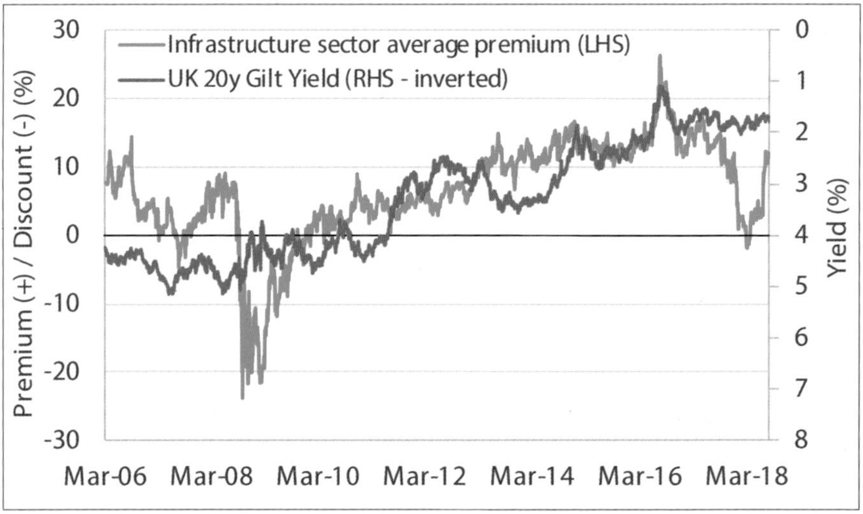

Source: Winterflood Securities, Morningstar, Thomson Reuters. Data to 31 August 2018.

ASSESSING THE RISKS ACCURATELY

As chart 4 also demonstrates, events in 2017 and 2018 served as a reminder that the asset class is not entirely 'risk-free', as some investors seemed to assume. The historic correlation between the funds' premium ratings and movements in government bond yields broke down. The change was particularly in evidence in the social infrastructure sub-sector. A number of factors contributed to this reassessment of the risks.

In September 2017 John McDonnell's pledge, at the Labour Party conference, to bring PFI contracts "back in-house" negatively impacted share prices for funds investing in social infrastructure. PFI contracts have been a political football for a number of years. Although it was unclear how this would translate into policy if Labour were to gain power, it served as a reminder of the political risk borne by infrastructure funds. PFI contracts include terms for early termination and some funds published estimates of the potential negative impact on NAVs, up to 16%, if the entire portfolio were to suffer such a fate.

Other potential risks came to the fore following the tragic fire at Grenfell Tower, with funds prompted to review cladding and fire safety at the buildings within their projects. In 2018, counterparty risk came into focus with the collapse of Carillion, which provided sub-contracted services to projects owned by funds in the social infrastructure sub-sector. Funds incurred frictional costs in finding replacement service providers and in some cases revenues from projects were delayed as lenders put projects into lock-up. Although no fund suffered a negative impact of more than 2% of NAV, their significant premium ratings disappeared and several moved to trade on discounts to NAV for the first time in several years.

John Laing Infrastructure also saw its rating and NAV negatively impacted by political developments following the Catalan independence referendum in 2017 which made it difficult for the fund to refinance the debt in the Barcelona metro project, which was its largest asset at the time. As well as political risk, this investment also highlighted the foreign exchange exposures that some funds now have, although these are often partially hedged. At launch, most funds in the sector primarily focused on UK assets. However, as demand has increased for infrastructure assets in the UK and pricing has become more competitive, some funds have expanded their search for new assets to include countries outside the UK as well as other infrastructure sectors.

In addition to John Laing Infrastructure's investment in the Barcelona Metro, other examples include HICL INFRASTRUCTURE's large investment in Affinity Water, a water utility, and increased exposure to demand-based assets such as toll roads where revenue fluctuates with traffic volume, in contrast to earlier so-called availability-based PFI/PPP assets (if the asset is available, payments are received). Funds in other sectors, such as FORESIGHT SOLAR and NEXTENERGY SOLAR, have also expanded overseas with investments in Australia and Italy respectively. It is important to monitor such changes and to assess whether managers have the requisite skills and capacity to produce the expected returns from expanded remits, sometimes known as 'style creep'.

GEARING AND POWER PRICE RISK

The perceived strength of government-backed contracted revenues from PFI projects and availability-based assets has supported relatively high levels of debt, often in the region of 80% or 90% of the total enterprise value of the project. This allows equity investors to boost their returns, but means that there is a relatively slim level of margin if things go wrong. There have been examples of projects where social infrastructure funds have had to write off their equity investment, although the impact on overall NAVs has been small.

Gearing levels for renewable energy assets are lower given that part of asset revenues come from sales of electricity, which are less certain. Historically, gearing has fallen into two categories: long-term gearing at the asset level, preferably fully amortising and for a term which is shorter than the life of the asset to remove any refinancing risk; and short-term gearing at the fund level, used as a bridge to equity when acquiring new assets in order to reduce cash drag on returns. However, as the renewable energy sector has matured, and revenues have reduced due to a falling power price, long-term gearing has been added at the fund level as well to enhance returns. It is therefore important to consider gearing levels across both the portfolio and fund level.

Chart 5: Movement in energy pricing since launch of infrastructure sector

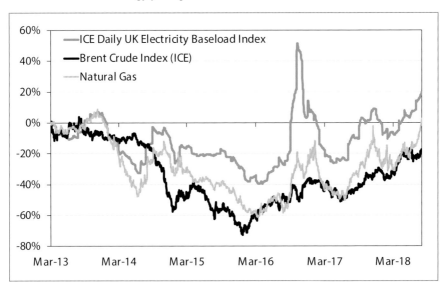

Source: Winterflood Securities, Bloomberg. Data to 30 August 2018.

For funds investing in renewable energy, exposure to the power price can impact NAVs. Long-term forecasts of power prices are one of the inputs into the modelling of cash flows for the purpose of the DCF model valuation. Since 2013, when most of the funds were launched, there has been a significant fall in the forecast for the long-term electricity price and it has had a significant negative impact on NAVs. This has been offset by positive impacts such as higher inflation, lower costs, higher gearing and increased demand for assets (lower discount rates).

We do not know what the power price will be over the next 20 years but based on the experience of the last five years it seems reasonable to assume that it is far from certain to follow the path that is currently forecast. All of the funds have a mixture of revenues from subsidies, which are usually linked to inflation, and revenue from the sale of electricity, but the proportions vary between funds and can change over time as the constituents of portfolios change. This may be an increasingly important variable to monitor as the reducing cost of solar technology begins to make subsidy-free solar farms economically viable, with these assets clearly having different risk/return characteristics.

One of the best performers in the sector has been 3I INFRASTRUCTURE, which is differentiated from its peers by its focus on operating companies that own their assets in perpetuity. The fund has an approach similar to private equity funds, but with a focus on infrastructure-related companies and an eye towards stable income rather than capital gains. However, the fund has had significant success in capital terms, as well as income, with investments in Eversholt Rail, AWG and Elenia, which were all sold at large uplifts to cost.

WHAT IS NEXT FOR THE SECTOR?

The infrastructure sector is a unique asset class, which is well suited to the closed-end structure of listed investment companies given the illiquid nature of the underlying assets. While there are open-ended infrastructure funds, they primarily invest in listed companies operating in infrastructure sectors such as utilities, construction or energy and so have very different characteristics. More recently there have been several open-ended funds launched with fund-of-fund mandates offering access to a diversified portfolio of listed infrastructure investment companies.

Given the expectation of modest and gradual increases in interest rates, investor demand for income is likely to remain. The listed infrastructure sector has delivered attractive and growing dividend streams, with low correlation to equity markets, and it therefore may be tempting for investors to view such funds as bond proxies. However, many of the sector's risk characteristics differentiate the asset class from bonds in important respects.

KIERAN DRAKE has been an investment trust analyst at Winterflood Securities since 2009. He leads the team's research on the infrastructure and hedge fund sub-sectors. He has a BSc and PhD in physics from the University of Warwick.

LISTED INVESTMENT COMPANIES INVESTING IN THE DEBT SECTOR

By INNES URQUHART

THE DEBT SECTOR has grown very significantly both in terms of the number of funds and assets over recent years, driven largely by the demand for income in a low-interest-rate environment. The majority of funds therefore provide attractive dividend yields.

Chart 1: Total market cap of listed investment company debt sector

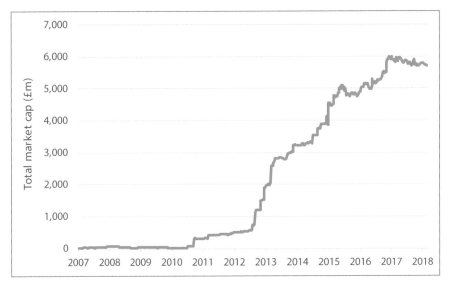

Source: Thomson Reuters

Chart 2: Historical yields in the debt sector

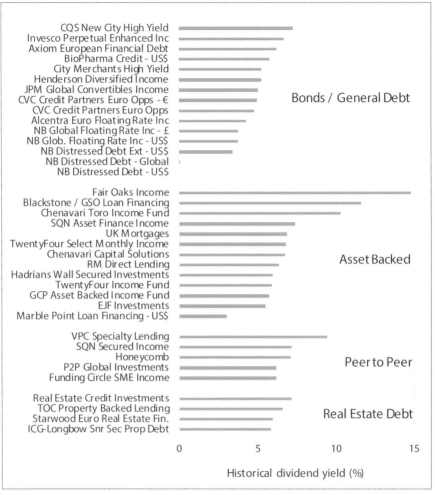

Source: Thomson Reuters as at 30 September 2018.

In general terms, the exposure that funds in the debt sector provide is to non-investment-grade credit and, as such, it is important to appreciate that the prospective returns they offer are not without risk. As with any fund, it is worth understanding the track record of the fund manager and how historical performance has been delivered. This can be difficult as many funds in the sector have been launched within the last five years and therefore have not experienced a full credit cycle.

The debt sector provides exposure to a wide range of underlying sub-sectors from across the broader credit spectrum, including high-yield bonds, leveraged loans, direct lending, asset-backed securities and leasing, as well as other specialist areas. Many of these assets are also relatively illiquid and are therefore well suited to the listed closed-ended fund sector. However, they can also be complex and it is therefore important to try and understand what they are actually investing in.

This can be difficult as some may not (or may not be permitted to) provide a huge amount of transparency in relation to portfolio holdings and many only report NAVs on a monthly basis. For example, while the use of gearing at the fund level is not particularly prevalent across the debt sector, assets such as CLO equity or bank capital transactions are inherently leveraged and consequently carry a higher level of underlying risk.

Key risks when analysing the debt sector are defaults and the impact of rising interest rates. However, a number of funds invest in 'floating rate' assets that should see the income they earn rise as interest rates rise. As with any other investment trust it is also important to understand the premium/discount to NAV at which you are buying the shares and how that compares with history, as well as any discount-control mechanism that the fund has in place.

It is also worth bearing in mind that the illiquid nature of many debt funds' underlying assets may make it difficult to manage any discount through regular share buybacks. This is not a sector where the average private investor can hope to add much value unless they have both time on their hands and relevant business or analytical experience.

INNES URQUHART, *a qualified chartered accountant, joined the investment trust research team at Winterflood Securities in 2012.*

PARTNERS

DYNAMIC AND FLEXIBLE –
THE BENEFITS OF INVESTMENT TRUSTS

The structure of investment trusts makes them worth considering for investors who are seeking potential investment opportunities in the UK and further afield – with due consideration of risk.

One company – dozens of opportunities

Investment trusts are companies that invest in other companies' shares. So, in effect, one investment trust provides instant exposure to a broad portfolio of investments – giving greater investment diversification than most private investors could achieve by investing in those companies directly.

And the choice of opportunities is wide. Aberdeen Standard's investment trusts invest in markets from the UK to Asia. Many trusts focus on capital growth but some also aim to generate income.

Our range also includes some very specialist choices that involve higher levels of risk and are designed to exploit the potential from specific markets and industry sectors.

Market expertise hired independently

Managing a portfolio of investments takes skill, resources and a thorough knowledge of the markets in which you invest. With an investment trust, our investment knowledge and experience becomes yours.

Most importantly, the fund managers are appointed by the trust's board and can be changed if the manager fails to perform. In other words, the fund managers constantly have to prove why they should be running the portfolio – a great incentive to keep delivering strong performance.

A structure for long-term vision

Investment trusts are often referred to as 'closed-end' funds because they have a fixed number of shares in issue which are bought and sold on the stock market. This structure allows the fund managers to take a long-term view of investments and invest in more specialist areas of the market, without the pressure to liquidate holdings if investors want their cash.

But please note that the share price of an investment trust is driven by market demand for the fixed number of shares in issue. This means the shares can trade at a price above (at a 'premium') or below (at a 'discount') the value of the trust's underlying portfolio or 'Net Asset Value'. At times there may be low demand for an investment trust's shares which may affect their price.

Gearing – increasing reward potential

As public limited companies, investment trusts have more freedom than other types of investment fund. For example, they can borrow money – a practice known as gearing or leverage. Investing the borrowings can potentially increase returns for shareholders – and can allow the fund managers to increase exposure to investment opportunities as and when they arise.

However, gearing can also potentially magnify investment losses and therefore needs to be sensibly managed. All of our investment trusts make clear whether they use gearing and how much. Highly geared investment trusts involve greater risk than trusts that have lower or no gearing.

Balancing risk and reward

As pooled investments, investment trusts generally offer a more diversified exposure to equities than owning an individual share. However, unlike a bank account or building society savings account, your capital is at risk. This risk varies trust by trust, according to the particular investment policy and approach of each. It is generally recommended to hold investment trust shares for at least five years so that losses from any short-term volatility can be recovered (although this is never guaranteed).

Accountability – have your say

When you buy shares in an investment trust, you become a shareholder and that gives you particular entitlements – just like any shareholder of a public limited company. You can expect the board of the investment trust to work in your best interests. You are entitled to receive the investment trust's annual report and accounts. You get full voting rights and can attend Annual General Meetings (AGMs).

The AGM is an opportunity for investors to hear the report from the Chairman and Board of Directors and vote on the resolutions presented for your trust and typically hear a presentation by the trust's fund manager. Share Plan investors are sent details of the AGM automatically with the trust's annual report. So you can have an active say in how your investment is managed.

Important features to remember

As we've explained, the company structure of an investment trust has lots of advantages but there are implications you need to be aware of:

The trust's share price can fall as well as rise – just like any publicly traded share

Any income payments ('dividends') can vary and are not guaranteed.

The share price won't necessarily reflect the underlying portfolio

Unlike funds such as OEICs and unit trusts, the trust's shares may be worth more or less than the underlying portfolio, depending on market demand. This is because there is a fixed number of shares in issue.

Gearing can increase risk

Gearing provides a flexible way to increase potential returns. It also increases risk and trusts that use a lot of gearing can see significant swings in value. Be sure you are comfortable with the level of gearing in a trust before you invest.

Share price liquidity

At times there may be low demand for shares which may affect their price.

Important – Risk factors

The value of investments and the income from them can go down as well as up and you may get back less than the amount invested. Past performance is not a guide to future results. Investment may not be appropriate. Investment trusts are specialised investments and may not be appropriate for all investors. We recommend that you seek financial advice prior to making an investment decision.

Issued by Aberdeen Asset Managers Limited which is authorised and regulated by the Financial Conduct Authority in the UK. Registered Office: 10 Queen's Terrace, Aberdeen AB10 1YG. Registered in Scotland No.108419. A member of the Aberdeen Asset Management group of companies. Aberdeen Standard Investments is a brand of the investment businesses of Aberdeen Asset Management and Standard Life Investments.

Find out more at – www.invtrusts.co.uk

ABOUT ARTEMIS

Independent and owner-managed, Artemis is a leading UK-based fund manager. It manages some £29.7bn* of clients' money across a range of funds, two investment trusts, a venture capital trust and both pooled and segregated institutional portfolios.

Since its foundation in 1997, the firm's aim has always been to offer exemplary performance and client service. All Artemis' staff share these two precepts – and the same flair and enthusiasm for fund management.

Artemis' fund managers can only invest in their own and their colleagues' funds, which aligns their interests directly with those of Artemis' investors. Whatever markets are doing, there are opportunities for active managers to make above-average returns. Artemis' fund managers only buy a share if they think it is undervalued, and not because it represents a big proportion of the index. Artemis respects benchmarks – but is not driven by them. This produces 'high conviction' portfolios which differ markedly from those of competitors and benchmark indices.

Artemis has a history of recruiting and training fund managers with proven skills – and an excellent record of retaining fund managers. Artemis' managers have the freedom to invest without the constraints of a single house style or process. Yet Artemis' policy of co-investment gives its fund managers every reason to share their views with each other. Open, communicative and always keen to debate investment ideas, Artemis' managers immerse themselves in their markets. They do this through research (both their own and external), conferences, meetings with analysts, economists and industry experts, and with the management of companies, and also in formal and informal conversations with each other.

---

*   Source: Artemis as at 30 September 2018.

Artemis operates a 'knowledge management system' (called Delphi, as in the Greek oracle). Delphi stores all this information and analysis so that it can be shared across the firm.

Some of Artemis' fund managers also use proprietary stock-screening systems, which narrow down the number of stocks to be examined in more detail. This allows the managers to concentrate their time, knowledge and skills on the most promising investments.

Keeping bureaucracy to a minimum, Artemis allows its managers to concentrate on what they do best – selecting the right stocks or bonds for clients. Artemis' investment teams have a collegiate approach. Drawing on each other's experience and knowledge, sharing ideas and insights between teams, specialist units operate with support from the wider business towards a common goal.

Artemis is a Limited Liability Partnership (LLP) and currently has 29 partners who are fund managers and other key individuals at the firm. Affiliated Managers Group (AMG) and the management of Artemis own 100% of the equity of the business. This is a financial partnership: AMG takes a share of the revenues produced by Artemis, but does not get involved in the day-to-day running of the business. Artemis believes that a LLP is the ideal structure for an investment management business. It means freedom from the (often) short-term demands of shareholders; and it allows Artemis to focus entirely on trying to meet or exceed its clients' needs. The partnership enables Artemis to manage generational change, whilst also attracting new talent.

Artemis' growth has been largely organic, and the partnership is firmly committed to remaining independent. The firm's aim is likewise unchanged: superior, long-term returns for the people whose money Artemis manages.

ABOUT FIDELITY INTERNATIONAL

Fidelity International provides world-class investment solutions and retirement expertise to institutions, individuals and their advisers – to help our clients build better futures for themselves and generations to come.

As a private company, we think generationally and invest for the long term. Helping clients to save for retirement and other long-term investing objectives has been at the core of our business for nearly 50 years.

We offer our own investment solutions and access to those of others, and deliver services relating to investing. For individual investors and their advisers we provide guidance to help them invest in a simple and cost-effective way. For institutions, including pension funds, banks and insurance companies, we offer tailored investment solutions, consultancy, and full-service outsourcing of asset management to us. For employers, we provide workplace pension administration services on top of, or independently from, investment management. We are responsible for total client assets of £315.6bn from 2.4m clients across Asia Pacific, Europe, the Middle East and South America.

OUR INVESTMENT APPROACH

Investing requires a continuous research commitment to build a deep understanding of what is driving industries and individual businesses. This is where our global research capabilities with over 400 investment professionals and research staff around the world come in: Fidelity International is committed to generating proprietary insights and our analysts work together across asset classes, e.g. combining insights from equity, credit, macro and quantitative research, to form a 360° view on the health and prospects of companies.

- Our analysts carry out their research on the ground – visiting the shop floor, speaking to customers, competitors, suppliers, and independent experts to form conviction.

- Over the course of a year, our portfolio managers and analysts attend more than 16,000 company meetings – or one every eight minutes on average between them.

- We commission over 250 bespoke surveys and reports a year to understand the market potential of companies' product and service innovations.

OUR UK INVESTMENT TRUST BUSINESS

Fidelity has over 25 years' experience managing investment companies, and manages around £3.3bn in assets across five investment trusts. These are all focused on equity growth strategies. Fidelity won the Premier Group category in *Money Observer*'s 2016 Investment Trust Awards and was highly commended in 2017 and 2018.

As a major platform distributor, Fidelity is able to offer its own investment trusts and those managed by third parties to professional investors and retail investors alike through a range of different product wrappers. Fidelity also promotes its range of trusts directly to institutions and wealth managers through its highly experienced in-house sales teams.

Past performance is not a reliable indicator of future results. This information is not a personal recommendation for any particular investment. If you are unsure about the suitability of an investment you should speak to an authorised financial adviser. Assets and resources source: Fidelity International, 30 June 2018. Third-party trademark, copyright and other intellectual property rights are and remain the property of their respective owners. Issued by Financial Administration Services Limited, authorised and regulated in the UK by the Financial Conduct Authority. Fidelity, Fidelity International, The Fidelity International logo and F symbol are trademarks of FIL limited.

JUPITER
Asset Management

ABOUT JUPITER

Jupiter was founded in 1985 and has since become one of the UK's most respected and successful fund management groups. From our origins as a manager primarily of investment trust and private client portfolios, we expanded into institutional fund management before mutual funds became the key engine of growth.

In 2007, Jupiter's employees bought the Jupiter Group from its parent company Commerzbank through a management buyout supported by private equity firm TA Associates, and other minority investors. In June 2010 Jupiter listed on the London Stock Exchange. Many of our fund managers and other employees continue to hold shares in the Company and in addition, we encourage our fund managers to invest their own money into Jupiter funds, helping to create what we believe to be a stable environment in which the interests of our fund managers and other employees are aligned with those of our customers.

DIRECTORY

We list here trusts which had a market capitalisation of at least £100m in the last week of October 2018. The table shows the ticker and Sedol number of the trust, its name and sector and, where relevant, whether it constitutes a member of a market index (most are). Searching for the tickers on industry websites is the quickest way to find out more details of individual trusts and should make it easy for you to find links to the relevant trust's or investment management companies' websites as well.

EPIC	SEDOL	NAME	AIC SECTOR	MARKET CAP (£M)	INDEX
III	B1YW440	3i Group PLC	Private Equity	8,099	FTSE 100
SMT	BLDYK61	Scottish Mortgage Investment Trust PLC	Global	6,771	FTSE 100
FRCL	346607	Foreign & Colonial Investment Trust PLC	Global	3,589	FTSE Mid 250
RCP	736639	RIT Capital Partners PLC	Flexible Investment	3,065	FTSE Mid 250
PSH	BS7JCJ8	Pershing Square Holdings Ltd	Hedge Funds	2,973	FTSE Mid 250
HICL	B0T4LH6	HICL Infrastructure Company Ltd	Spec: Infrastructure	2,764	FTSE Mid 250
ATST	B11V7W9	Alliance Trust PLC	Global	2,417	FTSE Mid 250
INPP	B188SR5	International Public Partnership Ltd	Spec: Infrastructure	2,150	FTSE Mid 250
BBOX	BG49KP9	Tritax Big Box REIT PLC	Property Spec	2,142	FTSE Mid 250
3IN	BF5FX16	3i Infrastructure Ltd	Spec: Infrastructure	1,982	FTSE Mid 250
WTAN	974406	Witan Investment Trust PLC	Global	1,811	FTSE Mid 250
TEM	882929	Templeton Emerging Markets Investment Trust PLC	Global Emerging Mkt	1,695	FTSE Mid 250
MNKS	3051726	Monks Investment Trust (The) PLC	Global	1,660	FTSE Mid 250
SYNC	B8P59C0	Syncona Ltd	Spec: Biotech/ Life Sciences	1,653	FTSE Mid 250
PCT	422002	Polar Capital Technology Trust PLC	Spec: Tech Media, Telecom	1,593	FTSE Mid 250
MRC	BF4JDH5	Mercantile Investment Trust (The) PLC	UK All Companies	1,479	FTSE Mid 250
CLDN	163992	Caledonia Investments PLC	Global	1,478	FTSE Mid 250

EPIC	SEDOL	NAME	AIC SECTOR	MARKET CAP (£M)	INDEX
UKW	B8SC6K5	Greencoat UK Wind PLC	Spec: Renewable Energy	1,475	FTSE Mid 250
CTY	199083	City of London Investment Trust (The) PLC	UK Equity Income	1,390	FTSE Mid 250
MYI	611190	Murray International Trust PLC	Global Equity Income	1,361	FTSE Mid 250
WWH	338530	Worldwide Healthcare Trust PLC	Spec: Biotech/ Life Sciences	1,320	FTSE Mid 250
FGT	781606	Finsbury Growth & Income Trust PLC	UK Equity Income	1,301	FTSE Mid 250
LMP	B4WFW71	Londonmetric Property PLC	Property: UK	1,271	FTSE Mid 250
TRIG	BBHX2H9	The Renewables Infrastructure Group Ltd	Spec: Renewable Energy	1,254	FTSE Mid 250
EDIN	305233	Edinburgh Investment Trust (The) PLC	UK Equity Income	1,235	FTSE Mid 250
TRY	906409	TR Property Investment Trust PLC	Property Securities	1,231	FTSE Mid 250
SEQI	BV54HY6	Sequoia Economic Infrastructure Income Fund Ltd	Spec: Infrastructure	1,177	FTSE Mid 250
PIN	414850	Pantheon International PLC	Private Equity	1,131	FTSE Mid 250
UKCM	B19Z2J5	UK Commercial Property Trust Ltd	Property: UK	1,121	FTSE Mid 250
GCP	B6173J1	GCP Infrastructure Investments Ltd	Spec: Infrastructure	1,106	FTSE Mid 250
FCPT	B4ZPCJ0	F&C Commercial Property Trust Ltd	Property: UK	1,100	FTSE Mid 250
HVPE	BR30MJ8	Harbourvest Global Private Equity Ltd	Private Equity	1,089	FTSE Mid 250
ASL	6655	Aberforth Smaller Companies Trust PLC	UK Smaller Comp	1,085	FTSE Mid 250

EPIC	SEDOL	NAME	AIC SECTOR	MARKET CAP (£M)	INDEX
RSE	BBHXCL3	Riverstone Energy Ltd	Spec: Commodities, Natural Res	1,056	FTSE Mid 250
FCSS	B62Z3C7	Fidelity China Special Situations PLC	Ctry Spec: Asia Pacific	1,039	FTSE Mid 250
BNKR	76700	Bankers Investment Trust PLC	Global	1,012	FTSE Mid 250
JMG	341895	JPMorgan Emerging Markets Inv Trust PLC	Global Emerging Mkt	969	FTSE Mid 250
JAM	BKZGVH6	JPMorgan American Investment Trust PLC	North America	959	FTSE Mid 250
VEIL	BD9X204	Vietnam Enterprise Investments Ltd	Ctry Spec: Asia Pacific	949	FTSE Mid 250
PNL	682754	Personal Assets Trust PLC	Flexible Investment	909	FTSE Mid 250
FEV	BK1PKQ9	Fidelity European Values PLC	Europe	884	FTSE Mid 250
JEO	19772	Jupiter European Opportunities Trust PLC	Europe	861	FTSE Mid 250
BBGI	B6QWXM4	Bilfinger Berger Global Infrastructure SICAV SA	Spec: Infrastructure	861	FTSE Mid 250
HRI	422864	Herald Investment Trust PLC	Spec: Small Media, Comms, IT	820	FTSE Mid 250
FCS	17505	F&C Global Smaller Companies PLC	Global	818	FTSE Mid 250
PHP	BYRJ5J1	Primary Health Properties PLC	Property Spec	811	FTSE Mid 250
BTEM	133508	British Empire Trust PLC	Global	797	FTSE Mid 250
PLI	679842	Perpetual Income & Growth Investment Trust PLC	UK Equity Income	793	FTSE Mid 250

EPIC	SEDOL	NAME	AIC SECTOR	MARKET CAP (£M)	INDEX
TMPL	882532	Temple Bar Investment Trust PLC	UK Equity Income	793	FTSE Mid 250
NRR	BD7XPJ6	NewRiver REIT PLC	Property: UK	789	FTSE Mid 250
GSS	B4L0PD4	Genesis Emerging Markets Fund Ltd	Global Emerging Mkt	751	FTSE Mid 250
HGT	392105	HgCapital Trust PLC	Private Equity	741	FTSE Mid 250
NBLS	B3KX4Q3	NB Global Floating Rate Income Fund Ltd	Spec: Securitised Debt	729	FTSE Mid 250
BGFD	48583	Baillie Gifford Japan Trust (The) PLC	Japan	720	FTSE Mid 250
FSV	BWXC7Y9	Fidelity Special Values PLC	UK All Companies	673	FTSE Mid 250
JFJ	174002	JPMorgan Japanese Investment Trust PLC	Japan	664	FTSE Mid 250
SDP	791887	Schroder AsiaPacific Fund PLC	Asia Pacific Excl Japan	642	FTSE Mid 250
BRSC	643610	BlackRock Smaller Companies Trust PLC	UK Smaller Comp	634	FTSE Mid 250
SCIN	782609	Scottish Investment Trust PLC	Global	628	FTSE Mid 250
EFM	294502	Edinburgh Dragon Trust PLC	Asia Pacific Excl Japan	624	FTSE Mid 250
JII	345035	JPMorgan Indian Investment Trust PLC	Ctry Spec: Asia Pacific	618	FTSE Mid 250
VOF	BYXVT88	VinaCapital Vietnam Opportunity Fund Ltd	Ctry Spec: Asia Pacific	611	FTSE Mid 250
WPCT	BVG1CF2	Woodford Patient Capital Trust PLC	UK All Companies	702	FTSE Small Cap
LWDB	3142921	Law Debenture Corp (The) PLC	Global	679	FTSE Small Cap

EPIC	SEDOL	NAME	AIC SECTOR	MARKET CAP (£M)	INDEX
APAX	BWWYMV8	APAX Global Alpha Ltd	Private Equity	636	FTSE Small Cap
NESF	BJ0JVY0	NextEnergy Solar Fund Ltd	Spec: Renewable Energy	635	FTSE Small Cap
RDI	B8BV8G9	RDI REIT PLC	Property: Europe	631	FTSE Small Cap
HSL	906506	Henderson Smaller Companies Investment Trust PLC	UK Smaller Comp	622	FTSE Small Cap
DIGS	B8460Z4	GCP Student Living PLC	Property Spec	610	FTSE Small Cap
FSFL	BD3QJR5	Foresight Solar Fund Ltd	Spec: Renewable Energy	607	FTSE Small Cap
SOI	B0CRWN5	Schroder Oriental Income Fund Ltd	Asia Pacific Excl Japan	604	FTSE Small Cap
P2P	BLP57Y9	P2P Global Investments PLC	Spec: Securitised Debt	594	FTSE Small Cap
BRWM	577485	BlackRock World Mining Trust PLC	Spec: Commodities, Natural Res	592	FTSE Small Cap
ICGT	329200	ICG Enterprise Trust PLC	Private Equity	582	FTSE Small Cap
JESC	BMTS0Z3	JPMorgan European Smaller Companies Trust PLC	Europe Smaller Comp	579	FTSE Small Cap
SRE	B1W3VF5	Sirius Real Estate Ltd	Property: Europe	573	FTSE Small Cap
ESP	BLWDVR7	Empiric Student Property PLC	Property Spec	567	FTSE Small Cap
SLPE	3047468	Standard Life Private Equity Trust PLC	Private Equity	538	FTSE Small Cap
JLEN	BJL5FH8	John Laing Environmental Assets Group Ltd	Spec: Renewable Energy	519	FTSE Small Cap
NBPE	B28ZZX8	NB Private Equity Partners Ltd	Private Equity	509	FTSE Small Cap

EPIC	SEDOL	NAME	AIC SECTOR	MARKET CAP (£M)	INDEX
MRCH	580007	Merchants Trust (The) PLC	UK Equity Income	503	FTSE Small Cap
SCAM	787369	Scottish American Investment Co (The) PLC	Global Equity Income	502	FTSE Small Cap
BGS	BFXYH24	Baillie Gifford Shin Nippon PLC	Japan Smaller Comp	494	FTSE Small Cap
EWI	291633	Edinburgh Worldwide Investment Trust PLC	Global	483	FTSE Small Cap
IEM	3123249	Impax Environmental Markets PLC	Spec: Environment	474	FTSE Small Cap
MUT	611112	Murray Income Trust PLC	UK Equity Income	473	FTSE Small Cap
CREI	BJFLFT4	Custodian Reit PLC	Property: UK	471	FTSE Small Cap
TFIF	B90J5Z9	TwentyFour Income Fund Ltd	Spec: Securitised Debt	471	FTSE Small Cap
PCTN	B0LCW20	Picton Property Income Ltd	Property: UK	463	FTSE Small Cap
ATT	339072	Allianz Technology Trust PLC	Spec: Tech Media, Telecom	462	FTSE Small Cap
BSIF	BB0RDB9	Bluefield Solar Income Fund Ltd	Spec: Renewable Energy	461	FTSE Small Cap
SLS	295958	Standard Life UK Smaller Companies Trust PLC	UK Smaller Comp	449	FTSE Small Cap
UEM	BD45S96	Utilico Emerging Markets Ltd	Global Emerging Mkt	449	FTSE Small Cap
TRG	906692	TR European Growth Trust PLC	Europe Smaller Comp	439	FTSE Small Cap
NAS	643900	North Atlantic Smaller Companies Inv Trust PLC	North America Smaller Comp	423	FTSE Small Cap
HFEL	B1GXH75	Henderson Far East Income Ltd	Asia Pacific Excl Japan	417	FTSE Small Cap

EPIC	SEDOL	NAME	AIC SECTOR	MARKET CAP (£M)	INDEX
BBH	BZCNLL9	BB Healthcare Trust PLC	Spec: Biotech/ Life Sciences	413	FTSE Small Cap
LXI	BYQ46T4	LXI REIT PLC	Property: UK	412	FTSE Small Cap
RICA	B018CS4	Ruffer Investment Company Ltd	Flexible Investment	412	FTSE Small Cap
SWEF	B79WC10	Starwood European Real Estate Finance Ltd	Spec: Securitised Debt	399	FTSE Small Cap
HSTN	B0PPFY8	Hansteen Holdings PLC	Property: Europe	397	FTSE Small Cap
ADIG	129756	Aberdeen Diversified Income & Growth Trust PLC	Flexible Investment	394	FTSE Small Cap
JPGI	BYMKY69	JPMorgan Global Growth & Income PLC	Global Equity Income	393	FTSE Small Cap
JCH	342218	JPMorgan Claverhouse Investment Trust PLC	UK Equity Income	385	FTSE Small Cap
CSH	BD8HBD3	Civitas Social Housing PLC	Property Spec	385	FTSE Small Cap
THRL	B95CGW7	Target Healthcare REIT Ltd	Property Spec	383	FTSE Small Cap
CCPG	B9MRHZ5	CVC Credit Partners European Opportunities Ltd	Spec: Securitised Debt	383	FTSE Small Cap
BIOG	38551	Biotech Growth Trust (The) PLC	Spec: Biotech/ Life Sciences	381	FTSE Small Cap
RGL	BYV2ZQ3	Regional REIT Ltd	Property: UK	378	FTSE Small Cap
LWI	536806	Lowland Investment Co PLC	UK Equity Income	372	FTSE Small Cap
DIVI	B65TLW2	Diverse Income Trust (The) PLC	UK Equity Income	368	FTSE Small Cap
SOHO	BF0P7H5	Triple Point Social Housing REIT PLC	Property Spec	362	FTSE Small Cap

EPIC	SEDOL	NAME	AIC SECTOR	MARKET CAP (£M)	INDEX
NAIT	29362	North American Income Trust PLC	North America	361	FTSE Small Cap
SLI	3387528	Standard Life Investments Property Inc Trust Ltd	Property: UK	360	FTSE Small Cap
PSDL	BVG2VP8	Phoenix Spree Deutschland Ltd	Property: Europe	359	FTSE Small Cap
DIG	340609	Dunedin Income Growth Inv Trust PLC	UK Equity Income	357	FTSE Small Cap
THRG	891055	Blackrock Throgmorton Trust PLC	UK Smaller Comp	354	FTSE Small Cap
MXF	B1DVQL9	MedicX Fund Ltd	Property Spec	351	FTSE Small Cap
SQN	BN56JF1	SQN Asset Finance Income Fund Ltd	Spec: Leasing	348	FTSE Small Cap
JEMI	B5ZZY91	JPMorgan Global Emerging Markets Income Trust PLC	Global Emerging Mkt	347	FTSE Small Cap
IIT	81168	Independent Investment Trust (The) PLC	Global	346	FTSE Small Cap
FCIF	BYYJCZ9	Funding Circle SME Income Fund Ltd	Spec: Securitised Debt	341	FTSE Small Cap
AAIF	B0P6J83	Aberdeen Asian Income Fund Ltd	Asia Pacific Excl Japan	340	FTSE Small Cap
EUT	329501	European Investment Trust PLC	Europe	339	FTSE Small Cap
BHMG	B1NP514	BH Macro Ltd	Hedge Funds	334	FTSE Small Cap
AAS	10076	Aberdeen Asian Smaller Companies Investment Trust PLC	Asia Pacific Excl Japan	333	FTSE Small Cap
GABI	BYXX8B0	GCP Asset Backed Income Fund Ltd	Spec: Securitised Debt	330	FTSE Small Cap

EPIC	SEDOL	NAME	AIC SECTOR	MARKET CAP (£M)	INDEX
ELTA	308544	Electra Private Equity PLC	Private Equity	317	FTSE Small Cap
FCI	346328	F&C Capital and Income Investment Trust PLC	UK Equity Income	314	FTSE Small Cap
SREI	B01HM14	Schroder Real Estate Investment Trust Ltd	Property: UK	312	FTSE Small Cap
BUT	149000	Brunner Investment Trust PLC	Global	312	FTSE Small Cap
PAC	667438	Pacific Assets Trust PLC	Asia Pacific Excl Japan	300	FTSE Small Cap
JAI	132077	JPMorgan Asian Investment Trust PLC	Asia Pacific Excl Japan	295	FTSE Small Cap
BHGG	B2QQPT9	BH Global Ltd	Hedge Funds	295	FTSE Small Cap
ATR	871079	Schroder Asian Total Return Investment Company PLC	Asia Pacific Excl Japan	294	FTSE Small Cap
FEET	BLSNND1	Fundsmith Emerging Equities Trust	Global Emerging Mkt	293	FTSE Small Cap
VSL	BVG6X43	VPC Specialty Lending Investments PLC	Spec: Securitised Debt	291	FTSE Small Cap
RAV	B0D5V53	Raven Property Group Ltd	Property Spec	285	FTSE Small Cap
BRGE	B01RDH7	BlackRock Greater Europe Investment Trust PLC	Europe	279	FTSE Small Cap
HINT	B3PHCS8	Henderson International Income Trust PLC	Global Equity Income	275	FTSE Small Cap
BRFI	B3SXM83	Blackrock Frontiers Investment Trust PLC	Global Emerging Mkt	274	FTSE Small Cap
CGT	173861	Capital Gearing Trust PLC	Flexible Investment	270	FTSE Small Cap
SST	783613	Scottish Oriental Smaller Companies Trust PLC	Asia Pacific Excl Japan	261	FTSE Small Cap

EPIC	SEDOL	NAME	AIC SECTOR	MARKET CAP (£M)	INDEX
PCGH	B6832P1	Polar Capital Global Healthcare Growth & Income PLC	Spec: Biotech/ Life Sciences	258	FTSE Small Cap
SJG	802284	Schroder Japan Growth Fund PLC	Japan	257	FTSE Small Cap
FAS	332231	Fidelity Asian Values PLC	Asia Pacific Excl Japan	257	FTSE Small Cap
RECI	B0HW536	Real Estate Credit Investment PCC Ltd	Spec: Securitised Debt	257	FTSE Small Cap
PCFT	B9XQT11	Polar Capital Global Financials Trust PLC	Spec: Financials	254	FTSE Small Cap
USA	BDFGHW4	Baillie Gifford US Growth Trust PLC	North America	254	FTSE Small Cap
JRS	3216473	JPMorgan Russian Securities PLC	Ctry Spec: Europe	249	FTSE Small Cap
FPEO	3073827	F&C Private Equity Trust PLC	Private Equity	248	FTSE Small Cap
BGUK	791348	Baillie Gifford UK Growth Fund PLC	UK All Companies	246	FTSE Small Cap
HEFT	526885	Henderson European Focus Trust PLC	Europe	243	FTSE Small Cap
NCYF	B1LZS51	CQS New City High Yield Fund Ltd	UK Equity & Bond Income	241	FTSE Small Cap
HAN	7879728	Hansa Trust PLC	Flexible Investment	240	FTSE Small Cap
JMF	235761	JPMorgan Mid Cap Investment Trust PLC	UK All Companies	238	FTSE Small Cap
ANII	604877	Aberdeen New India Investment Trust PLC	Ctry Spec: Asia Pacific	233	FTSE Small Cap
FCRE	B012T52	F&C UK Real Estate Investment Ltd	Property: UK	231	FTSE Small Cap
LTI	3197794	Lindsell Train Investment Trust (The) PLC	Global	231	FTSE Small Cap
HMSF	B13YVW4	Highbridge Multi-Strategy Fund Ltd	Hedge Funds	228	FTSE Small Cap

EPIC	SEDOL	NAME	AIC SECTOR	MARKET CAP (£M)	INDEX
ABD	BBM56V2	Aberdeen New Dawn Investment Trust PLC	Asia Pacific Excl Japan	228	FTSE Small Cap
IBT	455934	International Biotechnology Trust PLC	Spec: Biotech/ Life Sciences	226	FTSE Small Cap
EPIC	BNGMZB6	Ediston Property Investment Co PLC	Property: UK	225	FTSE Small Cap
JPS	316581	JPMorgan Fleming Japanese Smaller Cos Inv Tr PLC	Japan Smaller Comp	220	FTSE Small Cap
SLET	603959	Standard Life Equity Income Trust PLC	UK Equity Income	219	FTSE Small Cap
HNE	419929	Henderson EuroTrust PLC	Europe	218	FTSE Small Cap
HHI	958057	Henderson High Income Trust PLC	UK Equity & Bond Income	216	FTSE Small Cap
TIGT	370866	Troy Income & Growth Trust PLC	UK Equity Income	211	FTSE Small Cap
KIT	491206	Keystone Investment Trust PLC	UK All Companies	208	FTSE Small Cap
MNP	537241	Martin Currie Global Portfolio Trust PLC	Global	205	FTSE Small Cap
ASLI	BD9PXH4	Aberdeen Standard European Logistics Income PLC	Property: Europe	203	FTSE Small Cap
JPS	BSFWJ54	JPMorgan Fleming Japanese Smaller Cos Inv Tr PLC	Japanese Smaller Companies	203	FTSE Small Cap
CCJI	BYSRMH1	CC Japan Income & Growth Trust PLC	Japan	202	FTSE Small Cap
FJV	332855	Fidelity Japanese Values PLC	Japan	200	FTSE Small Cap
MTU	BZ1H9L8	Montanaro UK Smaller Companies Inv Tr PLC	UK Smaller Comp	192	FTSE Small Cap
JETG	B18JK16	JPMorgan European Growth Investment Trust PLC	Europe	189	FTSE Small Cap

EPIC	SEDOL	NAME	AIC SECTOR	MARKET CAP (£M)	INDEX
MWY	B6VTTK0	Mid Wynd International Inv Trust PLC	Global	186	FTSE Small Cap
SCF	791586	Schroder Income Growth Fund PLC	UK Equity Income	184	FTSE Small Cap
WPC	365602	Witan Pacific Investment Trust PLC	Asia Pacific Incl Japan	184	FTSE Small Cap
CMHY	B6RMDP6	City Merchants High Yield Trust Ltd	UK Equity & Bond Income	182	FTSE Small Cap
IAT	453530	Invesco Asia Trust PLC	Asia Pacific Excl Japan	179	FTSE Small Cap
SMIF	BJVDZ94	TwentyFour Select Monthly Income Fund Ltd	Spec: Securitised Debt	175	FTSE Small Cap
PHI	666747	Pacific Horizon Investment Trust PLC	Asia Pacific Excl Japan	174	FTSE Small Cap
SCP	610841	Schroder UK Mid & Small Cap Fund PLC	UK All Companies	174	FTSE Small Cap
JMI	741600	JPMorgan Smaller Companies Investment Trust PLC	UK Smaller Comp	174	FTSE Small Cap
JUSC	BJL5F34	JPMorgan US Smaller Companies IT PLC	North America Smaller Comp	173	FTSE Small Cap
JMC	343501	JPMorgan Chinese Investment Trust PLC	Ctry Spec: Asia Pacific	171	FTSE Small Cap
BRLA	505840	BlackRock Latin American Investment Trust PLC	Latin America	171	FTSE Small Cap
STS	B09G3N2	Securities Trust of Scotland PLC	Global Equity Income	168	FTSE Small Cap
ASIT	BYPBD39	Aberforth Split Level Income Trust PLC	UK Smaller Comp	167	FTSE Small Cap
HDIV	BF03YC3	Henderson Diversified Income Trust PLC	Global High Income	159	FTSE Small Cap

EPIC	SEDOL	NAME	AIC SECTOR	MARKET CAP (£M)	INDEX
RESI	BYSX150	Residential Secure Income PLC	Property Spec	158	FTSE Small Cap
SERE	BY7R8K7	Schroder European Real Estate Investment Trust Ltd	Property: Europe	156	FTSE Small Cap
IPU	B1FL3C7	Invesco Perpetual UK Smaller Companies Investment Trust PLC	UK Smaller Comp	153	FTSE Small Cap
MAJE	555522	Majedie Investments PLC	Global	151	FTSE Small Cap
IVI	358572	Invesco Income Growth Trust PLC	UK Equity Income	150	FTSE Small Cap
AEFS	B6116N8	Alcentra European Floating Rate Income Fund Ltd	Spec: Securitised Debt	148	FTSE Small Cap
JUS	346340	Jupiter US Smaller Companies PLC	North America Smaller Comp	147	FTSE Small Cap
JETI	B17XWW4	JPMorgan European Investment Trust PLC	Europe	145	FTSE Small Cap
MTE	454351	Montanaro European Smaller Companies Trust PLC	Europe Smaller Comp	141	FTSE Small Cap
SEC	B0BDCB2	Strategic Equity Capital PLC	UK Smaller Comp	135	FTSE Small Cap
SQNX	BFXYHJ1	SQN Asset Finance Income Fund Ltd C Shares NPV	Spec: Leasing	131	FTSE Small Cap
EPG	3386257	EP Global Opportunities Trust PLC	Global	128	FTSE Small Cap
RDL	BW4NPD6	Ranger Direct Lending Fund PLC	Spec: Securitised Debt	126	FTSE Small Cap
LBOW	B8C23S8	ICG-Longbow Senior Secured UK Property Debt Investments Ltd	Spec: Securitised Debt	124	FTSE Small Cap

EPIC	SEDOL	NAME	AIC SECTOR	MARKET CAP (£M)	INDEX
MCP	569512	Martin Currie Asia Unconstrained Trust PLC	Asia Pacific Excl Japan	122	FTSE Small Cap
VIN	848471	Value & Income Trust PLC	UK Equity Income	122	FTSE Small Cap
ATS	435594	Artemis Alpha Trust PLC	UK All Companies	121	FTSE Small Cap
JGCI	B96SW59	JPMorgan Global Convertibles Income Fund Ltd	Spec: Securitised Debt	118	FTSE Small Cap
MPO	BGDYFV6	Macau Property Opportunities Fund Ltd	Property: Asia Pacific	117	FTSE Small Cap
EGL	BD3V464	Ecofin Global Utilities And Infrustructure Trust PLC	Spec: Utilities	116	FTSE Small Cap
BRNA	B7W0XJ6	Blackrock North American Income Trust PLC	North America	115	FTSE Small Cap
HAST	121600	Henderson Alternative Strategies Trust PLC	Flexible Investment	107	FTSE Small Cap
MCT	B15PV03	Middlefield Canadian Income Trusts Investment Company PCC	North America	101	FTSE Small Cap